ADMIRAL OF THE BLUE

IAIN GORDON

Admiral of the Blue

THE LIFE AND TIMES OF
ADMIRAL JOHN CHILD PURVIS
1747-1825

Pen & Sword
MARITIME

First published in Great Britain in 2005 by
Pen & Sword Maritime
An imprint of
Pen & Sword Books Ltd
47 Church Street
Barnsley
South Yorkshire
S70 2AS

ISBN 1 84415 294 4

A CIP catalogue record for this book is
available from the British Library

Printed and bound in England
By CPI UK

Pen & Sword Books Ltd incorporates the Imprints of Pen & Sword Aviation,
Pen & Sword Maritime, Pen & Sword Military, Wharncliffe Local history,
Pen & Sword Select, Pen & Sword Military Classics and Leo Cooper.

For a complete list of Pen & Sword titles please contact
PEN & SWORD BOOKS LIMITED
47 Church Street, Barnsley, South Yorkshire, S70 2AS, England
E-mail: enquiries@pen-and-sword.co.uk
Website: www.pen-and-sword.co.uk

Contents

Maps & Plans

List of Plates

Permission to reproduce illustrations used in this book is gratefully acknowledged as follows:

Between pages 80/81:

   (i)   Toulon Harbour from Mount Faron.
         Napoleone Buonaparte. ©*National Maritime Museum.*
         Admiral Lord Hood. ©*National Maritime Museum.*

  (ii)   Toulon Harbour. ©*National Maritime Museum.*
         Captain Sir Sidney Smith. ©*National Maritime Museum.*
         French memorial on Balaguier.

 (iii)   Tour de la Balaguier.
         Main gateway of Balaguier.
         Fort Napoleon on the site of 'Little Gibraltar'.

  (iv)   H.M.S. *Victory* and the British Fleet off Bastia 1794.
         ©*National Maritime Museum.*
         Genoese watchtower, Corsica.
         The Citadel at San Fiorenzo.

   (v)   Admiral Hotham's Action off Genoa March 1795.
         ©*National Maritime Museum.*
         Vice-Admiral Fremantle. ©*National Maritime Museum.*

  (vi)   Lord Howe, Lord St Vincent and Lord Nelson.
         Mrs. A.A.G. Carmichael.

 (vii)   Blackbrook Cottage, Fareham.
         George Purvis and his wife Renira.
         ©*Jane Austen Memorial Trust.*

(viii)   H.M.S. *London.* ©*National Maritime Museum.*
         Admiral Sir John Colpoys. ©*National Maritime Museum.*
         Captain Edward Griffith. ©*National Maritime Museum.*
         Richard Parker, mutineer. ©*National Maritime Museum.*

Between pages 176/177:

(i) Admiral-of-the-Fleet Sir Francis Austen.
  Mrs. A.A.G. Carmichael.
  Admiral Sir William Cornwallis.
  ©National Maritime Museum.
  H.M.S. *Dreadnought. ©National Maritime Museum.*

(ii) Lord Collingwood. *©National Maritime Museum.*

(iii) Cadiz from the air.
  ©Editorial Escudo de Oro SA, 08004 Barcelona.
  Admiral Alava. *Museo de Cadiz*
  (Detail of an oil painting by Sir Thomas Lawrence.)
  Contemporary engraving of The Siege of Cadiz
  ©Editorial Escudo de Oro SA, 08004 Barcelona.

(iv) The Carraca Arsenal.
  Military prison in the Arsenal.
  Plaza de Armas, Carraca Arsenal.

(v) The old Suaso Bridge.
  The site of Fort Louis, Trocadero.
  Declaration of Loyalty by the citizens of Cadiz. *Museo de Cadiz. (Detail of an oil painting by Ramón Barcaza.)*

(vi) View from Castillo de Santa Catalina.
  Site of Fort Matagorda.
  Ruins of Castillo de Santa Catalina.

(vii) Vice-Admiral J.B. Purvis. *Mrs. W.H.A. Purvis.*
  Revd. R.F. Purvis. *Mrs. C.G.F. Purvis.*
  Captain J. Scott. *Eric D. Scott, Esq.*
  Vice-Admiral J.C. Purvis 2. *©Royal Geographical Society.*
  Sir William Purves Bart. *Mrs. W.H.A. Purvis.*
  Darsham House. *Mrs. O. Reeve.*

(viii) Vicar's Hill House, near Lymington.
  St. Leonard's Church, Whitsbury. *W.J. Purvis, Esq.*

Conventions

On 11th October 1805, ten days before the Battle of Trafalgar, the Admiralty issued an edict that, henceforth, the Royal Naval day should conform with the civil day and start at midnight instead of at noon as had previously been the practice. So deep-rooted was the old tradition, that it was some time before the new system was universally adopted in ships of the Fleet. This explains the frequent discrepancy of one day in the accounts of events from different sources and the same discrepancy between British and French or Spanish records prior to October 1805. In this book, the dates given are those recorded by Admiral Purvis. Similarly, the 'Order of Battle' tables are as they were written down by Purvis, at the time and on the spot, and may be found to differ, in minor detail, from information subsequently compiled by historians.

Spelling in quotations has not been altered and I have tried to avoid the use of 'sic' as far as possible; readers should be aware, however, that there were small contemporary differences in spelling (e.g. 'chase' was often written as 'chace'). Punctuation has, to some extent, been modernised in the interests of clarity but the more generous and expressive use of initial capitals, which was the style of the time, has been retained (who can deny that 'Horrible Carnage' is not the richer for its use of initial capitals?); indeed, the Publishers have kindly allowed me to adopt a more old-fashioned style in this respect throughout the book despite today's preference for minimalism. Hence, we have the return of Lieutenants, Flag-Officers and Fleets and Squadrons where the reference is specific.

An ellipsis . . . indicates a deliberate omission; the same in square parentheses [...] indicates an illegible word or words; a [word] or [several words] in square parentheses indicates my best guess or a considered link to make sense of a passage. "Double quotation marks", again unfashionably, are used for direct quotations.

The ranks of Admirals can be confusing to people unfamiliar with the period: there were, effectively, nine successive 'grades' of Admiral starting with Rear-Admiral of the Blue Squadron, then of the White, then of the Red; then the same three levels for Vice-Admiral, and then the same for Admiral, with Admiral-of-the-Fleet the tenth and final step at the top. Promotion, however, was by seniority and not by merit as it is today. Many Admirals of the period, ostensibly on the Active List though unemployed, were simply bumped up the promotion ladder by the need to create competent, serving Flag-Officers from the Captains' list below them; they were Admirals by name but had never actually 'hoisted their Flag' — that is to say commanded a Squadron or Fleet at sea. Purvis was a 'proper' Admiral who flew his Flag at sea as a Rear-Admiral and as a Vice-Admiral of the Red; his subsequent promotions were automatic after he had retired from active duty.

Ships of the Royal Navy were seldom prefixed by H.M.S. as they are today; I have used this, however, in the Index and in certain other places in the book in the interests of clarity. The number following the name of a warship — e.g. *London*, 98, — referred to the number of guns she carried (excluding carronades). Warships were classified into six 'rates' as shown below. The first four rates were sufficiently powerful to take their place in the line-of-battle in a formal fleet engagement and were therefore known as ships of-the-line or line-of-battle ships. The most common work-horse of the Battle Fleet was the 74-gun third-rate which would be referred to as a 'seventy-four'.

THE RATING OF BRITISH WARSHIPS c.1800

		Rate	No. of Guns	Approx. Crew
SHIPS OF THE LINE	THREE GUN DECKS	1st	100+	850+
		2nd	90-98	750-850
	TWO GUN DECKS	3rd	70-84	500-750
		4th	50-70	350-400
FRIGATES	SINGLE GUN DECK	5th	30-50	200-300
		6th	20-30	120-200

Below the 6th-rates came the sloops-of-war, brigs, gun-brigs, bomb-vessels, fireships, schooners and cutters. The larger of these would usually be commanded by Commanders; the smaller by Lieutenants.

Preface

Few people, other than serious writers and readers of naval history, will ever have heard of Admiral John Child Purvis. The names of the great sea commanders of that remarkable 100 years between 1750 and 1850, when Britannia truly ruled the waves, scream from the pages of the British chronicle like a crescendo of boatswains' pipes — Howe, Jervis, Nelson, Hood, Collingwood, Duncan, Cochrane, Cornwallis, Saumarez, Smith, Troubridge, Pellew, Keppel. Their reputations are secure; their deeds are known, or should be, by every British schoolboy.

But for every one of these acknowledged and undisputed heroes there were 10,000 sea officers, sailors and marines whose names are not remembered. The sheer scale of the Navy of that period is difficult to visualise: the Royal Navy today has 102 ships manned by 14,171 officers and men; of these, seven are aircraft carriers and 'Vanguard' class ballistic submarines — the 'capital' ships of the modern age.[1] In 1806, the year that Admiral Purvis first hoisted his Flag, there were 590 British warships in commission of which 120 were battleships,[2] or ships of-the-line as they were known, and there were 124,172 seagoing personnel.[3] (It would be invidious to examine the number of civil servants evidently required to support these two vastly disparate fleets!)

Purvis was what would be referred to in the Navy as a 'Pusser-Built' officer meaning that he stuck rigidly to established naval procedures and regulations; meticulous attention to duty, respect for the hierarchy and total obedience to orders were the hallmarks of his career. There is little evidence of his having possessed a sense of humour; to him, the defence of the realm was far too serious a business to permit of levity. Yet what he may have lacked in this respect he more than made up for in strength of character, professional competence and complete dependability; throughout his service, his superiors knew that whatever task they set him would be carried out thoroughly, conscientiously and with strict adherence to their instructions. The Navy could not have functioned without such officers. Lord Collingwood knew his worth and chose him as his second-in-command in the Mediterranean when he desperately needed the support of a Flag-Officer upon whom he could really depend: "I shall be very happy in having so excellent a second,"[4] he wrote to Purvis.

Lord Nelson's unique tactical genius and astonishing bravery have excused him in the eyes of posterity for his frequent disregard of orders; but no fighting service could support too many such individualists and Nelson might, perhaps, in one of his less vainglorious moments, have conceded that the success of British seapower in the late 18th- early 19th-centuries must be, at least equally, attributed to the actions of the thousands of officers and men who simply did their jobs well; officers like Admiral Purvis.

It has been said of the infantry soldier in war that 1% of his time is spent in fighting and 99% in waiting. So it was with the Royal Navy; the great sea battles were generally the culmination of months, sometimes years, of endless patrolling and blockading and fortunate was the sailor who ever got to witness an enemy fleet downwind and at close range. Purvis, in common with the great majority of sea officers, was never present at a major fleet engagement though he saw plenty of action just the same. As Master and Commander of a sloop-of-war in the War of American Independence, he fought, and won, an individual duel with a more-heavily armed French corvette which brought him promotion to Post-Captain; as a battleship captain in the French Revolutionary and Napoleonic Wars he commanded four successive ships of-the-line; he was in action in the Siege of Toulon where he was probably the first British officer to directly confront the young Captain of Artillery, Napoleone Buonaparte, who was to be the focus of British military and naval attention for the next twenty years. It was no doubt this early encounter which fomented the deep respect which Bonaparte always had for the Royal Navy. Later, Captain Purvis was engaged in the Reduction of San Fiorenzo and Bastia and in both of Admiral Hotham's undistinguished Mediterranean actions of 1795. Then, under the command of the legendary Sir John Jervis (to whom his younger brother, George, was secretary for many years) he was an eyewitness to the transformation of the Fleet by that great man and the introduction of the controversial 'Mediterranean Discipline'.

In 1797, during the final throes of the Spithead Mutiny, Purvis was given command of the *London*, the most seriously disaffected ship in the Channel Fleet which had seen some of the worst violence of the Mutiny. With a "surly, sulky and murmuring crew who would scarcely weigh the ship's anchor or loosen her topsails"[5], he returned to Channel patrols and the Blockade of Brest and within ten months had restored the ship to an efficient fighting unit which was ready to rejoin Lord St. Vincent's crack Mediterranean Fleet. In an age of brutal discipline and widespread sedition in the King's ships, he was necessarily a strong disciplinarian; but his discipline was always tempered with humanity and with that greatest of all British qualities — fairness.

Later, as a Flag-Officer, Rear-Admiral Purvis returned to blockading, this time off Cadiz; in command of the Cadiz Squadron during 1807/08 he was continuously at sea for one year and seven months without once dropping an anchor and without once being blown through the Gut of Gibraltar. The strain of such an extended period of seatime is difficult to conceive today. As Collingwood's second-in-command, Purvis left us a fascinating record of the day-to-day duties of a Flag-Officer of the time — the sort of duties which are seldom chronicled: the difficulties and necessary subterfuges for keeping his Squadron supplied with fresh beef; the continual demands for surveys of rotten sails, rigging and provisions; the maintenance of health and discipline and the convention of Courts Martial for such dissimilar offences as mutiny, on the one hand, and breaking wind in the gunroom mess on the other. These, rather than the disposition of battle fleets, were the daily concerns of an average Flag-Officer of the period.

So, with his long experience, seamanship, administrative competence and total dependability, Purvis gave his Commander-in-Chief the first-class support he so badly needed. But he was not simply a good second-in-command: when Bonaparte invaded Spain and the balance of naval power in the Mediterranean was threatened by the possibility that France would capture the Spanish Fleet in Cadiz, Rear-Admiral Purvis recognised the danger and acted immediately on his own initiative; there was no time to wait for orders.

With Lord Collingwood at the other end of the Mediterranean, it was then Purvis's responsibility to undertake the extremely difficult operational and diplomatic task of preparing Cadiz for siege and ensuring that the Spanish ships would not fall to France; a task which had to be undertaken without offending the sensibility of a mistrustful and temporizing ally: "It will require much delicacy of conduct and skill," Collingwood wrote to him, "but it cannot be in better hands than yours."[6] His trials and frustrations were legion and his training and experience in the Navy had done little to prepare him for the world of statecraft and intrigue in which he found himself. Yet he never faltered in his purpose and was never seduced by Spanish flattery from his address of that nation's naval and military shortcomings which he knew it was his duty to confront.

On Lord Collingwood's death in 1810, Vice-Admiral Purvis became, albeit briefly, Commander-in-Chief Mediterranean. His foresight and tenacity had saved the Spanish ships from capture by the French, had bolstered the Spanish determination to resist and had prepared the city to withstand the long siege under which it never capitulated and under which the famous 1812 liberal Constitution of Spain was conceived and born.

Admiral Purvis's contribution to the defeat of Bonaparte was considerable yet he never received an honour from his sovereign. While he was always ready to lobby for the advancement of his sons and his protégés, it was not in his nature to push himself forward. It is probable that he was content in the knowledge that he had done his job well; talking of recognition in a letter to his son, Richard, in 1816 he wrote: ". . . even without such inducements, there is a self satisfaction in knowing you have always deserved that which may not ultimately fall to your lot."[7] It is also a consequence of his modest nature and diffidence that we have no image of John Child Purvis; we know what his sons and his brother, George, looked like but the Admiral never had his portrait painted — not even a miniature. However, one can learn far more of a man's character from his words and recorded deeds than from his picture.

This book, which follows my biography of the Admiral's younger son, Richard,[8] inevitably contains some overlap and repetition and for this I apologise to readers of both books — it would have been difficult to give a full picture of the Admiral's life without repeating certain excerpts from his correspondence; and difficult to tell Richard's story without reference to the career of his illustrious father. I am, again, deeply indebted to Admiral Purvis's descendants for allowing me to do this and for giving me full access to his private papers. Also to the Trustees of the National Maritime Museum for their permission to quote freely from the Purvis archive in their custody; such excerpts, with their permission, are not individually referenced but may be readily located by consulting the schedule at Appendix 'A'.

I must also thank my friends Ronald Dunning, a descendant of George Purvis, for his thorough genealogical research and guidance on computer and internet matters; and John Brain for many hours of research, the translation of Spanish documents and correspondence and for acting as my interpreter and negotiator in Cadiz. Finally, I must again thank the charming and helpful staff of the Caird Library and Manuscript Archives at the National Maritime Museum for their attention and assistance during the seven years it has taken me to read the entire collection of Admiral Purvis's papers.

IAIN GORDON
BARNSTAPLE, DEVON, APRIL 2005

PART 1

Captain

CHAPTER 1

Early Days

Monday 19th August 1782
H.M.S. Duc de Chartres
off the coast of Virginia, America.

As dawn broke, a cry from the lookout in the foretop sent the Officer-of-the-Watch racing up the rigging to join him. Braced firmly against the roll of the ship, the officer extended his telescope and focussed on the point on the north-western horizon which the seaman was indicating with an outstretched arm. It was, indeeed, a sail though, at this distance and in the half-light of dawn, it was not possible to say more. Descending again to the deck, the officer summoned a seaman of the duty watch to call the Captain.

Captain John Child Purvis was on deck within minutes. He ascended the rigging to join the lookout in the foretop where he remained for nearly twenty minutes studying the distant sail as the dawn haze cleared. The *Duc de Chartres* was on a southerly course making about one knot in the light east-south-east wind against the steady, two-knot northerly flow of the Gulf Stream. She had thus idled through the night under reefed topsails, drifting very slowly northwards so that, at dawn, she would be in a commanding, up-wind position for the approaches to Chesapeake Bay and might, with good fortune, spot just such a quarry at first light.

By 0600 the reefs had been shaken out, the ship had come about and was set on a course of north-by-east with all sail set to intercept the stranger. The wind increased from force two to force four and the *Duc de Chartres* gathered way to a smart four knots. By 0800 the other vessel was clearly visible to the ship's company which lined the leeward rail to catch sight of her at the top of each rise in the swell and to speculate as to what she might be. It was clear that she was standing in for land with a press of sail and if, as it appeared, she was making for the entrance to Chesapeake Bay, the chances were that she was French.

Only five days earlier, they reminded one another, they had been in a similar frenzy of anticipation as they had chased and overhauled an unidentified brig in a fresh gale off Cape Hatteras. The *Duc* had been flying then in an astonishing, high, confused sea with lightning flashing around the mastheads of the two combatants. The *Duc* had engaged her prey and fired off fifteen shots before it declared itself as a prize of the *Fair American*, a New York privateer. This chase, they knew, could end with a similar disappointment but they must be prepared for all eventualities.

By 1000 the *Duc de Chartres* had cleared her decks for action; her guns were prepared and every man was ready to take his battle station. If the wind held on his starboard quarter, Captain Purvis calculated that he would intercept his target before the change of the forenoon watch. She was a small warship, larger then his own sloop and mounting twenty-two guns as opposed to his own sixteen; but such odds had never dismayed the Royal Navy.

At 1030 the commander of the other ship, realising that he could not, now, outrun his pursuer, took in his studding sails and hauled his wind to close with the *Duc de Chartres*. At 1100 as the two ships approached each other, Captain Purvis ordered his studding sails taken in and made the Private Signal, the secret reply to which, or lack of it, would identify the ship as friend or foe. There was no reply. In turn, the other ship hoisted a red flag at her main peak which was not recognised or acknowledged by the *Duc de Chartres*. The formalities were now over and the two ships established as enemies. At noon the chase hoisted the French ensign and pendant identifying herself as a French warship. Four minutes later she opened fire with her 6-pounders.

Captain Purvis was not to be enticed into a reckless and ineffective exchange of fire at the limit of his range and continued on his course to close the enemy. For twenty-six minutes he bore down on his prey, with the French shot falling about the British ship, until at 1230 precisely the *Duc de Chartres* hauled her wind, laid herself at point-blank range alongside the enemy ship and opened fire.

For one hour and ten minutes the two ships pounded each other remorselessly. The French, as was their wont, shot high to demolish the enemy's rigging and thus impair its mobility. The British, as was their practice, swept the enemy's decks to kill men and destroy morale. At 1340 the French had had enough and struck their colours. The ship was the Corvette de l'Roi *L'Aigle* commanded by Capitaine Limoine Prineuf who had been killed, together with twelve of his men, during the action. Two Lieutenants and a further thirteen men had been seriously wounded. The *Duc de Chartres* had suffered severe damage to her spars, rigging and sails but she had not lost a man.

The *Aigle,* they were told, had left the Cape thirteen days earlier and had been bound, as Captain Purvis had surmised, for Chesapeake Bay. Her normal complement was 160 men, as opposed to the *Duc*'s 125, but she had only 138 aboard during this engagement. The afternoon was spent in transferring the French prisoners into the *Duc de Chartres* and in rigging jury spars, repairing rigging and swapping or replacing sails damaged in the fight. Having placed a prize crew aboard *L'Aigle* and completed sufficient repairs to his own ship to enable him to limp home, Captain Purvis made sail and ordered a course for New York. He judged that the action had taken place some thirteen leagues east-by-south of Cape Henry, Virginia.

* * *

Captain Purvis, as we have referred to him thus far, and as he would have been addressed by his crew and other contemporaries, did not actually hold the rank of Captain in the Navy. His rank was Master and Commander but, because he was in command of a small warship, of which he was the captain, he held the courtesy title of

Captain. He aspired, naturally, as did all commanders of minor men-of-war, to the next important step in his career when he would be 'made Post' — promoted to the rank of Post-Captain when he would be eligible to command a ship of-the-line, a post-ship, and could style himself Captain Purvis at all times.

It had been a long and hard struggle to reach his present position. Though he had been at sea since the age of fourteen, he had lacked the active patronage which was so necessary for rapid promotion in the Navy and, despite an exemplary record, had had to wait until the age of thirty-one for his Lieutenant's commission and thirty-four for his first command.

Born in Stepney on 13th March 1747, he had spent his first seven years in an Admiralty house which came with his father's job as Secretary to the Sick and Wounded Board. In 1754 his father was appointed Clerk of the Cheque and Storekeeper to the naval dockyard in Harwich where the family spent the next seven years until young John went to sea as a boy in H.M.S. *Arrogant* in 1761.

His great-grandfather, George Purves, had been the younger son of a younger son of Sir William Purves Bart., a landowner in the Scottish Borders and H.M. Solicitor-General for Scotland. George Purves migrated to England around the year 1670 and went to sea eventually becoming Captain, and probably part-owner, of an armed merchantman trading with the American colonies. He certainly prospered and in 1712 had bought the estate and recently-built mansion house of Darsham in Suffolk thereby founding the Darsham line of the Purves family which was to be continuously involved in the armed service of the Crown over the next two centuries.

George Purves's eldest son, another George, adopted the anglicised version of the family name, Purvis, and became a Post-Captain and Commissioner of the Navy as well as serving as Member of Parliament for Aldeburgh in Suffolk. His eldest son, Charles Wager Purvis, became a Rear-Admiral and inherited the Darsham Estates on his father's death. George, a younger son, started life as his father's clerk at the Admiralty and from there progressed through a series of increasingly responsible appointments as an Admiralty official which led him, as we have seen, to Stepney and then to H.M. Dockyard at Harwich.

   This George Purvis married Mary Oadham, daughter of Catesby
Oadham, a Member of the Council of Madras, who had done well
for himself in the service of the Honourable East India Company.
Though George, as a younger son, brought little in the way of
wealth to the marriage, his wife inherited the estates of Porters in
Essex and Bockenden Grange in Warwickshire from her cousin
Lady Clifton. These, in due course, were passed down to their eldest
son, Richard, also a Captain in the Navy.
   During his early years at sea, John Child Purvis received little
from his father in the way of financial support or assistance in
advancing his prospects. As a senior Admiralty official, George
Purvis must have come into contact with powerful men and
influential senior officers but there is no record of his ever having
used his position, as was the universal practice of the age, to further
the careers of any of his three sons.
   John Child Purvis served in the *Arrogant*, on the coast of Spain,
from April 1762 to August 1763. It was at the tail end of the Seven
Years War in which Britain had thwarted French ambitions in North
America and India and had established an overwhelming naval
supremacy in European waters. In 1761 Spain had foolishly entered
the war on France's side which cost her the almost immediate loss
of her two principal sources of overseas wealth: the Havannah
[Cuba] in the West Indies was captured by a British force in August
1762 together with a squadron of Spanish warships and over 100
richly-laden merchantmen. This was followed in October by the
capture of Manila, an equally important source of Spanish revenue
in the east. The Treaty of Paris in 1763 ended the Seven Years War
but left both France and Spain with severely wounded pride which
would, inevitably, have to be avenged at a later date. When the
peace was signed, John Child Purvis had acquired eight months
service as an Able Seaman and eight months as a Midshipman
during which time, according to his Captain, John Amherst, "he
behaved himself with great sobriety, dilligence [sic] and care and
always obedient to command". This was to be the pattern of his
service for the next fifteen years of peace as he found himself
relegated to the despairing pool of 'oldsters' — the elderly
Midshipmen without patronage who lay stranded in their rank as
they watched their younger, and frequently less able, compatriots

rise above them through the pressure of influential relatives or friends. It was probably during these years of despair and indigence that the young John Purvis denounced within himself the custom of primogenital inheritance and determined that, should he ever have sons of his own, which seemed unlikely with his present professional prospects, he would treat them equitably and would move heaven and earth, within his sphere of influence, to further their careers.

At last, on 11th February 1778, Purvis was offered a Lieutenant's commission in the *Invincible*, Flagship of Commodore John Evans and commanded by Captain Antony Parry. His first two months aboard were spent in Portsmouth Harbour and at the beginning of May the ship was moved out to anchorage in Spithead to prepare for the Royal Review.

At 1000 on Monday 4th May, in fair weather with light winds, the Royal Yacht *Augusta* came out of the harbour attended by the Admirals and Captains of the Fleet in their barges. As they passed through the anchored Fleet, each ship fired off a 21-gun salute and at 1100 King George III went aboard the Flagship, *Prince George*, when Admiral Keppel's Flag was hauled down and the Royal Standard, Admiralty Flag and Union Flag were hoisted in its place. The whole massed Fleet then fired a further 21-gun salute. The following day the same procedure was repeated and, in the afternoon, the Queen made a tour of her own when she received similar compliments from every ship in the Fleet. Their Majesties then returned to harbour to the thunder of yet another 21-gun salute. King George was obviously impressed by what he had seen, and heard, as within days each ship received the King's gift comprising, in the *Invincible*'s case: 180 lbs. of beef, 1,350 lbs. of flour, 112 lbs. of suet, 246 lbs. of raisins and 300 gallons of rum "all of which was in consideration of the Review at Portsmouth".

Invincible weighed anchor on 10th May and moved to St. Helens to continue more mundane and less rewarding duties. Britain had been at war with her American colonies since 1775 and the serious defeat of a British army at Saratoga in October 1777 persuaded France that it was time to seek revenge for her humiliations in the Seven Years War. In March 1778 the British Government was advised that France now recognised the sovereignty and independence of the thirteen United States of America and had signed an alliance with the colonists. The war thus assumed a new global dimension and the following month a French squadron of twelve ships of-the-line and five frigates, commanded by the Comte d'Estaing, broke out of the Channel and sailed for North America.

It was therefore decided to form a squadron of thirteen ships of-the-line, including *Invincible*, and one frigate, from the Channel Fleet, to sail for American waters in support of Lord Howe's squadron of six of-the-line *[Table A]*.

TABLE A. VICE-ADMIRAL BYRON'S SQUADRON FOR AMERICA — 9th June 1778

Rate	Ship	Commander	Guns	Men	Division
3rd	*Conqueror*	Captain Graves	74	600	**VAN** *Hyde Parker Esq. Rear-Admiral of the Blue*
3rd	*Sultan*	Captain Thurlock	74	600	
3rd	**Royal Oak**	**Rear-Admiral Parker** **Captain Evans**	74	615	
3rd	*Albion*	Captain Bowyer	74	600	
3rd	*Bedford*	Captain Affleck	74	600	**CENTRE** *Hon. John Byron Vice-Admiral of the Blue*
3rd	*Russell*	Captain Drake	74	600	
2nd	**Princess Royal**	**Vice-Admiral Byron** **Captain Blair**	70	770	
3rd	*Culloden*	Captain Balfour	74	600	
3rd	*Grafton*	Captain Wilkinson	74	600	
3rd	*Monmouth*	Captain Collingwood	64	500	**REAR** *John Evans Esq. Commodore*
3rd	**Invincible**	**Commodore Evans** **Captain A. Parry**	74	615	
3rd	*Cornwall*	Captain Evans	74	600	
3rd	*Fame*	Captain Colby	74	600	

Frigate: *Guadaloupe*

This Squadron, commanded by Vice-Admiral Hon. John Byron, sailed for America on 9th June and encountered appalling weather in mid-Atlantic. At midnight on Thursday 13th August during a strong gale, *Invincible*'s mainmast sprung close down to the wedges on the lower gun deck. Taking up the mainsail and lowering the yard did not improve matters and the order was given to cut away the mainmast. This was completed at 0400 shortly after which the mizzen mast went. Then at 0500 the foremast went close to the fo'c'stle deck, killing a Midshipman, Edward Willson. For the next four days the crew worked around the clock raising sheerlegs for fitting jury masts for the fore and main and rigging them. The longboat's mast was put into service as a mizzen topmast.

Two weeks later on 3rd September the ship limped into St. John's Harbour, Newfoundland. Five crew members had been lost on the voyage out and a further two were killed over the next two months during which the ship was re-rigged, a new foremast made on shore and the hull recaulked. On 31st October *Invincible* sailed from St. John's as part of the escort for a convoy to England and anchored at Spithead on 23rd November having lost a further two crew members on the homeward passage. It had been an unlucky voyage for Lieutenant Purvis in his first appointment as a commissioned officer but one which had taught him much about crisis management and the need for resourcefulness in the face of persistent adversity.

On 23rd January 1779 *Invincible* entered Portsmouth Dockyard where the ship's company spent the next two months in clearing out the ship — sails, stores, ballast, etc. — in preparation for a complete dockyard refit which would include copper-sheathing the bottom. Then on 29th March Vice-Admiral George Darby hoisted his Flag in the *Britannia,* commanded by Captain Charles Morice Pole, and Purvis was appointed as fourth Lieutenant.

The first six days of April were spent in trying to move *Britannia* from Portsmouth Harbour to anchorage in Spithead. On Friday 2nd April the pilot came on board and the signal for assistance was made. Fifty men each from *Formidable, Duke, Valiant* and *Robust* reported on board but the attempt had to be abandoned. The next day they were joined by a party of thirty-five marines from Headquarters but still to no avail. It was the same on the 4th, 5th and 6th — the wind was not favourable and the ship was making one inch of water every hour; but on the 7th the weather improved and they were able to slip the bridles and come to sail. At 1500 the ship anchored in Spithead. Two days later she sent her boats in response to a distress signal from the *Resolution* which had run ashore on the Dean in trying to enter harbour.

Britannia remained at anchor in Spithead until June 1779 when Spain, now anxious to redress her grievances against Britain, joined the war on the side of France. Political polarization among the senior ranks in the Navy had created a situation in which none of Britain's available top Admirals was prepared to take command of the Channel Fleet. Admiral Keppel had resigned his command following the indignity of a politically-motivated Court Martial earlier in the year and Admirals Howe and Barrington were both sufficiently at loggerheads with Lord North's Tory government to refuse to serve. The elderly Sir Charles Hardy had therefore been dug out of retirement to command the force, of which *Britannia* was a part, tasked with blocking an imminent Franco-Spanish invasion.

The French Admiral d'Orvilliers, commanding a massive invasion fleet comprising thirty French and thirty-six Spanish ships of-the-line, was heading up-Channel. At one point the enemy fleet got between the south coast of Britain and Hardy's Channel Fleet causing the civil population in the south of England considerable alarm; by Royal Proclamation all horses and cattle in the coastal areas were driven inland and those coastal residents who could afford to move soon followed them. However, the invasion fleet was ill prepared with insufficient water and provisions and was plagued by a vicious fever which was decimating its crews. On 29th August *Britannia* and the other ships of the Channel Fleet were sighted by d'Orvilliers's huge force. Outnumbered by more than two to one, Hardy had no alternative but to withdraw up-Channel pursued by the Franco-Spanish fleet which, soon afterwards, gave up the attempt and dispersed to its own home ports.

By October, with England still trembling at how close she had come to invasion, the Channel Fleet had been strengthened to forty-six ships of the line. With frigates and other craft, the fleet now comprised eighty-eight sail *[Table B]*.

This enormous force, with *Britannia* as Vice-Admiral Darby's Flagship of the Van Division, weighed anchor from Spithead on 23rd October 1779 alternating between the anchorages at Torbay and Spithead at the end of each Channel patrol.

Then on Monday 13th December, while trying to weigh anchor at Spithead in a fresh gale, *Britannia* ran out of control narrowly missing the *Sandwich* and driving at full force into the *Victory*, the Commander-in-Chief's Flagship. The damage to *Britannia*'s spars and rigging necessitated a five-month stay in the dockyard, alongside the *Essex*, hulk, from where she rejoined the Fleet on 8th June 1780 and resumed Channel patrols.

In March the following year, a Grand Fleet under the command of Vice-Admiral Darby, was formed to escort a large convoy of

TABLE B. ADMIRAL SIR CHARLES HARDY'S CHANNEL FLEET
23rd October 1779

Rate	Ship	Commander	Guns	Men	Division
3rd	*Resolution*	Sir Challoner Ogle	74	600	
3rd	*Invincible*	Samuel Cornish	74	600	
3rd	*Alfred*	William Bayne	74	600	**VAN**
2nd	*Formidable*	John Stanton	90	750	**DIVISION**
1st	**Britannia**	**Vice-Admiral Darby**			
		Captain Charles M. Pole	100	872	*George*
2nd	*Union*	John Dalrymple	90	750	*Darby Esq.*
3rd	*Alexander*	Rt. Hon. Ld. Longford	74	600	*Vice-Admiral*
3rd	*Marlborough*	Taylor Penny	74	600	*of the Blue*
3rd	*Intrepid*	Hon. Henry St. John	64	500	

Frigates: *Scarborough, Ambuscade, Crescent, Champion, Hydra, Triton.*
Sloop: *Bonetta.* **Fire Ships:** *Infernal, Pluto.* **Cutters:** *Tapaguer, Nimble.*

Rate	Ship	Commander	Guns	Men	Division
3rd	*Culloden*	George Balfour	74	600	
3rd	*Buffalo*	Hugh Bromadge	60	420	**FIFTH**
4th	*Jupiter*	Francis Reynolds	50	350	**DIVISION**
3rd	*Defence*	James Cranston	74	600	
1st	**Royal George**	**Rear-Admiral Sir John Ross**			*Sir John*
		Captain John Colpoys	100	867	*Ross Bart.*
3rd	*Thunderer*	Hon. R. B. Walsingham	74	600	*Rear-Admiral*
3rd	*Monarch*	Adam Duncan	74	600	*of the Blue*
3rd	*Arrogant*	John Cleland	74	600	
3rd	*Bienfaisant*	John McBride	64	500	

Frigates: *Diana, Pandora.*

Rate	Ship	Commander	Guns	Men	Division
3rd	*Cumberland*	Joseph Peyton	74	600	
3rd	*Courageaux*	Rt. Hon. Ld. Mulgrave	74	600	**CENTRE**
3rd	*Triumph*	Philip Affleck	74	600	**DIVISION**
2nd	*Duke*	Sir Charles Douglas Bart.	98	750	
1st	**Victory**	**Admiral Sir Charles Hardy**			*Sir Charles*
		Captain Richard Kempenfelt			*Hardy*
		Captain Henry Collins	100	894	*Admiral*
3rd	*Foudroyant*	John Jervis	80	700	*of the White*
3rd	*Princess Amelia*	George Walters	80	650	*and*
3rd	*Terrible*	Sir Richard Bickerton Bart.	74	600	*Commander-*
3rd	*Berwick*	Hon. Keith Stewart	74	600	*in-Chief*
3rd	*Edgar*	John Elliott	74	600	

Frigates: *Southampton, Lizard, Phoenix, Stag, Amazon, Quebec, Apollo.*
Brig: *Drake.* **Sloop:** *Cormorant.* **Fire Ships:** *Firebrand, Incendiary.*
Cutters: *Kite, Griffin, Rattlesnake.*

Rate	Ship	Commander	Guns	Men	Division
4th	*Isis*	John Raynor	50	350	
3rd	*Shrewsbury*	Mark Robinson	74	600	**FOURTH**
3rd	*Saint Albans*	Richard Onslow	64	500	**DIVISION**
2nd	*Namur*	Charles Fielding	90	750	
1st	**Prince George**	**Rear-Admiral Digby**		.	*Robert*
		Captain Philip Patton	90	767	*Digby Esq.*
3rd	*Valiant*	Samuel G. Goodall	74	650	*Rear-Admiral*
3rd	*America*	Samuel Thompson	64	500	*of the Blue*
3rd	*Ramillies*	John Montray	74	600	
3rd	*Centaur*	John N. P. Nolt	74	600	

Frigates: *Richmond, Porcupine, Andromeda.* **Cutter:** *True Briton.*

Rate	Ship	Commander	Guns	Men	Division
3rd	*Hector*	Sir John Hamilton Bart.			
4th	*Romney*	George Johnston	50	530	**REAR**
3rd	*Canada*	Hugh Dalrymple	74	600	**DIVISION**
2nd	*Queen*	Alexander [Jervis]	90	767	
2nd	**London**	**Rear-Admiral Graves**			*Thomas*
		Captain	90	767	*Graves Esq.*
3rd	*Egmont*	John Carter Allen	74	600	*Rear-Admiral*
3rd	*Prudente*	Thomas Burnet	64	500	*of the Blue*
2nd	*Blenheim*	Broderick Hartwell	90	750	
3rd	*Bedford*	Edmund Affleck	74	600	

Frigates: *Brilliant, Media, Amphitrite, Pegasus, Camel.* **Brig:** *Helena.*
Cutters: *Rambler, Flying Fish.* **Fire Ships:** *Salamander, Furnace.*

Rate	Ship	Commander	Guns	Men	Division
TABLE C. VICE-ADMIRAL DARBY'S FLEET FOR THE RELIEF OF GIBRALTAR 22nd March 1781					
3rd	*Marlborough*	Taylor Penny	74	600	**VAN** ⚓ *Robert Digby Esq. Rear-Admiral of the Red*
3rd	*Courageux*	Rt. Hon. Ld. Mulgrave	74	650	
3rd	*Nonsuch*	Sir James Wallace Kt.	64	500	
2nd	*Formidable*	John Cleland	90	750	
2nd	***Prince George***	**Rear-Admiral Digby Captain Williams**	**90**	**750**	
2nd	*Ocean*	George [Durry?]	90	750	
3rd	*Repulse*	Sir Digby Dent Kt.	64	500	
3rd	*Canada*	Sir George Collier Kt.	74	600	
3rd	*Defence*	James Cranston	74	600	
Frigates: *Monsieur, Crescent.* **Fire Ship:** *Firebrand.* **Cutter:** *Peggy.*					
3rd	*Bellona*	Richard Onslow	74	600	**CENTRE** ⚓ *George Darby Esq. Vice-Admiral of the White and Commander-in-Chief*
3rd	*Bienfaisant*	Richard Braithwaite	64	500	
2nd	*Queen*	Hon. Fred. Maitland	90	750	
3rd	*Foudroyant*	Rear-Admiral Kempenfelt Captain John Jervis	80	700	
1st	***Britannia***	**Vice-Admiral Darby Captain Jas. Bradby**	**100**	**887**	
2nd	*Duke*	Sir Charles Douglas Bart.	98	750	
3rd	*Valiant*	Samuel Goodall	74	600	
3rd	*St. Albans*	Charles Inglis	64	50	
3rd	*Fortitude*	Sir Richard Bickerton Bart.	74	600	
3rd	*Lyon*	Hon. Will. Cornwallis	64	500	
Frigates: *Kite, Pheasant, Minerva, La Prudenta, Flora, Emerald.* **Fire Ships:** *Lightning, Harpy.* **Cutters:** *Sandwich, Dorset, Hawk, Folkestone, Goodintent.*					
3rd	*Alexander*	Rt. Hon. Ld. Longford	74	600	**REAR** ⚓ *Sir John Ross Bart. Rear-Admiral of the Red*
3rd	*Dublin*	Samuel Uredale	74	600	
3rd	*Medway*	Harry Harmood	60	420	
2nd	*Namur*	Herbert Sawyer	90	750	
1st	***Royal George***	**Rear-Admiral Ross Captain John Bourmaster**	**100**	**650**	
2nd	*Union*	John Dalrymple	90	750	
3rd	*Inflexible*	Rowland Cotton	64	500	
3rd	*Edgar*	Erasmus Gower	74	600	
3rd	*Cumberland*	Joseph Peyton	74	600	
Frigates: *Ambuscade, Vestal.* **Fire Ship:** *Furnace.* **Cutter:** *Amelia.*					

transports to relieve Gibraltar which was again under heavy siege and had not been supplied since the previous February *[Table C]*.

The British occupation of this fortress since its capture by Admiral Hawke in 1704 had been a constant thorn in Spanish flesh and remains so to this day. The Rock had undergone a succession of sieges and blockades; indeed, Lieutenant Purvis's grandfather, Captain George Purvis, commanding the *Dursley Galley*, a 20-gun frigate, had been there as part of Admiral Wager's relief force in the siege of 1727.[1] With the movement of officers, Lieutenant Purvis had by now become First Lieutenant of *Britannia*, the Commander-in-Chief's Flagship, which sailed from St. Helen's on 13th March 1781 in company with the relief force of merchantmen. Further supply ships joined off the Irish coast and the convoy headed south across the Bay of Biscay.

At 0500 on Wednesday 28th March, dawn revealed the *Valiant* in sight ahead and two strange sail to the south. The Admiral despatched the *Marlborough* and the *Cumberland* to chase them. The wind increased to a fresh gale and a signal was made for the Fleet to close up. *Britannia* took in her fore topsail and two frigates were despatched astern to herd the convoy into a tighter formation. By noon *Marlborough* and *Cumberland* were out of sight in the chase.

The following morning the wind had not abated and at 0700 *Marlborough* and *Cumberland* returned bringing with them a prize they had taken — the *Duc de Chartres*, a French privateer from St. Malo mounting 24 guns. The convoy continued south in the strong gale and heavy seas which, next day, broke through *Britannia's* stern windows necessitating emergency repairs.

On the morning of Monday 9th April with the Fleet closing the approaches to Gibraltar Bay, Admiral Darby sent for Lieutenant Purvis and told him that he intended putting the *Duc de Chartres* into commission as a British sloop-of-war and putting him in command in the rank of Master and Commander. His orders were to supply the prize with provisions and cordage from the Flagship, then return to England with the French prisoners and a skeleton prize crew for a refit before entering general service. Two days later Captain Purvis went aboard his new command with his officers and "put in hand some essential repairs, swaid the top mast up and clapt on some good hull lashings". They took on some water from the *Furnace* and the following day, as Admiral Darby's Fleet anchored in Gibraltar Bay, the *Duc de Chartres* set sail for England. Twice during the voyage home she was chased by French ships of-the-line when Captain Purvis discovered that his little sloop had a tidy turn of speed and could show a clean pair of heels to any lumbering two-decker. One of the ships was flying English colours as she approached but Captain Purvis was not to be fooled that easily —

he had seen her earlier with the French ensign and pendant. On 6th May the *Duc de Chartres* challenged a brig flying English colours which, in reality, was a Tartar privateer which Captain Purvis believed might have lately been a British cutter, the *True Briton*. Shots were exchanged but the Tartar thought better of it and fled.

The *Duc de Chartres* entered Mounts Bay on 8th May and a pilot came on board to moor the ship off Penzance where the *Aurora* and the *Squirrel* were already lying at anchor. Captain Purvis went ashore with the despatches and to make arrangements for the French prisoners to be received at Penzance. An absence of wind kept them moored in Mounts Bay for nine days but on the 16th there was enough to enable them to make sail and proceed up-Channel. The following day they sighted a vast crowd of forty-five sail to windward which was soon identified as Admiral Darby's Grand Fleet returning from Gibraltar. The *Duc de Chartres* closed the Fleet and made the Private Signal. At 0500 the following morning, there being no wind, Captain Purvis was rowed to the Flagship where he delivered his despatches to Admiral Darby. Three days later they anchored in Spithead and on the 27th the pilot came on board to take the ship into Portsmouth Dockyard where she was moored alongside the *Milford*, hulk, to be cleared out prior to her refit.

Four months later, on 7th October 1781, newly rigged and painted and the damages inflicted by the *Marlborough* and *Cumberland* repaired, H.M.S. *Duc de Chartres* stood to sea in company with the *Astraea*, the *Rotterdam* and a convoy of fifty-four sail bound for the American Station. The passage was uneventful, proceeding slowly at the pace of the slowest merchantmen until 1st December, between Bermuda and the American coast, when a Spanish privateer of 12 guns and fifty men was sighted. After a four-hour chase she struck to the *Astraea*. A Midshipman and six seamen were put aboard the prize and the *Duc de Chartres* received thirteen prisoners. The convoy entered Charlestown [Charleston] Harbour on 21st December where they found the *Santa Monica* which had come in dismasted and was engaged in making new masts from trees they had cut down for the purpose. The *Blonde* lay alongside her with her main yard secured to act as a crane for stepping the *Santa Monica*'s masts. The *Carysfort* was fitting out alongside Gadson's Wharf and also the *Sandwich*, "a ship bought into the

Service to guard the harbour, having large cannon for this purpose".

For the first six months of the year 1782 the *Duc de Chartres* was employed in escorting small convoys up and down the coast between New York, Georgetown, Charlestown, Savannah and, in June, to Bermuda. Captain Purvis was constantly on the lookout for a prize which would make his reputation and, perhaps, his fortune. Several were challenged but all turned out to be spoken for as prizes of other ships. As prize-money was shared by every member of a ship's company, the excitement of a chase was felt by all as was the disappointment if it turned out to be fruitless.

* * *

So, on 20th August 1782, as the *Duc de Chartres* sailed northwards for New York, her prize following in her wake, her ship's company was in a high state of euphoria — not least her Captain who had shown himself worthy of his command; who had joined that select band of commanders who had cornered and challenged an enemy more powerful than his own ship and had beaten it into submission. The victory was the sweeter in the knowledge that he had done it without losing a single member of his own crew. After twenty-one years of hard fagging with little recognition or reward, his opportunity had come to show what he was made of; and he had not failed; he had engaged the enemy closely with that dogged determination which had marked the British sailor through the centuries — a quality which was esteemed by the British people and, more importantly, recognised by the high command.

It was a quality which was surely in his blood. Seventy-four years previously in 1708, his grandfather, who was serving as First Lieutenant in Admiral Sir Charles Wager's Flagship in the West Indies, had been given command of the *Dunkirk*'s prize, a sloop of 24 guns. He, too, had found his Frenchman and had given chase. The French ship, desperate to escape, ran aground off Cape Francois on the north coast of Hispaniola [Haiti], and the pilot of the *Dunkirk*'s prize ran his charge on to a rock ledge where she started to sink. George Purvis was not to be deterred and prepared to attack his prey in the ship's boats. He ordered three of his wrecked ship's guns to be moved ashore and mounted on a makeshift platform from where they engaged the enemy. Some twenty of his men deserted believing that they were being led to certain death; the rest of the men followed their commander in the boats to attack the enemy who, witnessing with disbelief the strength of their opponents' resolution, declined to fight them hand-to-hand and struck their colours as the British approached. George Purvis and his men kedged their prize off the shore and sailed her triumphantly to Jamaica where he was made Post-Captain and given command of the *Coventry*, frigate, on 22nd May 1709.[2]

His grandson's achievement, if less spectacular, had, on balance been more successful as Captain John Child Purvis was bringing back his Frenchman and his own ship, damaged but serviceable, and with his full complement of 125 men and the same number of French prisoners. Would this, Captain Purvis barely dared to wonder, have earned him, likewise, that step so vitally important to his career in the Royal Navy — promotion to Post-Captain?

At 0500 on Saturday 24th August 1782, the *Duc de Chartres* and her prize stood off Sandy Hook at the mouth of New York Harbour and made the signal for a pilot who came on board within the hour. At 0900 they turned in to Sandy Hook and anchored. At 1400 the following day they crossed the bar and sailed down the line of moored British warships. The first was the *Lion* and, as they approached her, they saw that her whole ship's company was lining the rail to applaud their triumphant return. As they passed, three rousing cheers rang across the water followed by whoops, whistles and taunting shouts of good-natured derision; but the envy and approbation on the faces of their fellow-countrymen was clear enough.

Next was the *Astraea* which had enjoyed her own moment of glory when she had brought in her Spanish privateer last October and was now happy to voice a similar tribute to her erstwhile fellow escort. The same from the *Rhinoceros* and then — a moment of particular pride and delight for Captain Purvis — the old *Britannia* in which he had been serving as First Lieutenant only seventeen months previously; he recognised several of the faces at her rail as the Britannias roared their tumultuous welcome. Further inshore, the crews of two British fireships waved and cheered. Sadly, the joy

of the occasion was marred when one of the *Duc*'s seamen, Robert
Skinner, fell from the main yard and was drowned.

At 1700 the two ships passed Staten Island Bluff and one hour
later anchored in the East River abreast the dockyard to an equally
boisterous welcome from the ships riding there — *Warwick, Santa
Margaretha, Assurance* and *Racoon*. As soon as they were moored,
the French prisoners were sent to the prison ship in the harbour.

The following day as the crew began unbending sails and
stripping the masts preparatory to their being sent ashore for repair,
Captain Purvis received two visitors on board the *Duc de Chartres*
— Rear-Admiral Hon. Robert Digby, to officially congratulate him,
and Prince William Henry, Duke of Clarence, the King's third son
(and future King William IV). The Prince, who had himself served
as a boy in the old *Invincible,* was anxious to hear every detail of
the engagement with *L'Aigle*. One can only speculate as to what the
Admiral, or the Prince, may have intimated unofficially to him as
they took a glass of Madeira in the Captain's small, cramped cabin
that day but, five days later on 1st September, it was announced that
John Child Purvis had been made Post — he was now a full-blown
Post-Captain, Royal Navy.

By the time the *Duc de Chartres* was ready for sea again at the end
of September 1782, Britain's war with her American colonies was
all over bar the shouting. For seven years she had been engaged in
a war, the justice of which was questionable to many British people,
against an enemy which, to her surprise, had proved itself to be
every bit as competent in arms as Britain herself. Besides, the
colonists were mainly of British stock and shared too many British
attributes to engender the depth of animosity which is necessary for
any sort of serious military commitment. Several senior officers of
the Royal Navy, though welcoming any command against the
French, Spanish or Dutch, had declined to serve against the
American colonists.

Since the fall of Lord North's Tory ministry in March, Britain had
been suing for peace and had evacuated all her garrisons except for
New York and Charlestown. In November the Treaty of Paris was
signed which recognised the United States of America and ended
the war between Britain and her former colonies — to become

effective as soon as hostilities with the Franco-Spanish Alliance had ended. Both these countries, which had rallied to America's cause in order to injure Britain and avenge their wounded pride had, in the event, gained nothing: France had suffered another humiliating defeat at the Battle of the Saints in the West Indies earlier in the year and Spain had lost the sources of her overseas revenue. Both nations had lost credibility as European sea powers for the time being.

The Treaty of Versailles in January 1783 ratified the peace with the United States and ended hostilities with France and Spain. Florida and Minorca were restored to Spain but Britain retained Gibraltar. France gained nothing.

On 10th April 1783 with the British naval and military withdrawal from the United States well under way, Captain Purvis laid up the *Duc de Chartres* in the North River, New York, from where she was later sold, and took passage back to England where he was destined to remain ashore on half pay for the next ten years of peace.

CHAPTER 2

Toulon

Thursday 29th August 1793
H.M.S. Princess Royal
Toulon, France

Asignal from Lord Hood's Flagship, the *Victory*, at 0800 had ordered the Fleet to enter the outer harbour of Toulon. Working in against a fresh north-westerly wind, the British ships had passed into La Grande Rade and now lay at anchor under the guns of Fort la Malgue which was manned by 1,500 British soldiers and 200 seamen and marines who had been landed two days earlier under the command of Captain Hon. George Elphinstone of the *Robust*.

Captain John Child Purvis stood on the quarterdeck of his own command, the *Princess Royal*, a second-rate ship of-the-line of 98 guns, and surveyed the vast concourse around him. There were twenty-two ships of-the-line and twenty-nine other vessels — frigates, sloops, brigs, fireships and a hospital ship, the *Dolphin*. There was the old *Britannia* in which he had served fourteen years earlier on the American Station; and the *Amphitrite*, frigate, which he had commissioned earlier in the year and commanded on her passage from Woolwich to Spithead; and the *Colossus*, 74, commanded by Charles Morice Pole, his old Captain in the *Britannia*; and there was the *Agamemnon*, 64, commanded by one

of the youngest Captains in the Fleet, the thirty-five year-old
Horatio Nelson who, having had the right influence, had made Post
at the unusually early age of twenty-one.

Captain Purvis, without such influence, had had to wait until the
age of thirty-four for his promotion and had been extremely
fortunate that his chance had, at last, come during the final stages of
the previous war. Within months of his making Post, peace with
France and Spain had been signed and he, with the majority of sea
officers, including Nelson, had found himself ashore on half-pay.
The difference between a Captain's and a Lieutenant's half-pay
meant the difference between being able to lead the life of a
gentleman, albeit not without restraint, and a miserable, scrimping
existence which usually entailed a degree of dependence upon
family and friends.

His ten years ashore had not been uneventful: on 11th October
1784 he had married Catherine Sowers. Catherine was twenty-
seven years old with a background similar to his own. She had been
born in Deptford where her father, John Sowers, was an Admiralty
official and, at the time of the marriage, held the senior appointment
of Clerk of the Cheque in Portsmouth Dockyard which was, at the
time, the largest industrial complex in the world. The newlyweds
had rented a modest house in Havant and ten months later, on 1st
August 1785, Catherine had presented him with a baby daughter
whom they christened Catherine. The infant only lived for three
months and died on 10th November. Seven months later, on 27th
June 1786, Catherine had a son, John, who died the same day.

The following year Captain Purvis took a short lease on Vernon
Hill House in Bishops Waltham, which had been built for and
previously occupied by Admiral Vernon. Here, on 12th August,
Catherine gave birth to another son whom they christened John
Brett Purvis. The following year the family moved from Bishops
Waltham to Wickham where Captain Purvis had bought a house at
which, on 4th January 1789, another son was born and christened
Richard Fortescue Purvis. But four children in four years was too
much for poor Catherine who died on 3rd February 1789, one
month after Richard's birth, and was buried in the churchyard of
Kingston Church, Portsmouth, where she had been married five
years previously.

In the nearby village of Southwick lived one Daniel Garrett, a gentleman of considerable means, abundant good nature and more than one unmarried daughter, the eldest of whom, Mary Longhurst Garrett, was married to the widowed Captain Purvis on 11th March the following year. Within twelve months she presented him with a son, George, who died in infancy, to be followed by a daughter born on 26th May 1792 who was christened Mary Emily Oadham Purvis.

By this time, Europe was again in turmoil. The War of American Independence had left France with her pride wounded and her economy plundered. It had, however, inspired her people, who lived in misery and poverty under an effete monarchy and a privileged aristocracy, to rise up against the order which oppressed them. In 1789 the French Revolution broke out and renewed war between Britain and France became inevitable.

With some four-fifths of Britain's ships of-the-line 'in ordinary', that is laid up in reserve, a programme of recommissioning was started and those half-pay Post-Captains who were alert to the situation, including Captain Nelson and Captain Purvis, started lobbying the Admiralty for a ship. Purvis travelled regularly to London where he would sit, with other Captains, in an ante-room at the Admiralty awaiting the chance to present his case.

Then in January 1793 the French King Louis XVI was executed by the revolutionaries. Britain promptly expelled the French ambassador in London and the revolutionary government responded with a declaration of war on Britain. Captain Purvis was promised the command of a ship of-the-line but, before this, he was ordered to commission the frigate *Amphitrite* and bring her down from Woolwich, where she was lying, to Spithead where she was to be put into service with the Channel Fleet. It was a duty which sounded simple enough.

The *Amphitrite* was a sixth-rate frigate of 24 guns which had been launched from Deptford Dockyard fifteen years earlier on 28th May 1778. By the standards of the time she was a comparatively new ship but when Captain Purvis went aboard her on Friday 1st February 1793, he found the ship was nothing but a bare hulk with no masts and nothing in her but twenty-two tons of iron ballast. Over the next six weeks he had to fit her out, provision her, crew her and get her to sea none of which was to be achieved without much difficulty and frustration. The first week was spent in taking in and levelling the ship's full quantity of ballast to a total of fifty tons of iron and seventy tons of shingle. The only men he could obtain to undertake this work were eighteen naval pensioners who were boated down daily from the Royal Hospital at Greenwich. On 6th February his First Lieutenant, Spencer Phips, came on board to be joined the following day by the second Lieutenant, William Henry Webley, but despite assurances from the Navy Board that riggers from the Woolwich Dockyard had been ordered to rig the ship, the work was simply not getting done. On 14th February Purvis felt it necessary to write to the Master Attendant of the Woolwich Dockyard to enquire why the Board's directions were not being complied with:

Sir — On the 6th Inst. I recd. a letter from the Navy Board to acquaint me they had directed the officers of Woolwich Yard to employ their riggers on board H.M.S. Amphitrite under my command since which they have worked for the ship not more than three hours. I have therefore to request that you will pleased to give me your reasons why the Navy Board's orders in this particular are not attended to that I may be furnished with the means of representing the same to the Admiralty. I am the more particular in addressing you by letter from my not having had any assistance from the riggers all this day.

The following day twenty-eight seamen from the King's yacht, the *Royal Charlotte,* arrived on board and the rigging of the ship began in earnest as Captain Purvis wrote to the various authorities to obtain the necessary stores and provisions. From the Sick & Hurt Board he requested: "the usual proportions of Elixir of Vitriol and Doctor James's Fever Powder", and from John Newby Esq., Secretary of the Marine Society: "seven stout boys to serve in the capacity of servants on board His Majesty's Ship under my command".

The dockyard painters proved as difficult to procure as the riggers and on 25th February, in desperation, Captain Purvis wrote to the Navy Board requesting that "the proportion of paint should be sent aboard that the crew of the ship may lay it on when there may be time and suitable weather for the purpose". That was, of course, assuming he had a crew; and here lay the greatest difficulty of all.

By the end of February the ship was provisioned with water, rations, boatswain's and carpenter's stores and was fully ballasted and rigged. She now only required her guns and gunner's stores and a crew to man her and it was soon made clear to Captain Purvis that he could expect no help from the authorities with the provision of men; it was up to him to recruit his own crew by his own resources. On 1st March, under the charge of a Thames pilot, the ship moved down-river to Long Reach where the guns and gunner's stores were taken aboard. For the first two weeks of March the ship's boats were employed in attempting to press a crew from the riverside towns and from inbound vessels coming up-river; but the longshoremen of the estuary were wise to the tactics of the press gangs and it was very difficult to find anyone at all. When they did return with two or three men, the chances were that they would have to release them the next day in response to a *habeas corpus* claiming that they were apprentices, indentured servants, or other holders of immunity from impressment. Charged by the Admiralty of having pressed Will Harris, a servant of Lord Onslow, and asked to report whether, at the time of his impressment, he was wearing Lord Onslow's badge, Captain Purvis replied:

I beg leave to acquaint you for their Lordships' information that he had not any badge. He had a certificate, it is true, setting forth his being so employed but from the great number of imposters we daily meet with I certainly did think this one of the many and that he was a very fit person to serve in His Majesty's Navy. I request you will likewise represent to their Lordships that on the 2nd inst. I impress'd two able seamen, Geo. Guthrie and Robt. Mason, and on the 14th I received an Habeas Corpus under the signature of Lord Kenyon which obliged me to deliver them up on a supposition of their being apprentices altho' they had refused to produce their indentures at the time of their being impress'd and each of them between 20 and 30 years of age and from every circumstance I am clearly of opinion they ought not have been taken from the Service.

Acting on a tip from a seasoned impressment officer, Captain Purvis sent boats to lie in wait for the colliers from the northern coal ports inbound up the Thames; but the seamen on the colliers, facing the same danger six to eight times a year, knew exactly how to hide from the press. After two abortive weeks with his boats out every day and night and only a handful of men to add to his crew, Captain

Purvis, again in desperation, wrote to Vice-Admiral John Dalrymple, Commander-in-Chief, the Nore:

I almost despair of benefiting the Service from the men I may raise on this occasion. I have every reason to think my officers have not neglected any means within their power to find out the places of concealment on board the colliers yet I have obtained only four men and those servants who only just come within the meaning of the instructions. The Fox having left the Nore I beg you will please to direct me how I am to proceed.

The solution was ultimately contained in an order from the Admiralty for the *Amphitrite* to use her boats to ambush an incoming convoy of East Indiamen from which to press the men she needed. The convoy was being escorted by the *Regulus*, a 44-gun frigate commanded by Captain James Hewett, whose cooperation Captain Purvis solicited in a letter on 23rd March:

Sir — In consequence of orders from the Lords Commissioners of the Admiralty and Directions which I have since recd. to use every endeavour to impress all the seamen belonging to your convoy, I think it necessary to inform you that the plan of operation is to draw the convoy between the ships at the Nore and the Buoy of the Mouse and when I judge that they are sufficiently advanced for the better executing the orders, I shall hoist an English Red Ensign at the fore top gallant masthead which is the signal established for the convoy to be brought to and all the ships' boats to act. You will therefore please to use your endeavours not only to facilitate the orders above mentioned but likewise impress yourself as many of the seamen of the convoy as possible and give directions to the commander of the Speedwell to do the same.

Thus, crewed largely by unfortunate seamen who had just completed a nine-month passage and had probably not been home or seen their families for the better part of two years, the *Amphitrite* sailed for Spithead where she dropped anchor on 4th April 1793.

The following day Captain Purvis transferred to his new command, the *Princess Royal,* and read his Commission to the assembled ship's company. *Princess Royal* was a second-rate line-of-battle ship of 98 guns, seven months older than the *Amphitrite* having been launched from Portsmouth Dockyard on 18th October 1773. Bearing in mind the difficulty he had had in acquiring his crew for *Amphitrite*, it is not surprising that he took several of his key personnel with him to *Princess Royal*.

On 11th April they took aboard ninety men of the 30th Regiment of Foot to act as marines and on the 16th, in company with a convoy of sixty-two sail, *Princess Royal* left Spithead for Gibraltar to receive the Flag of Rear-Admiral Samuel Granston Goodall and thence to join Lord Hood's Mediterranean Fleet off Toulon.

In the port of Toulon the French Mediterranean Fleet, consisting of thirty-one ships of-the-line and twenty-seven frigates, lay inactive due to the divided political allegiances of its crews and of the townspeople of this important naval base and arsenal. The Commander-in-Chief, Rear-Admiral le Comte de Trogoff, was a staunch royalist while his second-in-command, Rear-Admiral Saint-Julien, was an ardent republican.

On arrival outside the port, Admiral Hood received royalist envoys from Marseilles who assured him that the inhabitants of Toulon were strongly for the monarchy and that a delegation from the town would shortly come on board to endorse this assurance. In the meantime, the envoys reported, the townspeople were expecting an imminent attack by the army of the National Convention and had no more than eleven days provisions with which to withstand any form of siege. When this second delegation failed to appear, Admiral Hood sent one of his officers, Lieutenant Edward Cooke, ashore to meet with the Royalist Committee and establish their position. The Committee explained that their previous delegation had been prevented from going aboard the *Victory* by Saint-Julien's people but that the townspeople had declared for Louis XVII and were ready to surrender the port and its Fleet to Lord Hood in return for Britain's assistance. On his way back to his boat, Cooke was arrested but was rescued by a royalist mob and the following day Captain Baron d'Imbert of the *Apollon,* 74, who had been appointed Royalist Special Commissioner, confirmed to Hood that Louis XVII had been proclaimed in Toulon and that the townspeople had placed themselves under his command.

Thus reassured, Admiral Hood prepared to land troops to man Fort la Malgue and ordered all French ships to move into the inner harbour and land their powder; any ships failing to obey this order would be regarded as enemies and would be dealt with accordingly. At this proclamation, Saint-Julien and some 5,000 French seamen abandoned their ships and retired ashore from where they could cause the occupation forces the maximum nuisance.

TABLE D. VICE-ADMIRAL LORD HOOD'S MEDITERRANEAN FLEET AT TOULON — August 1793		
Ship	Commander	Guns
Victory	Vice-Admiral Samuel Lord Hood	
	Rear-Admiral Sir Hyde Parker	
	Captain John Knight	100
Britannia	Vice-Admiral William Hotham	
	Captain John Holloway	100
Windsor Castle	Vice-Admiral Phillips Cosby	
	Captain Sir Thomas Byard Kt.	98
Princess Royal	Rear-Admiral Samuel Granston Goodall	
	Captain John Child Purvis	98
Saint George	Rear-Admiral John Gell	
	Captain Thomas Foley	98
Alcide	Commodore Robert Linzee	
	Captain John Woodley	74
Terrible	Captain Skeffington Lutwidge	74
Egmont	Captain Archibald Dickson	74
Robust	Captain Hon. George Keith Elphinstone	74
Courageux	Captain Hon. William Waldegrave	74
Bedford	Captain Robert Man	74
Berwick	Captain Sir John Collins Kt.	74
Captain	Captain Samuel Reeve	74
Fortitude	Captain William Young	74
Leviathan	Captain Hon. Hugh Seymour Conway	74
Colossus	Captain Charles Morice Pole	74
Illustrious	Captain Thomas Lenox Frederick	74
Ardent	Captain Robert Manners Sutton	64
Diadem	Captain Andrew Sutherland	64
Intrepid	Captain Hon. Charles Carpenter	64
Agamemnon	Captain Horatio Nelson	64
Saint Albans	Captain James Vashon	64

FRIGATES:
Romney, 50, Capt. Hon. William Paget.
Inconstant, 36, Capt. Augustus Montgomery.
Romulus, 36, Capt. John Sutton.
Juno, 32, Capt. Samuel Hood.
Lowestoft, 32, Capt. William Wolseley.
Mermaid, 32, Capt. John Trigge.
Castor, 32, Capt. Thomas Troubridge.
Nemesis, 28, Capt. Lord Amelius Beauclerk.
Amphitrite, 24, Capt. Anthony Hunt..

Aigle, 36, Capt. John Nicholson Inglefield.
Leda, 36, Capt. George Campbell.
Isis, 32, Capt. George Lumsdaine.
Aimable, 32, Capt. Sir Harry Burrard Bart.
Meleager, 32, Capt. Charles Tyler.
Aquilon, 32, Capt. Hon. Robert Stopford.
Dido, 28, Capt. Sir Charles Hamilton Bart.
Tartar, 28, Capt. Thomas Fremantle.

OTHERS:
Dolphin, 44, Hosp. Ship, Com. Jas. May.
Camel, 20, St. Ship, Com.Benjamin Hallowell.
Bulldog, 14, Com. George Hope
Speedy, 14, Com. Charles Cunningham.
Conflagration, 14, F.S., Com. Edward Brown.
Tisiphone, 12, Com. Thomas Byam Martin.

Gorgon, 44, St. Ship, Com. Chas. Patterson.
Eclair, 20, Com. George Henry Towry.
Fury, 14, Com. Frank Sotheron.
Scout, 14, Brig, Com. Joseph Hanwell.
Vulcan, 14, F.S, Com. John Matthews.
Weazel, 12, Com. William Taylor.

On 28th August the British Fleet was joined by seventeen Spanish ships and various other naval and military contingents from Naples and Sardinia. Captain Purvis sent all the *Princess Royal*'s soldiers aboard the *Robust* for service in the shore batteries together with a contingent of one Lieutenant, a Midshipman and forty-five seamen, which the Admiral had ordered from every British ship, to serve as gunners in the forts. The troops were landed and took possession of Fort la Malgue without opposition. On the same day Rear-Admiral Goodall was appointed Governor of Toulon.

At the end of August, the advance guard of a republican army from Marseilles, which city they had recently, and bloodily, purged of royalist support, was defeated and driven back from Ollioules by a British and Spanish force under Captain Elphinstone. This force was drawn from the defenders of Fort la Malgue necessitating a further contribution of two officers and thirty seamen from each of the British ships to take their places. *Princess Royal* was now so short of officers that when an order was received to send a party ashore to dismount a battery on the south-west side of the Cepét Peninsula, Captain Purvis had to lead it himself; nine cannons, a 36-pounder and a 13-inch mortar were spiked up and thrown down on to the rocks below.

Despite their defeat at Ollioules, the revolutionary government in Paris knew that resistance in Toulon had to be crushed at any price. A Bourbon enclave on the south coast would not only give Britain effective control of the western Mediterranean but could threaten the very survival of the new French order. The army from Marseilles, under Citizen-General Carteaux, a policeman in civilian life, was therefore reinforced to 32,000 men and a further force of 5,000, under Citizen-General Lapoype, was summoned from the east. These two forces converged upon and encircled the town and, during the first half of September, aided by the renegade French seamen, caused perpetual annoyance to the occupation forces though doing nothing significant to bring about their eviction. Lord Hood eventually decided that it would be worth the sacrifice of a few French warships to be rid of the troublesome seamen; so on 17th September some 7,000 of them, together with their officers, were repatriated to their home ports in four of the French ships one of which ran aground and sailed again two days later.

On the previous day an event had occurred which was to change
the whole course of the siege. Carteaux's Artillery Commander had
been wounded and had been replaced by a young Captain of
Artillery called Napoleone Buonaparte. Two days later the French
opened two new batteries at the head of the north-west arm of the
harbour where Lord Hood had positioned a British-manned French
frigate, the *Aurore, 36,* and two armed pontoons, one of which was
manned by two Midshipmen and forty seamen from *Princess Royal,*
to cover Fort Malbousquet and defend the head of the harbour. In
addition to this, Captain Purvis had to arm and keep manned from
his ship another armed pontoon mounting four 24-pounders
covering the isthmus leading to Cap Cepét.

A third republican battery was shortly afterwards opened by
Captain Buonaparte and, now under proper command, the enemy
artillery began to achieve a new power and accuracy. The *Saint
George,* Flagship of Rear-Admiral Gell, was moved up to assist the
Aurore. Four seamen were killed and seventeen wounded when a
lower-deck gun burst in the *Saint George.* The enemy were now
firing red-hot shot. *Princess Royal*'s pontoon had two of its guns
disabled, two men killed and a Midshipman and four men wounded.
The other pontoon was so badly damaged that it sank at its
moorings.

Up until now, Captain Purvis in the *Princess Royal* had been
involved in a number of activities with a large number of his crew
seconded to man the armed pontoons, to act as gunners in the forts
or as labourers on the defensive works being constructed ashore.
His carpenters were in constant demand for work ashore or for
repair work in other ships which had been damaged in action.
However, on Monday 23rd September the Admiral ordered
Princess Royal to move up the harbour to the action zone to take
over from the *Saint George* which was sailing for Genoa as
Flagship of an allied squadron. Captain Purvis "sent to all the ships
in the Fleet to borrow launches, hawsers, etc. but could get none",
so his move had to be postponed until the following day when,
having fired a 21-gun salute to mark the anniversary of the King's
Coronation, he began to warp his ship up the harbour until it was
close to the *Saint George,* under the enemy's batteries. Here he
moored with four anchors to hold the ship broadside to the shore:

"the Best Bower in 5 fathoms to the N.W., the Small Bower in 6 fathoms to the S.E. with springs to the rings of both anchors and stream anchors out on the starboard bow and larboard quarter."

The *Princess Royal* was cleared for action and carronaded the town of La Seyne throughout the night and, the following day, opened up with her lower-deck guns. A Spanish line-of-battle ship joined to assist in the bombardment. The enemy batteries were now returning a steady fire which was finding its mark "but the Spanish ship having received a shot or two haul'd off and left us".

There was then established a daily pattern of engagement which was to continue for the next six weeks during which *Princess Royal* exchanged fire with the enemy almost every day losing many of her men and being much cut up in the process. Each day Buonaparte's batteries on the La Seyne to Toulon road, which were temporary fortifications of fascines, sandbags and earthworks, were destroyed by the *Princess Royal*'s bombardment and the French gunners killed or driven out; then each night, under cover of darkness, the French pioneers would move in and rebuild the fortifications so the batteries were ready for action the following morning. During the night *Princess Royal* would fire into the town of La Seyne "by way of keeping up the alarm and harassing the enemy tho' much mischief was done to the poor inhabitants".

At 0400 on 1st October, Purvis heard musket fire and the sound of a battle from Mount Faron which towers above Toulon on the northeast side of the town. At 0730 he heard that the republicans had captured the heights and, later in the day, he and the crew of *Princess Royal* had a grandstand view as an allied army of 3,500 scaled the heights and drove the republicans from their newly-acquired position: "the French gave way and fell on their rear who almost immediately began to retreat down a precipice from the redoubt exposing themselves to the fire of Fort Pharon and our victorious army who cut them to pieces many falling down the hill and driving others before them."

Some 200 republicans were killed in this engagement for the loss of twelve allied troops killed and twenty wounded. However, the euphoria of this victory was to be short lived.

The defences of Toulon consisted of a fifteen-mile long ring of detached forts encircling the heavily-fortified town and port. At the head of the promontory to the south of where the *Princess Royal* was moored were two allied-held forts, one at each corner, Fort L'Eguillette and the Tour de la Balaguier. It was immediately evident to Captain Buonaparte that in the control of the former lay the key to control of the whole harbour; but to convince his amateurish citizen-commanders was another matter. A half-hearted attempt by the republicans to storm L'Eguillette merely served to alert the allied command to its tactical importance. They responded with the immediate construction of new defensive works on Mont Caire, the high ground in the centre of the promontory, in which were mounted twenty cannon and four mortars. This they called 'Fort Mulgrave' but, so strong and seemingly impregnable were the works, the French knew it as 'Le Petit Gibraltar'.

Following an adverse report on the treatment of British sick and wounded in the hospital on Cepét, Rear-Admiral Sir Hyde Parker directed Captain Purvis to pay an inspection visit, when time and duty permitted, and report back to him. With his ship short-handed and engaged in operations, it was three weeks before he could implement the Admiral's instructions which he did on the morning of 7th October; but he could find no fault: "I have this morning visited the hospital in Scipet and find that the men are taken proper care of and that there appears to be no cause of complaint whatever."

On 19th October Captain Buonaparte was promoted to Major and authorised to augment the republicans' wholly-inadequate siege train. Collecting big guns from fortifications all along the coast, as far away as Antibes, he eventually had at his disposal 194 assorted guns manned by sixty-four officers and 1,500 gunners, many of whom were retrained infantrymen. At this stage the republicans had some 30,000 men against the allies' effective force of 12,000 British, Spanish, Neapolitan, Piedmontese, Sicilian and Maltese — with all the command difficulties endemic within such a mixed-nationality force. Buonaparte could not, however, persuade Carteaux to adopt the assault plan which he knew would bring rapid victory. He had, though, established eleven new batteries which would be pivotal in the eventual assault on Fort L'Eguillette.

On 23rd October, as the daily exchange of fire between the La Seyne batteries and the *Princess Royal* commenced, two 32-

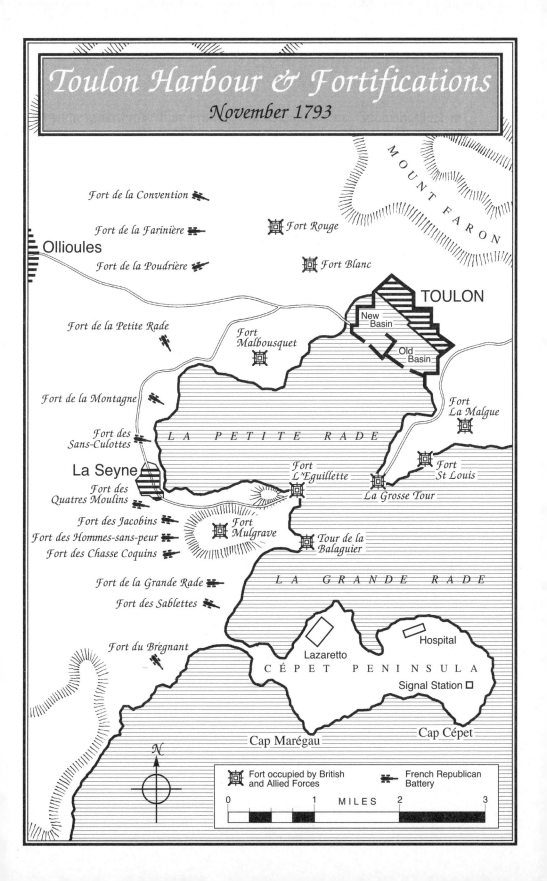

Toulon Harbour & Fortifications
November 1793

MOUNT FARON

Fort de la Convention

Fort Rouge

Fort de la Farinière

Ollioules

Fort Blanc

Fort de la Poudrière

TOULON

New Basin

Fort de la Petite Rade

Fort Malbousquet

Old Basin

Fort La Malgue

Fort de la Montagne

LA PETITE RADE

Fort des Sans-Culottes

Fort St Louis

La Seyne

Fort L'Eguillette

Fort des Quatres Moulins

La Grosse Tour

Fort des Jacobins

Fort Mulgrave

Fort des Hommes-sans-peur

Tour de la Balaguier

Fort des Chasse Coquins

Fort de la Grande Rade

LA GRANDE RADE

Fort des Sablettes

Fort du Brégnant

Hospital

Lazaretto

CÉPET PENINSULA

Signal Station □

Cap Cépet

Cap Marégau

N

Fort occupied by British and Allied Forces

French Republican Battery

0   1   MILES   2   3

pounders on the lower gun deck burst killing William Pearse, the
Master-at-Arms and three seamen — Robert Hamilton, Will
Parsons and Michael Eadey. Lieutenants Maston and Ellison and a
further twenty-nine seamen were wounded, many of them seriously.
The middle deck above the guns suffered considerable damage, one
of the beams being split to pieces and some of the knees and carling
ledges being displaced and broken, thirteen planks of the middle
deck broken and many others lifted from the beams. Captain Purvis
could not understand why the guns had burst: "Being 32-pounders
they were served with 13 lbs. of powder and never had more than
one Round Shot, tho' the instructions point out 14 lbs. of powder for
service."

On examining the wrecked guns, he noticed pieces of iron
resembling spike nails in the body of the metal which he thought
may possibly have weakened the guns. However: "To prevent in
future the risque of the like accidents I shall in future use only one-
third of the weight of the shot in powder."

Although *Princess Royal* was operating with more than 250 of her
officers and men seconded to shore and boat duties, the orders for
further secondments kept coming. A demand from Rear-Admiral
Sir Hyde Parker, on the same day as the gun bursts, for another
Midshipman for shore duties brought the following rejoinder from
Captain Purvis:

In consequence of having directions to send another Midshipman to Hauteur de
Grasse, I beg leave to represent that the Quarter Deck is so very much reduced
that I hope you will favour me by not requiring any more from me, particularly
while the two Lieutenants are rendered unable to do their duty.

The harbour of Toulon is periodically subjected to winds of great
violence and, under such conditions, it was necessary to let go the
springs and allow *Princess Royal* to swing to the wind thereby
bringing her closer to the shore than usual. The enemy batteries
would naturally take full advantage of this situation when the
British ship was often unable to return their fire effectively. On one
such occasion, on 3rd November, they managed to land a red-hot
shot through one of the lower gun ports disabling the gun by
knocking it off its trunnion and wounding five men. The shot went

through the middle gun deck where it was taken up in a bucket and thrown overboard. Captain Purvis reported to the Admiral: "It was perfectly red hot and burnt the deck as it rolled."

The shore batteries continued firing throughout the night and, although they did not manage to hit the ship again, Purvis was sure they were using hot shot "from seeing a fire in the battery and the particular noise the shot made when taking the water in the middle watch".

Two days later Lord Hood, realising that the increased efficiency of the republican artillery had now made *Princess Royal*'s position untenable, ordered Captain Purvis to kedge back out of range. Three days after this a party of seamen attempted to recover the best bower anchor and cable, which they had had to leave behind marked with a buoy, but the pontoon from which they were working came under such heavy fire from the enemy that they had to abandon the attempt and complete the recovery under cover of darkness. On the 9th eight shipwrights from other ships in the Fleet came aboard to start work on repairing the damage the *Princess Royal* had suffered and on the 14th the enemy opened fire on the British ships with a huge new gun which Captain Purvis was certain could throw a ball three miles.

The news that Marie Antoinette, Queen of France, had been guillotined in Paris reached the British Fleet at Toulon on 17th November and the order was issued for all officers to wear mourning dress for a period of three weeks.

Meanwhile, in the republican army, Carteaux had been replaced by Citizen-General Doppet, a dentist in civilian life, who proved no more competent than his predecessor; then, on 16th November the veteran General Dugommier was appointed and the republicans were at last under command of a professional soldier who surveyed and immediately understood the situation: "There is only one possible plan," he wrote to the Minister of War, "—Buonaparte's."[1]

On Sunday 24th a melancholy ceremony was conducted aboard the *Princess Royal* when the effects of those sailors who had been killed in action, or subsequently died of their wounds, were auctioned at the mast. Because the proceeds would go to the widows or dependants of their dead shipmates, the custom was that the members of the ship's company would bid far in excess of the actual value of each item — a tradition which continues in the Royal Navy to this day.

Six days later a strong force from Fort Malbousquet under the command of Lieutenant-General O'Hara, Commander-in-Chief of the allied land forces, stormed and captured the republican Fort de la Convention but, Captain Purvis recorded: "Unfortunately a party of the Royals whose zeal got the better of the rules of good order, pursued the fleeing troops of the enemy, and being followed by other troops of the Allied army, threw the whole into confusion." These troops, being cut off from the main body of the allies, were slaughtered by the republicans who then mounted a counter attack on the fort which they recaptured before the allies had had a chance to spike up the guns. Both Buonaparte and General Dugommier took part in this action which resulted in over 600 allied casualties and the capture of General O'Hara.

On 14th December the republicans, whose strength had now increased to 45,000 against the allies' 9,000, opened fire on Fort Mulgrave from the three batteries which Buonaparte had established to the north. There followed a violent, 48-hour artillery duel. The centre of the three French forts which was closest to the guns of Fort Mulgrave had suffered such crippling casualties that there was a reluctance to man it. Buonaparte ordered a sign to be erected at its entrance: *"Batterie des Hommes-Sans-Peur"*, the Battery of the Men without Fear. There was no shortage of volunteers thereafter. Throughout the bombardment Buonaparte commanded from the most exposed position aided by a fearless young Burgundian Sergeant, Andoch Junot, who would later become one of his most trusted Generals. Two days later, in a violent storm with heavy rain and gale-force wind, 7,000 republican troops stormed Fort Mulgrave. The first wave was repelled by the British and Piedmontese defenders. The second wave was led by Buonaparte on horseback; his horse was shot from under him and he continued on foot. Two hours of furious hand-to-hand fighting ensued with the French suffering more than 1,000 casualties; Buonaparte was wounded in the thigh by the deep thrust of an English Sergeant's bayonet. But the republicans' weight of numbers prevailed and at three o'clock in the morning 'Little Gibraltar' fell to be shortly followed by Fort L'Eguillette and the Tour de la

Balaguier. Some 250 of the British defenders were put to the sword including Midshipman Wilkie and nine seamen from the *Princess Royal*.

The French were now masters of Mont Caire from where they could pound the allied Fleet with their heavy artillery which, effectively, placed them in complete control of Toulon and its harbour. To the north of the town General Massena had captured the positions on Mount Faron and all allied troops were retiring to the town ready for evacuation.

Lord Hood called an immediate council-of-war with the allied commanders who decided that Toulon should be evacuated as soon as the remaining French ships had been removed or destroyed and the magazines blown up. At this point the ships of the Fleet would embark the remaining allied troops and as many of the royalist townsfolk as they could safely carry. Since her six-week action with the La Seyne batteries, *Princess Royal* had been making a great deal of water and, on 17th December, had been ordered into the inner harbour for recaulking. Captain Purvis had actually unmoored and was hove to outside the inner harbour entrance waiting for the pilot who, by sheer providence, failed to turn up. *Princess Royal* therefore returned to her mooring in La Petite Rade from where her boats were employed in taking the sick and wounded officers and men from the hospital on Cepét while the rest of the hands prepared the ship for sea.

The evacuation started the same night and continued throughout the following day in an orderly fashion with the exception of the Neapolitan troops manning Fort Malbousquet who panicked and let the side down with a gross display of cowardice. By the evening of the 18th all troops had been embarked with the exception of the Fort La Malgue garrison which was to remain in place until the port and ships had been fired. Coordination of this task was given to Sir Sidney Smith who was in Toulon as a volunteer in the *Swallow,* a small ship he had purchased and fitted out at his own expense. Together with three British and three Spanish gunboats, *Swallow* entered the western basin and, under continuous gunfire from the enemy, began preparations for the destruction of the French ships. The *Vulcan,* fireship, was towed in and placed among them and at 2200 on the 18th was fired together with the powder trains to the magazines and storehouses in the port. By the light of this mighty conflagration, the evacuation continued through the night. The Spanish contingent with Smith, tasked with scuttling the French ship *Iris,* 32, which was loaded with an enormous quantity of powder, decided instead, whether through panic or malice, to set fire to her. The resultant colossal explosion sank two nearby ships, including the British gunboat *Union*, with the loss of three seamen. Having dealt with the western basin, Smith then tried to enter the eastern basin but found that its entrance had been blocked. On his way out he destroyed two French seventy-fours, the *Héros* and the *Thémistocle,* moored in La Petite Rade. Only nine out of thirty-one of the French ships of-the-line had been destroyed with a further four carried off by the allies. With the frigates and corvettes, five out of twenty-seven were destroyed with fifteen being carried off.

During the night, the boats of the *Princess Royal* ferried civilian evacuees out to the ship: "The poor inhabitants are flocking aboard the ships in the greatest number, begging to be received."

The following morning all the boats of the Fleet were sent to Fort St. Louis to embark the La Malgue garrison, the last of the allied troops left ashore. *Princess Royal* took aboard a contingent of royalist French chasseurs, a company of Royal Artillery and the contents of "boats of all descriptions bringing on board troops and emigrants of all sorts — men, women and children", until Captain Purvis adjudged that any more would prejudice the safe working of his vessel and the lives of his own crewmen. At 1800 with a gentle breeze from the east-south-east, *Princess Royal* weighed anchor and, in company with the rest of the combined Fleet, began to work her way out of La Grande Rade.

The allied Fleet evacuated nearly 15,000 of the civil population of Toulon. Those who were left behind, men, women and children, were slaughtered without mercy by the revolutionary troops when they entered the town. Many were drowned as they struggled in the water to follow the departing boats. It is estimated that over 6,000 royalist civilians were murdered by their fellow countrymen at the end of this sad and bloody affair.

The 'Man of the Match' was undoubtedly Major Napoleone Buonaparte who was promoted to the provisional rank of Brigadier-General on 22nd December. His promotion was confirmed by the

Committee for Public Safety on 16th February 1794. It is probable that Captain Purvis never knew the name of the young French artillery officer who had organised the enemy shore defences with such devastating effect, with whom he had exchanged shot on a daily basis and whose skill and persistence had accounted for such serious damage to his ship and the lives of so many of his men. Had he heard the name, it would have meant nothing to him at that time; but it was a name which, before too long, would be spoken of with awe in every corner of Europe.

DISPOSITION OF THE FRENCH SHIPS
17th December 1793

In the Old Basin
Dauphin Royale, 118
Couronne (later *Ça Ira*), 80
Languedoc, 80
Tonnant, 80
Alcide, 74
Censeur, 74
Conquerant, 74
Genereuse, 74
Guerier, 74
Heureuse, 74
Mercure, 74
Souverain, 74
Hardie, 64, (Port Admiral)
Beudeuse, 32
Friponne, 32
Britonne, 24
Hospital Ship
Careening Punt
Masting Sheers

In the New Basin
Triomphant, 80
Centaure, 74
Commerce de Bordeaux, 74
Destin, 74
Dictateur, 74
Du Guay Trouin, 74
Le Lys, 74
Suffisant, 74
Iphigenie, 32
Serieuse, 32
Caroline, 20
Careening Punt

Moored in La Petite Rade
Heros, 74
Thémistocle, 74
Courageuse, 32
Iris, 32
Montreal, 32

CHAPTER 3

Corsica, Genoa and Hyères

Friday 20th December 1793
H.M.S. Princess Royal
Hyères Bay, France

S tanding at the quarterdeck rail of the *Princess Royal,* Captain Purvis surveyed the scene around him. The allied Fleet lay at anchor in Hyères Road, some fifteen miles east of Toulon, having worked its way round the Giens peninsula the previous day following its ignominious departure from Toulon. Among the moored men-of-war, a vast flotilla of boats was passing from one ship to another, laden with troops and civilian evacuees, dropping some here, others there, and at each stop taking on more passengers who were trying to get to other ships in the bay. The massive task of sorting out the 15,000-odd refugees had begun and the first priority was to try and assemble like with like and to reunite families which had been separated in the chaos of the evacuation. He recorded in his journal:

Boats employed transporting troops from one ship to another and berthing and disposing of the emigrants. Sending husbands to look for their wives in other ships and wives for their husbands and children. For the very short warning these poor people had occasioned the greatest confusion, many women even hanging by boats to secure passage to the ships leaving their property behind.

The sight and sound of the panic and terror they had left behind was something which Purvis would never forget. Nor would he forget the misery and despair of those who had been fortunate enough to escape the slaughter as they huddled, dazed and dispossessed, in every vacant space aboard the ship. He himself had managed to pack over 200 refugees aboard *Princess Royal* and this was in addition to the French chasseurs of Captain Hunter's company, the gunners of Captain Stephens's company of Royal Artillery and a mixed bunch of troops of other nationalities.

There was then the question of how to feed these extra mouths; the evacuation had been ordered and undertaken with such haste that the Fleet had had no time to take in extra provisions. Admiral Hood ordered all ships to reduce to two-thirds rations. Also by his order, the chasseurs and the gunners were to receive the same rations as the crew and were to be supplied with 'slops' under the same regulations as British seamen. The refugees fared less well: male refugees received the full allowance of food and two-thirds of wine; women and children got two-thirds the allowance of food and half of wine. However, on the 24th several bullocks were slaughtered for Christmas Day dinner and on that day, by Captain Purvis's decree, all refugees received full rations.

The additional people on board, for which the ship was never designed, inevitably led to a lapse in the traditionally high standard of cleanliness in ships of the Royal Navy. When her foreign guests had eventually been relocated, Captain Purvis therefore ordered the whole ship to be scrubbed with vinegar and fumigated.

Now that the British Fleet was denied the use of Toulon, it had only Gibraltar left as a Mediterranean base and this was really too far west to be of much use in the present operations against France. Corsica would serve well and Lord Hood's intelligence reported that not only were the Corsicans ripe for revolt against their French overlords, but that the republican troops on the island had run very short of provisions. Therefore, having detached a squadron to prevent any attempt to resupply the garrison from the French mainland, he established contact with the leader of the Corsican nationalists, General Pascal Paoli. Paoli, who had been largely responsible for the eviction of the Genoese some thirty years earlier, had initially supported the Girondins, the more moderate faction of the revolutionary movement, rather than the Jacobin extremists with whom his cooperation had been less than wholehearted. Consequently, a warrant for his arrest for 'counter-revolutionary activities' had been issued by the Revolutionary Council to which Paoli responded by declaring Corsica's secession from France. He was therefore delighted to receive Lord Hood's overtures and promised the support of his followers in an insurrection.

The British Fleet sailed on 25th January 1794 Captain Purvis having taken aboard a company of the 25th Regiment of Foot. Strong gales over the next four days dispersed the Fleet and at 0900 on the 29th, *Princess Royal*, under storm canvas and staysails, hauled into Porto Ferrajo on the north coast of Elba where she anchored together with several other ships of the Fleet.

On 3rd February Captain Purvis went aboard the *Victory* to sit on the Court Martial of Captain Anthony Hunt, lately commanding the *Amphitrite*, for the loss of his ship on some rocks south-west of Leghorn [Livorno] — a poignant duty for Purvis with his struggles to get the ship into commission the previous year no doubt still fresh in his mind. Hunt was acquitted as the rocks which had destroyed the *Amphitrite* were submerged and uncharted.

The following day a convoy of light transports arrived from Leghorn and *Princess Royal*'s boats were employed in ferrying troops from the warships to the transports which sailed for Corsica on 6th February escorted by *Alcide, Egmont* and *Fortitude;* and the frigates *Lowestoft* and *Juno.* The *Juno,* commanded by Captain Samuel Hood, had had a lucky escape in January when, unaware that Toulon was now in the hands of the republicans, had sailed into the inner road in the night and anchored just off the arsenal. Challenged by a gunboat, she had realised her mistake, loosed her sails, backed off and stood out to sea again under fire from every enemy battery around the harbour.

The *Princess Royal* arrived in San Fiorenzo [St. Florent] Bay on 9th February by which time the convoy had landed its troops, under the command of Major-General Dundas, and a joint land-sea attack was under way on a Genoese tower on the northern point of the bay. Some eighty-five of these fortified towers were built around the coast of Corsica by the Genoese in the 16th century to act as watch towers for Saracen raiders. Each was in sight of the next so a

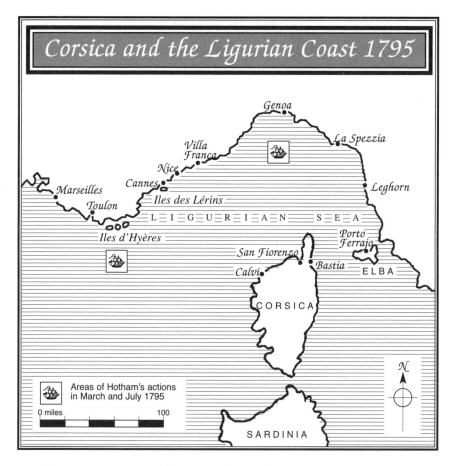

warning message could be passed around the island in one hour and some sixty of them survive to this day. The troops had taken up position on the landward side of the tower while the *Fortitude* and *Juno* bombarded it from the sea. The republican defenders, however, were not to be intimidated and put up a tremendous fight. At 1600, after two and a half hours of firing, the British ships withdrew having been badly mauled. Captain Purvis had witnessed the whole action: "I find the Fortitude suffered much injury from her engagement with the tower but more particularly by the explosion of some cartridges set on fire by the enemy's hot shot."

The *Fortitude* had six of her men killed and fifty-six wounded. But the bombardment from the landward side was too much for the gallant defenders who eventually surrendered to General Dundas.

For the next nine days *Princess Royal* patrolled the approaches to San Fiorenzo Bay [Golfe de St. Florent] where she anchored again on the 19th to learn that the British had stormed and captured the Redoubt de la Convention, the remaining significant republican stronghold:

I found that the redoubt to the westward of the town had been taken by our troops at 9 last night the enemy having been very much harassed by our fire from a battery of two 18-pounders and one 8-inch howitzer on the top of a mountain very near them. The enemy retired to a strong work consisting of a tower with a cannon on it, two or three batteries one of 4 x 24-pounders on a new construction — all which they abandoned before morning and fled to the town where there is a fortification. The two French frigates far within shot of our new posts.

However, at 1600 the republicans, having detained the officer and boat which had been sent to demand their surrender, set fire to one of the two frigates, the *Fortunée,* and allowed the other, the *Minerve*, which had been badly damaged in the action, to sink at her moorings. They then spiked up all their guns and retreated to Bastia leaving a detachment of gunners with five field pieces on a hilltop to the south-east of the harbour to cover their withdrawal.

The boats of the fleet were immediately sent to take possession of the other frigate (the Minerve) which by this time was fast aground and full of water having recd. some of our shot, the enemy having entirely left their caulkers at work on the lower deck. The boats having secured her from being set fire to proceeded to the town and garrison and took possession. Sent 10 prisoners on board the Aurora to proceed to Gibraltar. The remains of the French frigate Fortunée having burnt nearly to the water edge and floating to the northward, sent the boats of the fleet and towed her on shore by which means we shall save her guns, some anchors, etc.

As there was already a *Minerve* in the Royal Navy, the salvaged frigate was later commissioned into British service as the *San Fiorenzo*.

Lord Hood was now ready to proceed to Bastia whose massive and heavily-defended citadel could not be reduced by bombardment from the sea alone. Major-General Dundas, however, who was awaiting the arrival of 2,000 troops from Gibraltar, did not consider he would have sufficient strength for the job until his reinforcements were in place. On 24th February, Purvis sent all *Princess Royal*'s marines and sixty rounds of ball cartridge to the *Victory* which sailed the same day, in company with the *Juno*, to cruise off Bastia so Lord Hood could survey the situation and gather intelligence.

While they were away, *Princess Royal*'s long-overdue caulking was started while fifty of her seamen were sent to assist in fitting out the captured French frigate H.M.S. *San Fiorenzo*. When *Victory* and *Juno* returned two weeks later, the troops from Gibraltar had still not arrived and General Dundas remained adamant that he would not act without them. Lord Hood therefore decided to take matters into his own hands.

On 20th March Purvis sent his boats to water Nelson's *Agamemnon* which was to be sent to Bastia ahead of the main force. Lord Hood then embarked sufficient soldiers from the shore garrison to make good his deficiency in marines; *Princess Royal* took aboard part of the 69th Regiment of Foot. Nelson sailed on the 25th to be followed eight days later by *Victory, Egmont, Fortitude, Alcide, Inconstant, Princess Royal* and one transport with ordnance stores. They anchored off Bastia on 4th April where *Princess Royal*'s soldiers were transferred to *Agamemnon* which, together with *Alcide, Egmont* and *Fortitude*, was to land the troops on the coast to the north of the town.

About 1,250 men in all were landed, the troops under the command of Lieutenant-Colonel Vilettes and a contingent of seamen, including a Lieutenant, two Midshipmen and twenty-five sailors from *Princess Royal*, commanded by Captain Nelson. They were met by a party of General Paoli's Corsican partisans.

By 11th April the British land force and guns were in place and the Governor of the Citadel, General Lacombe Saint-Michel, had refused even to read an invitation to treat with Lord Hood. The British 24-pounders and mortars therefore opened a steady fire which was returned from the Citadel. The siege was to last for thirty-seven days.

Lord Hood had moored his Fleet in an arc just out of range of the enemy batteries and now sent the *Prosélyte,* a French bomb ship taken from Toulon, and two gunboats to bombard the Citadel from close inshore. The republicans answered with hot shot and at 1500 on the 12th the *Prosélyte* was hit and set on fire. Her commander, Walter Serocold, fought her most bravely but, when it was clear his ship could not be saved, he signalled for immediate assistance and Purvis and the other captains sent their boats in to take off the crew. By 1600 she was ablaze from stem to stern.

One of the ships which, in January, Lord Hood had detached from Hyères to prevent supplies reaching Corsica, was the *Ardent*, 64, commanded by Captain Robert Manners Sutton whose brother would later become Archbishop of Canterbury. She had last been sighted observing two French frigates and a convoy off Villa Franca [Villefranche] but had not been seen or heard from since. On 2nd May some grim news reached the Fleet at Bastia: "Rec'd intelligence of many pieces of wreck, etc., with the ship's name 'Ardent' marked on them floating off the coast of France near Toulon which gives us too much reason to conclude that the ship is blown up." She was never seen again and, whatever may have been her fate, there was not a single survivor to tell the tale.

Better news was received on the 16th when the Fleet learned of the capture in January of Martinique by a joint-service force commanded by Vice-Admiral Sir John Jervis and Lieutenant-General Sir Charles Grey. The British ships at Bastia fired a 21-gun salute by order of the Commander-in-Chief. This news was particularly welcome to Captain Purvis as his younger brother, George, was serving aboard the Flagship *Boyne* as Admiral Jervis's secretary.

Throughout the thirty-seven days of the siege, *Princess Royal*'s boats and men were continuously employed in supporting and provisioning the forces ashore. Her sailmakers made tents, her carpenters made tent poles and her seamen made endless quantities of wads for the guns. As well as ferrying stores from ship to shore during the day, her boats patrolled the harbour mouth at night to prevent any vessels sneaking in under cover of darkness with provisions for the beleaguered garrison. The carpenters made a special carriage for a small brass cannon to be mounted in the ship's launch which on 17th May intercepted a boat with forty sacks of flour trying to slip into the port. The flour was sent ashore the following day to the British batteries. On 20th May Lord Hood ordered a ceasefire and sent a boat in under Flag of Truce to parley with the French Governor. After four days of negotiations the surrender was completed, the British took possession of the forts and redoubts on the heights at the back of the town and the Fleet drew back to a better anchorage some two miles offshore. The republican troops in Bastia were taken off by the boats of the Fleet and the women and children were sent to Toulon in transports under Flag of Truce.

Though the republican stronghold of Calvi was yet to be captured, General Paoli felt the moment had now arrived for the island to declare its allegiance to Britain and on 19th June George III was proclaimed King of Corsica and Sir Gilbert Elliot (later Lord Minto) was appointed as his Viceroy.

Meanwhile, on 8th June, *Princess Royal* put to sea again in company with *Victory, Illustrious, Fortitude, Agamemnon* and *Scout,* in response to intelligence that a French Fleet had been sighted in the vicinity. The next day they joined up with the balance of the British Fleet comprising ten of-the-line and several frigates. On the 10th the French were sighted and a general chase was ordered. The French Fleet consisted of seven ships of-the-line and five frigates which the British had left behind at Toulon and which had now been refitted and were at sea under the command of Rear-Admiral Pierre Martin. The following day they were observed to be working in to Gourjean Bay [Golfe Juan].

French fleet of seven of the line and five frigates bearing NE by N working in for the land. Signal 54 to prepare for battle. At noon the whole fleet in chase of the French fleet some of which have anch'd in a bay to the west of Antibes called Gourjean Road and the others preparing to do the same.

Lord Hood drew up a plan to attack the French ships at their moorings the following day but it had to be abandoned partly due to unfavourable weather and partly because the enemy were so well supported by their own shore batteries.

On 11th June the Commander-in-Chief had detached *Agamemnon* and *Courageux* to start preparations for the siege of Calvi and on the 13th sailed himself, with part of the Fleet, to join Nelson, leaving *Princess Royal* and eight other ships of-the-line, under Vice-

Admiral William Hotham, to watch the French Fleet. However, during a spell of bad weather, Admiral Martin managed to slip out of Gourjean Bay and return to the sanctuary of Toulon. Admiral Hotham and his squadron sailed for Leghorn where they anchored on 19th June.

Princess Royal did not take part in the Siege of Calvi which lasted for fifty-one days with the republican garrison surrendering on 10th August. The British casualties included Commander Serocold, who had fought the *Prosèlyte* so gallantly at Bastia. He was one of two naval officers and five seamen who were killed. Nelson was blinded in his right eye when he was hit by some debris thrown up by a round shot. Corsica was now entirely in British hands.

Captain Purvis remained anchored at Leghorn until 21st July with ten Italian caulkers continuing their work on *Princess Royal*'s hull. On 4th July the Fleet fired a 21-gun salute on the orders of Vice-Admiral Goodall on hearing the news that Lord Howe had beaten a French fleet and had taken six of-the-line and sunk two. More detailed reports would eventually show that, in fact, six French ships were captured and only one sunk but this encounter, later to be known as 'The Battle of the Glorious First of June' was Britain's first decisive victory in a major fleet engagement with Revolutionary France and did much for the flagging morale of the Royal Navy in all theatres.

For the remaining months of the year 1794 *Princess Royal* patrolled off the south coast of France, mainly on the stretch between Nice and Cannes which would later be known as the 'French Riviera' or 'Côte d'Azur'. On 12th October Admiral Lord Hood departed for England in the *Victory* handing over command to Vice-Admiral Hotham and on the 16th *Princess Royal* said farewell to Vice-Admiral Goodall who, having obtained three months leave for the recovery of his health, struck his Flag and embarked on board the *Egmont* bound for Leghorn.

Early in November there was a mutiny in the *Windsor Castle* with the crew demanding the removal of their Rear-Admiral (Linzee), Captain (Shield), First Lieutenant (McKinlay) and Boatswain. Attempts to resolve the difficulty were fruitless. Captain Shield and Lieutenant McKinlay asked for a Court Martial on which Captain Purvis sat on 11th November. Both officers were honourably acquitted but Admiral Hotham gave in to the seamen's demands appointing a new Captain, First Lieutenant and Boatswain and even pardoning the mutineers. This feeble appeasement, as we shall see, was in sharp contrast to the way in which Sir John Jervis would later deal with mutiny and the incident is an indication of the poor state of discipline in the Mediterranean Fleet at this time.

Another Court Martial was to follow two months later. On 16th January in the course of a refit in San Fiorenzo Bay, the *Berwick,* 74, lay at anchor in a very heavy cross swell. The ship rolled so violently that she dismasted herself. Captain William Smith, his First Lieutenant and his Master were found guilty of negligence and dismissed from their posts. Captain Adam Littlejohn, who had just made Post, was appointed to command the *Berwick* with orders to rig jury masts and follow the Fleet to Leghorn but, as he left San Fiorenzo on 7th March, he ran straight into Admiral Martin's Fleet of fifteen sail of-the-line and six frigates. Three of the French frigates overpowered the jury-rigged *Berwick* and poor Captain Littlejohn lost, not only his newly-acquired command, but his life as well — the sole casualty of the engagement. (Nineteen years later his son was a Midshipman on board the *Shannon* during her historic fight with the American frigate *Chesapeake.*[1])

The object of Martin's foray into the Ligurian Sea was a half-hearted attempt to recapture Corsica and he had 5,000 troops embarked for that purpose. However, having captured the *Berwick* and seen that the British Fleet was not at San Fiorenzo, he changed his mind. Perhaps he had hoped to catch Hotham unawares and destroy the British ships at their moorings and feared that he, himself, might now be embayed if he attempted a landing.

The main body of the British was anchored at Leghorn where, on 9th March, Vice-Admiral Hotham received news that the French Fleet had been sighted near the Iles des Lérins, off Cannes. *Princess Royal* with the rest of the Fleet immediately weighed anchor and sailed to intercept them. During the night the Admiral received further intelligence that Martin was now in the Gulf of Genoa so he ordered a change in course from south-west to north-west and at daybreak the next morning his lookout frigates sighted the enemy beating in towards Cape Noli [Capo di Noli], clearly intending to return to Toulon.

At 0840 on Tuesday 10th Hotham signalled for all Flag-Officers and a boat from *Princess Royal* took Vice-Admiral Goodall to the Flagship from where he returned at 1100. At noon the *Inconstant* reported sighting a strange fleet to the westward and repeated the signal three times. For the next three days, in light and variable winds with periods of complete calm, the British Fleet struggled to get itself into a position from where it could close and engage the enemy. Each day a General Chase was ordered and subsequently annulled as the wind died leaving the ships wallowing in a heavy westerly swell, unable to maintain an orderly line of battle and within sight of their prey. At night every British ship was ordered to carry a light to avoid, as far as the weather would allow, dispersal of the Fleet in the darkness. On Thursday afternoon a fresh breeze sprang up and it looked like the opportunity had, at last, arrived. At 1600 the Admiral signalled for the Fleet to "Form the Order of Battle on the Larboard Line of Bearing" and then to "Give Chase and Engage the Enemy in Succession". At 1700:

Fresh breezes from the southward. In Chase but, when within random shot of the enemy, the wind headed us and failed. Endeavouring to reform the line. At sunset the French fleet W to SWbyS distant about 4 miles. Our fleet to the eastward of them forming the line.

During the night the French seventy-four *Mercure* lost her main topmast in a squall and was despatched by Admiral Martin to Golfe Juan with a frigate as escort. Then at 0800 the 80-gun *Ça Ira* ran aboard the ship ahead of her and lost her fore and main topmasts. By this time the wind was fresh and the British Fleet was in chase to the south-south-west. Captain Thomas Fremantle in the *Inconstant* was far ahead of the main body of the Fleet and, seeing the *Ça Ira* in trouble, closed on her and delivered a broadside into her port quarter as he passed. The French *Vestale*, 36, rushed to her aid, firing on the *Inconstant* and taking *Ça Ira* in tow but Captain Fremantle was not finished with her and, having come about, he passed down her leeward side and delivered a second broadside. But by this time the damaged Frenchman had cleared away the debris of her broken topmasts and rigging and was ready to return the *Inconstant*'s attack with a broadside of more than twice the weight which killed three seamen, wounded fourteen -nd damaged *Inconstant* to such an extent that she had to fall back. By this time Nelson in the *Agamemnon* had arrived and continued to harass the *Ça Ira* until several powerful French ships bore down on him and forced him to withdraw.

While this action was in progress, the *Bedford* and the *Egmont* had closed with the rear of the French line and were exchanging fire with three line-of-battle ships but at 1500 the wind shifted again, headed the British ships, and put an end to hostilities for the day.

At daybreak on Saturday 14th the French Fleet lay some four miles to windward of the British ships in a south-easterly direction but at 0530 the southerly breeze veered to the north-west placing the British Fleet up-wind of the enemy. During the night the French seventy-four *Censeur* had taken over the tow of the *Ça Ira* and both ships had drifted to leeward of the main body of their Fleet. The leading ships of the British Van were soon upon them and at 0645 Admiral Hotham gave the order for *Captain* and *Bedford* to "Engage the Enemy's Two Ships to Leeward". Five minutes later he urged them to "Engage Closer" but by this time *Captain* was receiving broadsides from both ships as she attempted to get into position to deliver one of her own and *Bedford* was close behind her. The two British seventy-fours exchanged broadsides with the French ships for well over an hour by which time they were so seriously damaged aloft that they had to be towed out of the line.

In the meantime, *Princess Royal, Illustrious* and *Courageux* had been ordered up to assist *Captain* and *Bedford* and had already drawn well ahead, and to leeward, of the rest of the Fleet. Admiral Martin, seeing this new danger to his damaged ships, ordered his Fleet to wear in succession on to the starboard tack and pass in line on the leeward side of the British Van thereby cutting off the British ships from *Ça Ira* and *Censeur*. Yet again, the wind failed at a critical moment and the French ships took an interminable time to pass their sterns through what little wind there was and lay off on the other tack. Then, whether through confusion or by a reluctance to lose what little advantage a windward position might offer, the Captain of the *Duquesne,* 74, the leader of the French Van, led the French line to windward of the British Van leaving the *Ça Ira* and *Censeur* exposed to its fire.

With practically no wind and moving at less than one knot, the *Duquesne,* followed by the *Victoire* and the *Tonnant,* drifted down the windward side of the British line at about a quarter of a mile's range and commenced a fierce exchange of fire with the *Illustrious, Courageux* and *Princess Royal.* As the British ships drew abreast of *Ça Ira* and *Censeur,* their starboard guns were brought into action as well.

0800. The Illustrious, Courageux and Princess Royal who had opened this fire some time before on the body of the enemy's fleet as they ranged along to windward, having about this time approached the crippled ship and her consort, opened their starboard fire upon them and continued to engage on both sides.

With no wind to separate them, the engagement continued for over an hour when, at 0945, the *Illustrious* lost her fore topmast to be followed fifteen minutes later by her mainmast which, in falling, brought down her mizzen too. Shortly afterwards the *Courageux* lost her main and mizzen and the *Princess Royal* her main topmast. Eventually the French line drifted out of range and the now-provident absence of wind prevented the French Fleet from coming in to finish off or capture the crippled British ships.

At 1100 *Ça-Ira* and *Censeur* struck to *Princess Royal.* The former had lost all her masts in the action and the main mast of the latter went overboard soon after she had capitulated.

Sent boats and brought on board the 1st and 2nd Captains of the Ça Ira, the Captain of the Censeur and principal land and sea officers from each of the prizes.

They had put up a gallant fight and, according to the French account of the battle, when Captain Coudé of the *Ça Ira* surrendered his sword to Vice-Admiral Goodall on the main deck of the *Princess Royal*, the Admiral insisted that he should accept his own sword in return "in recognition of your noble courage".[2]

At noon the enemy was standing to the north-west with very light airs from the north-east and was still firing on the British centre and rear until, at around 1400, the wind freshened and Admiral Martin withdrew to the west with all sail set. *Princess Royal* was badly damaged with holes from shot through both sides of her hull and her spars and rigging in a mess. *Illustrious* and *Courageux* were dismasted and unserviceable. In consequence, Admiral Hotham decided, to the dismay of many of his officers including Vice-Admiral Goodall and Captain Nelson, not to pursue the French with the words: "We must be contented. We have done very well."

In reality he had not done well. His Fleet had taken two French line-of-battle ships which must be countered by the loss of the *Berwick* and the crippled *Illustrious* which broke her tow, drove ashore and was wrecked a few days later. On balance he had gained nothing and had lost a rare opportunity to pursue and engage the French Fleet again.

There is one aspect of this affair on which the record should be set straight: almost every account of the engagement credits Nelson with the capture of the *Ça Ira* and fails to recognise the far greater part played by other ships. The *Ça Ira* and *Censeur* surrendered on the 14th to the *Princess Royal* which had three killed and eight wounded in her part of the action and not to the *Agamemnon* as is often stated. *Inconstant* also had three men killed; *Illustrious* and *Courageux* had twenty and fifteen killed respectively; *Captain* had three killed and *Bedford* seven. *Agamemnon* certainly engaged the *Ça Ira* for some three and a half hours on the 13th but this action was not in the same order of ferocity as her later encounters with the other six British ships involved. *Agamemnon* had no seamen killed in the engagement and it must be said that the reputation of Horatio Nelson, our greatest sailor and national hero of all time, has no need of other men's achievements to enhance it.

On 19th March *Princess Royal,* with the rest of the British Fleet and its two prizes, anchored in Porto Especia [La Spezia] to undertake emergency repairs before sailing for San Fiorenzo. From here the Fleet moved to Leghorn Roads where it anchored on 28th April.

Meanwhile, the French Fleet had returned to Toulon where Admiral Martin had been faced with mutiny in certain of his ships and had been reinforced with six of-the-line and three frigates from the French Channel Fleet at Brest. Fearing that this force, now equal in strength to his own, might try and break out into the Atlantic, Admiral Hotham decided to patrol the southern passage to the Strait of Gibraltar south of the Island of Minorca. With seventeen of-the-line, including *Princess Royal,* and five frigates, he therefore sailed from Leghorn on 9th May and cruised in the waters south of Minorca for six weeks, without sighting the French. On 14th June Hotham was joined by nine ships of-the-line — *Victory, Barfleur, Gibraltar, Saturn, Cumberland, Bombay Castle, Defence, Audacious* and *Culloden* — under Rear-Admiral Robert Man, thus restoring the British Fleet's superiority.

The Fleet returned to San Fiorenzo at the end of June from where, on 4th July, Hotham despatched Nelson, now flying the Broad Pendant of a Commodore in *Agamemnon,* with *Ariadne, Meleager, Moselle* and *Mutine* to search for Martin off the Ligurian coast west of Genoa. Three days later the French Fleet was sighted off Cape Melle [Capo Mele] and Nelson's little squadron headed back to Corsica with all sail set and the French in hot pursuit. As he passed Cap Corse at 0700 on the 8th, with the leading ships of the French Fleet almost upon him, Nelson began firing his guns to alert the British Fleet in San Fiorenzo Bay. However, when Admiral Martin drew abreast of the Punta di Canelle and saw twenty-two British ships of-the-line at anchor in the bay, he called off the chase and headed back towards Toulon.

Due to a strong onshore wind, *Princess Royal* and the rest of the British Fleet was not able to put to sea in pursuit until 2100 when a change in the wind enabled them to start working out of the bay. Having sailed on a westerly course for four days, they arrived off the Île du Levant where the Admiral received a report that the French Fleet had been seen south of Hyères only a few hours before. Setting a course to the south-west he ordered his Fleet to keep in close order and prepare for battle. As darkness fell, *Agamemnon* and *Diadem,* which were in the lead, were ordered to keep a good look out ahead and to carry lights. During a stormy night, several of the British ships split their topsails and at daybreak on the 13th the enemy were sighted to the east-south-east about five miles distant.

At 0455 the Admiral ordered the Fleet to wear in succession followed by the signal to form in the order of battle on the larboard line of bearing. At 0510 he ordered them to make more sail and called in all cruisers as the *Agamemnon* and the *Diadem* were detached from the main body of the Fleet. At 0530 he repeated the recall to *Agamemnon* and, shortly afterwards, ordered the Fleet to make all possible sail preserving the order of battle. At 0612, fearing, perhaps, that Commodore Nelson might have plans to act independently of the Fleet, the Admiral, for the third time, signalled *Agamemnon* to return and at 0655 to get in her station. Ten minutes later he signalled again for Nelson to make more sail and to get into station. At 0755 a General Chase was ordered and instructions to engage the enemy "as arriving up with them in succession".

With a brisk wind and regular signals from the Admiral to make more sail, the faster British ships drew ahead and the line became more and more extended. By noon, with the rear of the enemy line less than a mile from the leading British ships, the rear of the Fleet was still some eight miles behind. Then the wind, which until now had promised so well for a fast-moving engagement, dropped away to light and variable airs from the south with periods of calm. The *Victory* opened fire on the enemy rear at 1210 and was soon joined by *Cumberland, Culloden* and *Defence* who together began a running engagement with the three rearmost French ships. The *Princess Royal*, with every sail she could carry, bore down on the enemy line to take her part in the action. At 1300 Captain Purvis observed that *Culloden* had lost her main topmast and at 1345 saw the last ship in the French line, a 74-gun line-of-battle ship, heave to and strike to the *Cumberland*. Two French frigates, the *Justice* and *Alceste,* bore down to take the stricken ship in tow. One lowered a boat to take a tow line over to her but a well-aimed British shot cut the boat in half and the frigates were driven off. Shortly afterwards Purvis noticed that the French prize was on fire and at 1430 had to tack ship to avoid the burning wreck.

Observed great numbers of the enemy who had thrown themselves overboard to escape the flames of the ship on fire swimming in the water and floating on pieces of wood. Sent the boats to pick them up who brought on board the First Lieutenant and 34 men late belonging to L'Alcide.

At this point *Agamemnon*, *Blenheim* and *Captain* were just getting into action and *Cumberland,* having ignored her prize, had drawn abreast of the next rearmost French ship and was about to engage her. The French Van was some four miles to the north working its

way purposefully into Frejus Bay. Then at 1435, to the amazement
of every ship in the Fleet, Admiral Hotham signalled to
"Discontinue the Action". Captain Rowley of the *Cumberland*
could not initially believe that such an order had been issued until
the Admiral repeated it, directed personally with the *Cumberland*'s
pendants and accompanied by a cannon shot to attract attention.

One prize, it seemed, was sufficient for Admiral Hotham to regard
the engagement as a victory but his view was not shared by his
captains who felt cheated of yet another chance to inflict real
damage on the French Fleet. Nelson wrote to his wife: "Had Lord
Hood been here he never would have called us out of action", and
Sir Gilbert Elliot, Viceroy of Corsica, related to his wife how
Admiral Goodall had kicked his hat round the deck of the *Princess
Royal* in a frenzy of rage.

And the one prize was not to last long for at 1545 the *Alcide* blew
up and sank taking over 300 of her men with her. As the enemy
Fleet reached the comparative safety of Frejus Bay, Admiral
Hotham ordered the ships of his Fleet to close around him and sent
for artificers with their tools to come aboard the *Victory* to repair the
damage sustained by the Flagship.

For the next five months *Princess Royal,* as part of the main Fleet
operating from Leghorn and San Fiorenzo, patrolled the waters off
Toulon ostensibly to keep the French Fleet bottled up within. Yet on
14th September, when Hotham's Fleet was off Corsica, a squadron
of six ships of-the-line and three frigates under Rear-Admiral de
Richery managed to slip from the harbour and break out into the
Atlantic. This was particularly serious as a richly-laden convoy of
sixty-three merchantmen was then on passage from the Eastern
Mediterranean to Britain escorted by the *Bedford,* the *Fortitude,* the
captured French prize *Censeur,* which was under jury rig, six
frigates and a fireship.

Admiral Hotham, at anchor in San Fiorenzo Bay, learned of de
Richery's escape on 22nd September but it was not until 5th
October that he despatched six of-the-line and two frigates, under
Rear-Admiral Man, in pursuit. By this time, with the French some
three weeks ahead, there was little hope of catching up with them.
Meanwhile, the convoy had split into two halves one of which, with
the *Fortitude, Bedford* and *Censeur,* was intercepted off Cape St.

Vincent by de Richery who captured thirty of the thirty-one merchantmen. The *Censeur,* unable to manoeuvre under her jury rig, fought the French until she had expended all her powder and lost all three masts. Thus, Captain Purvis's hard-won prize from the action off Genoa was returned to French ownership after only seven months under the British flag.

On 1st November 1795 Vice-Admiral Hotham was relieved of his command and, after a short inter-regnum under Vice-Admiral Sir Hyde Parker, Admiral Sir John Jervis took over as Commander-in-Chief Mediterranean. He arrived off San Fiorenzo aboard the frigate *Lively* on Sunday 29th November and on the 30th Captain Purvis sent the *Princess Royal*'s boats to assist in towing the *Lively* into the bay. The following day the Princess Royals, together with the ships' companies of the other ships of the Fleet, were assembled on deck to welcome their new Commander with three rousing cheers. It was to mark the start of a new era in the Mediterranean Fleet.

CHAPTER 4

The Mediterranean Discipline

Tuesday 1st December 1795
H.M.S. Princess Royal
San Fiorenzo Bay, Corsica

The arrival of Sir John Jervis had a more personal significance for Captain Purvis as his brother, George, was aboard the *Lively* as the Admiral's secretary. The brothers had not seen each other for several years and, apart from the joy of a fraternal reunion, George would bring the latest news of family and friends back in England. As soon as the *Lively* had moored, he sent a boat to her with an invitation to his brother to dine with him aboard the *Princess Royal* as soon as his duties would allow.

An admiral's secretary in the 18th century navy was a powerful and influential figure acting, in effect, as the business manager of the squadron or fleet. He was generally his admiral's Prize Agent and chief negotiator in all matters pertaining to finance and supply. In more recent times, he would have been a senior commissioned officer in the Supply and Secretariat Branch supported by a staff of specialists but, in those days, he worked on his own and the position carried no rank although holders of the office would often have R.N. after their names. An admiral's secretary required education, tact and self-assurance as his job required him to communicate comfortably with senior officers, diplomats and politicians. Very often admirals' secretaries came from naval families as was the case with George Purvis whose two brothers were serving Post-Captains, whose father had been an Admiralty official and whose grandfather had been a Commissioner for the Navy. Before joining Sir John Jervis, George had been secretary to Admiral Lord Howe, one of the most universally-respected naval commanders of all time and the victor of 'The Glorious First of June'.

During and after dinner in the spacious Captain's cabin in the stern of *Princess Royal,* George brought his brother up to date with the news from home: during the six months he had spent in England after returning from the Caribbean in the *Boyne,* he had visited his brother's family in Wickham on several occasions. John's wife, Mary, was well and enjoyed the continual attention and support of her indulgent father, Daniel Garrett, who lived at Southwick, a short carriage ride away. The two boys, John now aged eight and Richard six, were fit, strong and full of energy though the little girl, Mary, seemed rather pale and delicate. There was never any question but that the two boys should follow their father into the Royal Navy and it was about time, George suggested, that the elder boy should have his name entered in a ship's register. Promotion required qualifying seatime and, where a boy enjoyed the necessary influence, it was the practice of the time to give him a head start by entering his name in a ship's books long before he reached the age when he was, officially, allowed to join a man-of-war. George therefore told his brother that as soon as the Admiral hoisted his Flag in the *Victory,* the name of John Brett Purvis would be borne in her books.

Not unnaturally, Captain Purvis also quizzed his brother about the character of their new Commander-in-Chief. He was a staunch Whig, George told him, who had entered Parliament in 1783 at the end of the American War but had resigned ten years later, for a seagoing command, on the outbreak of war with Revolutionary France. At the General Election of 1790, he had been returned as Member for Chipping Wycombe and, while Sir John had conducted his parliamentary business in London, George had looked after his affairs aboard the *Prince,* at Plymouth, and had provided him with regular reports on the ship's business.

His work had been varied; the Admiral expected to be kept posted on the state of morale in the Squadron and rejoiced when all was "quiet and harmonious". On one occasion, George told his brother, the Duke of Gloucester, who took a great interest in naval matters, asked Sir John for a detailed diagram of the Squadron's Line of Battle, describing each ship and showing their lines of bearing in three columns. Sir John expected his secretary to be able to prepare this from his own knowledge; but H.R.H. also required diagrams showing the evolution of wearing in three columns and the Admiral conceded that George might have to consult him, or another competent sea officer, when preparing this.[1]

Sir John entertained on a lavish scale with little thought of what it cost him. He enjoyed playing whist, with his secretary often called in to make up a foursome, and George told his brother how he and General Sir Charles Grey, the military commander in the West Indies, had trounced the Admiral and the Collector aboard the *Boyne* last August. George had got on well with General Grey who had invited him to ride with him ashore where they were escorted at all times by a troop of Dragoons.

On social occasions, Sir John Jervis could be a pleasant and amusing companion but when it came to efficiency and discipline he was ruthless. George warned his brother about some of his principal aversions: having himself a deep respect for any man, regardless of rank, who did his job well, Jervis would not tolerate any arrogance or lack of this same respect in his officers. When addressed by an officer or seaman, he would raise his hat and hold it above his head for the whole duration of the conversation and he would not allow any of his officers to merely touch their hat in a flippant and disrespectful fashion. Nor would he tolerate any officer to be improperly dressed. He had a mischievous streak, George said, and had his own ways of punishing such breaches of good manners to the discomfort and embarrassment of the perpetrator.

Paying no deference to social rank, he would bestow his interest by merit alone, much to the surprise of many aristocratic young officers who thought they would gain promotion solely by virtue of their birth. He was, however, fiercely loyal to the Service and to those who had served it well and would always give preference to the sons of old officers with good records. By the same token, any good officer who had fallen on hard times could be sure of his sympathy and his attention both to himself and to his sons. He had

	Rate	Ship	Commander	Guns	Men	Division
STARBOARD DIVISION	2nd	*Blenheim*	Capt. Thomas Lenox Frederick	90	738	**VAN SQUADRON**
	3rd	*Guiscardo* †	Commodore le Marquis Espluga			
			Capt. Chevalier Spannochi	74	600	*Marquis Espluga*
	3rd	*Courageux*	Capt. Benjamin Hallowell	74	640	*and Sir Hyde*
	3rd	*Zealous*	Capt. Lord John Augustus Hervey	74	590	*Parker*
	2nd	*Saint George*	Vice-Admiral Sir Hyde Parker			
			Capt. Thomas Foley	90	738	
	3rd	*Egmont*	Capt. John Sutton	74	590	
	3rd	*Samnita* †	Capt. Guillicine	74	600	**CENTRE**
	3rd	*Captain*	Capt. Smith	74	590	**SQUADRON**
	1st	*Victory*	Admiral Sir John Jervis			
			Capt. Robert Calder			*Vice-Admiral*
			Capt. George Grey	100	850	*Linzee under Sir*
LARBOARD DIVISION	1st	*Britannia*	Capt. Shuldham Peard	100	845	*John Jervis,*
	3rd	*Parthenope* †	Capt. Chevalier Marcocotti	74	600	*Commander-in-*
	3rd	*Culloden*	Capt. Thomas Troubridge	74	590	*Chief*
	2nd	*Princess Royal*	Vice-Admiral Robert Linzee			
			Capt. John Child Purvis	90	760	
	3rd	*Excellent*	Capt. Cuthbert Collingwood	74	590	**REAR SQUADRON**
	3rd	*Bombay Castle*	Capt. Thomas Sotheby	74	590	
	2nd	*Barfleur*	Vice-Adml Hon. Wm. Waldegrave			*Hon. William*
			Capt. James Richard Dacres	90	760	*Waldegrave*
	3rd	Gibraltar	Capt. Edward Pakenham	80	640	

TABLE E. SIR JOHN JERVIS'S MEDITERRANEAN FLEET 17th DECEMBER 1795

† Neapolitan

endless patience with conscientious people who tried hard, even if their performance was not impressive, but was contemptuous of idleness, carelessness and any form of lax discipline. One should never assume, George warned his brother, that one is out of his sight; he related how the Admiral was up at two o'clock every morning and, even when he was supposed to be sleeping, was constantly appearing on deck to see what was going on. Despite his sterling qualities, George said, he was a hard taskmaster and extremely difficult to work for.

The following day, Vice-Admiral Linzee hoisted his Flag in *Princess Royal* and on 13th December the Fleet, led by its new Commander-in-Chief in his Flagship *Victory,* left San Fiorenzo to cruise off Toulon. Over the next six months Captain Purvis was to witness the transformation of the Mediterranean Fleet, at last under the leadership of a dynamic commander.

Up until now there had been little cause for pride or self-satisfaction: the evacuation of Toulon might have been regarded as a partial success in so much as part of the French Fleet had been destroyed or carried off; but a total of sixteen line-of-battle ships and seven frigates and corvettes had been left intact for the enemy to use against the British again. It had been a classic case of 'too little, too late'. Corsica, admittedly, had been sieged and captured but, with extended supply lines and the French armies now threatening northern Italy, it was doubtful how long the British occupation could last. Most recently, Admiral Hotham's unexploited actions off Genoa and Hyères had left the officers and men of the ships involved with a deep sense of futility and frustration. What, they might have been excused for thinking, was the point of rigorous training when their commanders never gave them a fair crack at the enemy? Morale in the Fleet was consequently very low and the past year had seen a noticeable deterioration in discipline with increasingly frequent punishment for contempt of officers and neglect of duty.

Within days of putting to sea, Purvis and the other Captains of the Fleet began to feel the effect of their new Commander. Due to the severe damage she had received in Toulon, and later off Genoa, the *Princess Royal*'s hull was leaking badly, particularly in heavy seas. The recaulking that she had received in Corsica and at Leghorn had improved things slightly but the ship was really in need of a full dockyard refit. On 21st December strong gales beset the Fleet and did not abate for over a week. Throughout this period Captain Purvis had the hand pumps going continuously to try and keep on top of the ingress of water which made the ship sluggish to handle and difficult to keep in her station as the Admiral demanded:

The Commander-in-Chief observes with concern that the ships of the squadron do not preserve the prescribed distances from each other in the order of sailing, with the precision necessary for making a sudden impression upon the enemy, or to avoid accidents by falling aboard each other, which will happen continually if they do not keep their station correctly. . .

When the Fleet tacked, even during the night, the Admiral expected every one of his Captains to be on deck to ensure his ship did not miss stays (get caught with its head to the wind and unable to pay off on the new course). This could happen when a ship did not have sufficient way on her to turn her round through the eye of the wind and was caused, Sir John decreed, by some of his Captains being "too sparing with their mainsails". His order to ensure that Captains were on deck to oversee this manoeuvre was typical of the sardonic style with which they were to become only too familiar:

The Commander-in-Chief has too exalted an opinion of the respective Captains of the Squadron to doubt their being on deck when the signal is made to tack or wear in the night . . . and he directs that a sufficient quantity of canvas is clapped upon each ship to secure her staying, having observed with equal surprise and concern, that some of the fast sailing ships have frequently failed from this, while the worst going have stayed . . .

And that was not the end of it; as George Purvis had intimated, the Admiral would frequently come up on deck from his bed when the Squadron changed course in the middle watch to ensure that the Captains were themselves on deck and to observe their performance.

Aware of how scurvy, or other sickness, could render a ship unable to fight, health and hygiene was another of Jervis's pre-occupations. Now he ordered that all bedding should be shaken and aired once a week, tightened up on the arrangements for sick bays, harried the surgeons in the performance of their duties and ensured, sometimes against the dictates of the Navy Board, an adequate supply of fresh food and anti-scorbutics from local sources. Nor were the officers to enjoy any advantage in the issue of such: officers and men were to receive exactly the same amount of lemons and onions and a reluctance to eat the heads and tongues of slaughtered bullocks was addressed by the Admiral with an order that they should be eaten by the officers "by way of example".

Daily gun drill became obligatory with lower-deck guns being run out wherever sea conditions permitted. The morning scrubbing of decks had to be completed before daybreak so every ship was ready for action should an enemy be sighted at dawn. With supply becoming increasingly difficult and the French army gaining control of more and more of the Ligurian coast, the Commander-in-Chief demanded the utmost economy in food, water and boatswain's stores and heaven help any Master who relegated canvas or cordage which was still capable of being patched up and made serviceable for another purpose.

As far as the seamen were concerned, they soon learned exactly how they stood with 'Old Jarvie', as he was known by the sailors throughout the Fleet. They were required to give of their best at all times but knew, in return, that their Commander-in-Chief could be relied upon for fair treatment and that their welfare was always uppermost in his mind. They also knew that anyone guilty of desertion or the slightest hint of mutinous behaviour could expect no mercy. On the morning of 22nd April when the Fleet was off Cape Noli the order was given for all ships to close around the Flagship and heave to. Boats from each ship, fully manned and armed, were sent to lie alongside the *Egmont* in case any trouble should erupt in that ship during the forthcoming proceedings; then at 1015 two marines and one seaman were hanged from the yard-arm for desertion. As soon as the boats had returned to their ships, the Squadron resumed its patrol.

The following day the Admiral detached the *Agamemnon* and three other ships under the command of Commodore Nelson who, over the next month, captured several enemy transports, laden with stores and munitions, thus enhancing still further his already growing reputation. Sir John Jervis met Nelson for the first time shortly after his arrival at San Fiorenzo and, as had his predecessor Lord Hood, immediately recognised in him a commander of exceptional ability. However, his subsequent use of Nelson whenever a difficult and important job needed to be done began to cause considerable resentment from other, more senior, Flag-Officers. Among his fellow Captains, Nelson's preferment and independent spirit was already the subject of much good-natured complaint: "You did just as you pleased in Lord Hood's time," one of them said to him, "and the same in Admiral Hotham's and now again under Sir John Jervis; it makes no difference to you who is Commander-in-Chief."

For the next two months *Princess Royal* patrolled the coast off Toulon putting in to Adjaccio for four days on 17th May and then returning to San Fiorenzo ten days later. Here the Admiral decided that, in view of her condition, the *Princess Royal* should return to England for a full dockyard refit and therefore ordered Captain Purvis to proceed to Gibraltar from where he would pick up a convoy to escort back to Spithead. The convoy of fifty-six sail left

Gibraltar on 16th July escorted by *Princess Royal* and eight other warships including the *Agamemnon*, Nelson having transferred his Broad Pendant to the *Captain,* 74, in June.

During the six-week voyage back to England, Britain's situation in the Mediterranean deteriorated further. The armies of Captain Purvis's old adversary from La Seyne, Napoleone Buonaparte, now wishing to be known by the more-French version of his name, Napoleon Bonaparte, were sweeping the Austrians and Piedmontese aside and closing more of the Ligurian ports to the Royal Navy. On 27th June the British residents of Leghorn were evacuated by the boats of the *Inconstant* and later the same day the French occupied the town. Then on 19th August a Franco-Spanish Alliance was signed which effectively placed each country's Mediterranean Fleet at the disposal of the other, thereby gaining the balance of power over the British Fleet by about two to one. Sicily and Sardinia had declared their neutrality and on 24th July the Pope came to terms with Bonaparte, the papal treasure having been evacuated by two British frigates earlier in the month. It was thus only a matter of time before Britain would have to withdraw from Corsica and, with nowhere else to go, from the Mediterranean itself.

On 10th August, in the course of a very slow and stormy passage across the Bay of Biscay, Captain Purvis put his ship's company on two-thirds rations but The Lizard was sighted on the 23rd and three days later, with the convoy off Durleston Head, he felt able to restore the full issue.

The *Princess Royal* anchored in Spithead on 28th August where she remained for nearly two months awaiting a berth in the dockyard. On 19th September the *London,* flying the Flag of Vice-Admiral Colpoys, moored nearby. As he watched her swinging to her cable, Captain Purvis had no idea that she was to be his next command nor of the nefarious events which were to take place aboard her the following year.

On 22nd October the *Princess Royal* moved into Portsmouth Dockyard and the ship's company began emptying and derigging the ship for decommissioning. The work was completed within three weeks and at noon on Thursday 10th November 1796 the Pendant was struck and Captain Purvis went ashore to see his family for the first time in over three and a half years; but the joy of his homecoming was marred by the news that his little daughter, Mary, who George had told him was looking rather delicate and pale, had died aged only four shortly before his return to England.

Meanwhile, Spain had formally declared war on Britain on 8th October, following ratification of the Franco-Spanish Alliance, and on 2nd November Corsica was evacuated by the *Egmont* and the *Captain* under Nelson's control with the garrison and stores being moved to a temporary base at Porto Ferrajo on Elba.

With his supplies cut off and his men on half rations, with Bonaparte strengthening daily his grip on the Mediterranean and with Britain's erstwhile allies having either submitted or changed sides, Sir John Jervis had no option but to withdraw the major part of his Fleet from the Mediterranean. Leaving Nelson with a small detachment at Porto Ferrajo, he sailed from Gibraltar on 16th December for the Tagus. Britain's situation was dire indeed, but in just one year 'Old Jarvie' had instituted what was now spoken of with awe throughout the Royal Navy as 'The Mediterranean Discipline'. He had restored the Fleet to a healthy, efficient, well-trained and well-disciplined fighting force; now all it needed was a battle in which to prove itself and this opportunity came the following February.

Jervis's principal concern from his base on the Tagus was to prevent the consolidation of a French, Spanish and Dutch Fleet at Brest for an invasion of Britain. Early in February he received intelligence that a huge Spanish Fleet had left Cartagena under Admiral Don José de Cordova. The Spanish Admiral, with twenty-seven ships of-the-line and twelve frigates, had intended putting in to Cadiz before proceeding to Brest but strong easterly winds had blown him well out into the Atlantic. On the morning of the 14th as the Spaniards beat back towards Cadiz in very loose and undisciplined order, they found the tightly-controlled, highly-trained British Fleet, with roughly half their number of ships, lying in wait for them off Cape St. Vincent. The ensuing battle was a complete vindication of Sir John Jervis's draconian preparations: four Spanish ships of-the-line were captured and the badly-bruised remnants of Cordova's Fleet retired in disorder.

As part of the rewards for this decisive victory, Jervis was created Earl St. Vincent and Nelson, who had worn out of the line to prevent the two parts of the Spanish Fleet from joining up, was knighted and promoted to Rear-Admiral. George Purvis wrote to his brother two days after the battle:

Victory, off Lagos Bay, 16th February 1797

. . . We had been prevented by S.E. strong winds from getting upon our rendezvous off St. Vincent in search of the Spanish Fleet til the night of the 13th when we gained information of their position and heard their signal guns, on the morning of the 14th we got sight of several of them and La Bonne Citoyen, which was on the look out, made the signal for 25 sail of the line. I will give you an extract from my Minutes on the other side, but request you will not let it be known from whom they came; I regretted you were not commanding one of the fifteen line of battle ships which attack'd 27 of the enemy's of which there was one four decker and six three deckers with ten frigates; literally speaking the event of Valentine's Day was never before rivalled in the page of history; for all further particulars except the names of the captured ships, I must refer you to the Admiral's public account and gazette . . .[2]

With *Princess Royal* decommissioned, Captain Purvis now needed another ship. His father-in-law, Daniel Garrett, as well as his house at Southwick, also had a house in Penny Street, Portsmouth, and suggested that the Purvis family should live here during the Captain's time ashore so he would be better placed for the harbour and dockyard. Consequently, his family saw much more of him than they would have done at Wickham and John was able to take his two sons around with him pointing out the various ships and explaining the activities taking place on board. The elder boy, John, was now nearly ten. Thanks to the interest of his Uncle George, his name had been borne on the books of the *Victory* for ten months during the previous year; but now he was anxious to get to sea in reality. His father explained to him that he must be eleven years of age before, as the son of a serving officer, he could officially join a man-of-war and, although there was considerable abuse of this rule, Captain Purvis did not consider it would be in his son's interests to disregard the regulation. Life in the Navy was extremely hard and potential officers generally had a long, hard haul as boys, undertaking the duties of ordinary seamen, before they could hope to be appointed as Midshipmen.

Captain John Child Purvis spent six months ashore and in May 1797 was appointed to command H.M.S. *London,* a three-decked, 90-gun ship of-the-line. To understand the significance of this appointment, one must look for a moment at the events which preceded it.

Although, as we have seen, morale in the Mediterranean Fleet was high, particularly since the victory at Cape St. Vincent, it was at a very low ebb throughout the Navy in home waters. In mainland Europe the French republicans had crushed all remnants of royalist resistance and, now allied with the Spanish and the Dutch, could turn their attention on Britain, the only remaining threat to their supremacy in Europe. In December 1796, urged on by the Irish rebel (or patriot according to one's point of view), Wolfe Tone, who promised the support of a coincident Irish insurrection, a Franco-Spanish invasion fleet sailed for Bantry Bay on the west coast of Ireland. The plan went wildly wrong for them with their ships being dispersed by gales and returning to their home ports without a landing ever being effected. However, the British Channel Fleet had failed to intercept them on their outward journey which had invoked accusations of cowardice against Vice-Admiral Colpoys, who was commanding the squadron which should have been lying in their path, and of indolence against the Commander-in-Chief, Lord Bridport, who had taken three days to get to sea in pursuit of them.

Overlaid on these proceedings, a growing sense of injustice at their pay and conditions of service, exacerbated by the monotony of long periods at anchor in Spithead, had reached boiling point among the seamen of the Channel Fleet. An Able Seaman's pay at the time was less than one shilling a day — a rate which had been unchanged for over 100 years in spite of increasing prices and wages ashore, and was wholly inadequate for the family of a married man to live on; and to add insult to injury, the Army had recently been given a pay increase — a fact well known to the seamen as so many soldiers were serving as marines aboard ships of the Channel Fleet.

Respectful and reasonable petitions to the Admiralty to redress their very real grievances had been ignored and in April 1797 the seamen took matters into their own hands. On the morning of the 15th Lord Bridport ordered the Channel Fleet to weigh anchor and proceed to sea. The seamen of the *Queen Charlotte* manned the yards and gave three cheers which were answered by the crews of the other ships at anchor. This was the signal for the start of the Spithead Mutiny and the seamen of every ship in the Fleet refused to move.

The men's demands were for better pay, better and more food, improved treatment for the sick and an entitlement to shore leave after long periods at sea; to this was later added a demand for the King's pardon for all who had been involved in the mutiny. With the Navy inoperative and the country thus exposed to an unopposed invasion from the continent, Pitt's government acted quickly. The pay increase would have to be confirmed by Act of Parliament but the King's pardon was proclaimed without delay which satisfied the crews of the majority of ships which weighed anchor, as ordered, and moved to moorings at St. Helens.

However, as the days went on, the seamen began to fear that some of their grievances were being ignored by the government and, once again, the ships at St. Helens refused to move. A boat full of 'delegates' from St. Helens pulled up to Spithead to speak to the crew of the *London* which was still moored there. Seeing the boat approach, Admiral Colpoys ordered the crew below and mustered the marines and officers on the quarterdeck with orders not to allow the 'delegates' on board. Most of the seamen obeyed and went quietly below but a small party of the most dissident mutineers refused and assembled on the forecastle. When the 'delegates' drew alongside, the *London*'s marines barred their entry but, instead of pulling away, they started shouting encouragement to the *London*'s men on deck and at the gun ports. At this the party on the forecastle unlashed one of the ship's bow-chasers and began to slew it round to cover the quarterdeck; but the First Lieutenant, Peter Bover, saw what was going on and, pointing his loaded pistol at them, ordered them to stand away from the gun. Most of the party obeyed but a few of the hardest mutineers continued to turn the gun; one of them shouted at Lieutenant Bover daring him to shoot; he did, and the man fell mortally wounded. Open mutiny then broke out throughout the ship. The forecastle party rushed aft to attack the officers, and the marines on the quarterdeck threw down their muskets and joined the mutineers. The officers and marines at the hatchway fought a losing battle to prevent the rest of the crew from surging up on deck. The Admiral authorised the use of firearms, shots were exchanged and in the ensuing mêlée a Midshipman and a marine Lieutenant were wounded and four further seamen killed.

The mutineers soon had control of the ship and confined the officers and marines below. They decided, however, that the First Lieutenant, who had started the firing, should be hanged on the spot. A rope was rove to the fore yard and a noose placed around the neck of Lieutenant Bover who stood, quite fearlessly, though apparently at the point of death, berating his executioners as "the basest and most dastardly of cowards and traitors". At this point, Admiral Colpoys showed that, whatever else he may have been, he was certainly not a coward. Addressing the mutineers he accepted sole responsibility for the deaths and offered himself in place of Bover who, he explained, had been acting on his orders following explicit Admiralty instructions. Lieutenant Bover was a brave and popular officer and was eventually spared partly, perhaps, as a result of the Admiral's plea but possibly, as was later maintained by his family, through the intervention of one of the ringleaders of the mutiny, Valentine Joyce of the *Royal George,* who had sailed with Bover before and had a high regard for him.

The Spithead Mutiny was eventually laid to rest through the recall to duty of the aged but universally-trusted Admiral Lord Howe, 'Black Dick' to the men, who visited every ship and talked for hours at a time with the disaffected crews. As part of the 'settlement' many of the most unpopular officers were removed from their ships. In the *London*'s case, these included Admiral Colpoys; the Captain, Edward Griffith; and the chaplain, Revd. Samuel Cole, who was extremely unpopular and for whom some of the mutineers had advocated: "tar and feathers with a grating to launch him upon and a boat-hook and hammock for a sail." Admiral Colpoys never got another seagoing appointment and is commemorated, perhaps a little unfairly, in the sailors' song 'The Ballad of Bantry Bay':

> *The murdering Colpoys, Vice-Admiral of the Blue,*
> *Gave orders to fire on the London ship's crew.*
> *While the enemy of Britain was ploughing the sea,*
> *He, like a base coward, let them get away*
> *While the French and their transports sailed for Bantry Bay.*

The *London* had seen the worst violence of the mutiny and, even after it had officially been settled, feelings of injustice and resentment still ran high among her seamen several of whose shipmates had been killed during the trouble. They would require firm but delicate handling and it must have been clear to the Admiralty at the time that her new commander must be a resolute disciplinarian but, at the same time, an officer of manifest fairness, compassion, tact and professional competence. It speaks highly for John Purvis's reputation that he was selected for the command.

He came aboard on 15th May, the same day that the ship's company returned to its duties and the mutiny officially ended. His First Lieutenant was the gallant Peter Bover who had promised the crew that he would not desert them and, despite the pleas of his family and friends, returned on board to a rousing three cheers from the ship's company. He remained in the *London* as Captain Purvis's First Lieutenant until he was promoted to Commander the following year and was replaced by Lieutenant Francis Austen, a

	Rate	Ship	Commander	Guns	Men	Division
TABLE F. LORD BRIDPORT'S CHANNEL FLEET 15th MAY 1797						
STARBOARD DIVISION / VAN	3rd	*Impetueux*	Capt. Payne	74		
	2nd	*Duke*	Capt. John Holloway	90		
	3rd	*Terrible*	Capt. George Campbell	74		**VAN SQUADRON** ❧ *Vice-Admiral Sir Alan Gardner*
	1st	*Royal Sovereign*	**Vice-Adml Sir Alan Gardner Bt.** Capt. Bedford	100		
	3rd	*Robust*	Capt. Edward Thornbrough	74		
		[L'Clair]	Capt. John McDougall			
	3rd	*London*	Capt John Child Purvis	74		
		Fire Ship: *Megaera,* 14				
	3rd	*Minotaur*	Capt. Thomas Louis	74		**CENTRE SQUADRON** ❧ *Rear-Admiral Charles Morice Pole under Lord Bridport, Commander-in-Chief*
	3rd	*Defence*	Capt Thomas Wells	74		
	3rd	*Mars*	Capt. Alexander Hood	74		
	1st	*Royal George*	**Rear-Adml Charles Morice Pole** Capt. Bennet	100		
LARBOARD DIVISION	2nd	*Glory*	**Admiral Lord Bridport** Capt. James Brine	98		
	3rd	*Defiance*	Capt. T. Jones	74		
	3rd	*Marlborough*	Capt. J. Eaton	74		
	3rd	*Majestic*	Capt. George Blagdon Westcott	74		
		Frigates: *San Fiorenzo,* 38; *Phaeton,* 38; **Fire Ship:** *Incendiary,* 14				
	3rd	*Saturn*	Capt. Douglas	74		**REAR SQUADRON**
	3rd	*Monarch*	Capt. John Elphinstone	74		
	2nd	*Atlas*	Capt. Matthew Squire	98†		
	3rd	*Pompée*	Capt. James Vashon	80		
	1st	*Queen Charlotte*	Capt. Walter Locke	100		
	3rd	*Ramilles*	Capt. Sir Richard Bickerton Bt.	74		
		Frigates: *Unite,* 38; *Medusa,* 50				
		† *Atlas* was reduced from 98 guns to 74 in 1802				

future Admiral-of-the-Fleet and a brother of the author Jane Austen, who would remain in the post until 6th February 1799 when he was promoted into the *Petrel*. The fact that Captain Purvis had served under Jervis's 'Mediterranean Discipline' may, also, have influenced his selection to command the *London*.

The ship's company, including officers, boys and ninety marines, numbered 738. Of the 561 seamen, who worked the ship and manned the guns, 324 were English (including eighty-three Londoners), fifty-nine were Scots, sixteen were Welsh and 137 Irish. The remainder were a mixture of Swedes, Danes, Dutch, Portuguese, Germans and even included five Americans and four Frenchmen. Captain Purvis's task was now to weld this ill-assorted group of mainly-impressed men, many of them straight from the courts and prisons of the kingdom, into a cohesive and efficient fighting unit. Their attitude was still rebellious and insubordinate. On the evening before the ship sailed, the Captain of one of the other ships at Spithead, Captain Barrie, came on board the *London* to report to Captain Purvis some improper conduct by one of his boats' crews. Sensing the purpose of his visit, the men concerned gathered at one of the lower gun ports through which they dropped shot into Barrie's gig as it lay alongside until it sank.

The following day Captain Purvis got the ship to sea although, according to Jebediah Tucker, Lord St. Vincent's biographer, not without some difficulty: ". . . with perceptible agitation and audible murmuring the surly, sulky hands would scarcely weigh the ship's anchor or loosen her topsails."

By the time the *London* anchored in Torbay at the end of her first six-week Channel patrol under Captain Purvis's command, the Spithead part of the mutiny, which had meanwhile spread to the Nore, had effectively come to an end. Trial of the ringleaders was already under way and the Admiralty was anxious that their fate, and that of any others who might be guilty of the same crime in the future, should be known throughout the Navy. On 7th July Purvis and all other Captains in the Channel Fleet received orders to acquaint their ships' companies:

. . . that Richard Parker, the principal delegate of the mutineers at the Nore, was executed the 30th June on board the Sandwich, that 9 of the ship's company of the Leopard have been condemned to suffer death and that the remainder of those concerned in that mutiny will be brought to trial as expeditiously as possible. They are to point out to them the enormity of the crime of mutiny and the danger to which those who are guilty of it bring upon their country and themselves and to impress on their minds that it is the duty of every man to stand forward to resist all attempts at mutiny as not only those who are active in causing it but those who are not active in preventing it and suppressing it when begun are guilty of a very great crime for which they will deserve and must expect to suffer the severest punishment. They are to impress on them their Lordships' satisfaction at the good conduct of so considerable a part of the Royal Sovereign's ship's company and to represent that if the very great majority of good men in every ship were to conduct themselves in the same proper manner, the few ill disposed who may be among them would find it impossible to succeed in their wicked designs.

The main grievances of the Spithead and Nore mutineers having been redressed, the remaining disaffection in the Fleet was largely due to the preponderance of Irish seamen many of whom were criminals which the Irish courts had been glad to be rid of. These men were ready recruits to the cause of the 'United Irishmen' who were pledged to sedition and the seizure of the ships in which they served. Nor were their sanguinary ambitions confined to the murder of their officers as the oath they were required to swear attested:

"I swear to be true to the Free and United Irishmen who are fighting our cause against tyrants and oppressors, to defend their rights to the last drop of my blood and to keep all secret within my breast; and I do agree next time the ship looks out ahead at sea to carry her into Brest and to kill and destroy all the officers and every man who opposes, and to hoist a green ensign with a harp in it and afterwards to kill and destroy all protestants."

The London returned to Torbay on 25th August after her next patrol to receive orders from the Commander-in-Chief that the Acts of Parliament prohibiting the administration of such unlawful oaths were to be read aloud to the assembled ship's company who were to be made fully aware of the dangers of disregarding them. The following week two more mutineers were hanged aboard the Royal Sovereign after which Captain Purvis was ordered to read the 'Articles of War' to his crew "impressing on their minds upon that solemn occasion the fatal consequences that may arise from mutinous and disorderly behaviour that they may be restrained by the ignominy of their fate and warned by these examples".

The restoration of discipline and the establishment of a happy ship was not made easier for Captain Purvis by a shortage of officers. On 13th September, a week before he was due to sail again for Ushant, he wrote to Lord Bridport:

My Lord — The very bad weather we have lately experienced with the probability of a very long continuance of it as the season advances will, I trust, excuse me in representing to your Lordship the great and serious inconvenience I feel in the want of a sufficient number of officers to assist me in carrying on the duty of the ship. I am now two Lieutenants short of the established number and at this time have only three capable of duty, the rest being ill, two of which from that cause have done very little duty since their being appointed to the ship. Had I the advantage of experienced petty officers, I should not at this time have troubled your Lordship but I have not one mate or midshipman but what are youngsters and who have been at sea but a very short time. Your Lordship will see the necessity of this application when I inform you we have parted from two of our anchors and the cable we now ride by has been much injured by the Cleopatra's anchor.

Six days later he repeated his request but there were no replacements available and the *London*'s next six weeks off Ushant had to be endured with a grave shortage of officers and experienced petty officers and a sullen and less than willing crew. The weather did nothing to palliate Captain Purvis's difficulties with, as he had anticipated, violent autumn storms for most of the patrol and he must have been greatly relieved to drop anchor in Spithead on 14th November without having suffered major damage to his ship.

The *London* remained at anchor in Spithead until the middle of February 1798 when Captain Purvis received orders to join Lord St. Vincent in the Tagus. He was to collect and escort a large convoy of merchantmen from Falmouth and, to assist him in rounding it up, H.M. Cutter *Trial*, commanded by his brother-in-law, Lieutenant Henry Garrett, was placed under his command. On 24th February he briefed Henry on what he wanted him to do:

When the London shows a small St George's ensign at the main top masthead and fires a gun you are to make the best of your way to Falmouth and collect and bring out such vessels as may be inclined to take the advantage of the convoy to Oporto, Lisbon or Gibraltar and loose no time in joining me with them off the beforementioned port of Falmouth and in order to make the London more easily known I shall hoist a small St George's ensign at the fore top masthead.

On Monday 12th March the fleet of merchantmen came in from the eastward and the following day the *London* sailed from Spithead collecting the contingent that Henry Garrett had rounded up from Falmouth as they passed. The *Trial* was released to rejoin Sir Peter Parker and the convoy sailed for the Tagus where *London* anchored in twenty-one fathoms at 0500 on Sunday 25th March. Already at the anchorage off Lisbon were H.M. Ships *Culloden, Audacious, Gorgon, Speedy* and Lord St. Vincent's Flagship the *Ville de Paris* to which Captain Purvis immediately repaired to report himself to the Admiral. While he was on board, according to Tucker, a member of his boat's crew shouted up to one of the sailors at the lower gun ports of the Flagship: "I say there, what have you fellows been doing out here while we have been fighting for your beef and pork?" To which the sailor, very quietly, replied: "If you'll take my advice, you'll say nothing at all about all that here, for by God if Old Jarvie hears ye he'll have you dingle dangle at the yard-arm at eight o'clock tomorrow morning."

Over the next two days *London* took on board 2,307 lbs of fresh beef, 38 pipes of wine, 100 bags of bread and 48 firkins of butter and Purvis received the Admiral's orders, signed by his brother George, to proceed to join Sir William Parker off Cadiz "whose rendezvous is ten leagues west of the Tower of San Sebastian". Should he fall in with the *Bellerophon, Alexander, Swiftsure* or *Theseus*, he was to take those ships also under his command.

Before *London* left the Tagus, George was able to perform a further service for his brothers: John Purvis was carrying his nephew, Richard Oadham Purvis, (known in the family as 'Oadham' to avoid confusion), the eldest son of his eldest brother, Captain Richard Purvis R.N. Oadham was a Midshipman and his chances of being 'noticed' by Lord St. Vincent would be far better if he were aboard the Flagship. George therefore arranged a berth for him in the *Ville de Paris* to which he moved before the *London* sailed on 28th March in company with the *Audacious*.

TABLE G. LORD ST. VINCENT'S MEDITERRANEAN FLEET
28th MARCH 1798

Rate	Ship	Commander	Guns	Men	Division
2nd	*Blenheim*	**Rear-Adml. Thomas Frederick**			
		Captain Robert Campbell	**90**	**738**	
3rd	*Culloden*	Captain Thomas Troubridge	74	590	
3rd	*Minotaur*	Captain Thomas Louis	74	640	
3rd	*Theseus*	Captain Ralph Willett Miller	74	590	**STARBOARD**
3rd	*Defence*	Captain Thomas Wells	74	590	**SQUADRON**
2nd	*Prince George*	**Rear-Adml. Sir William Parker Bt.**			
		Captain William Bowen	**90**	**740**	*Rear-Admiral*
3rd	*Warrior*	Captain Henry Savage	74	590	*Sir William*
3rd	*Swiftsure*	Captain Benjamin Hallowell	74	590	*Parker Bt.*
3rd	*Bellerophon*	Captain Henry d'Esterre Darby	74	590	
3rd	*Goliath*	Captain Thomas Foley	74	590	
4th	*Leander*	Captain J. B. Thompson	50	313	
2nd	*London*	Captain John Child Purvis	90	738	
1st	*Ville de Paris*	**Admiral of the Blue**			*Lord St. Vincent*
		Lord St. Vincent			*Commander-in-*
		Captain Sir Robert Calder Bt.			*Chief*
		(Captain of the Fleet)			
		Captain George Grey	**110**	**841**	
3rd	*Orion*	Captain James Saumarez	74	590	
3rd	*Zealous*	Captain Samuel Hood	74	590	
3rd	*Gibraltar*	Captain William Hancock Kelly	80	640	
3rd	*Colossus*	Captain George Murray	74	640	**LARBOARD**
3rd	*Audacious*	Captain Davidge Gould	74	590	**SQUADRON**
3rd	*Hector*	Captain Peter Aplin	74	590	
2nd	*Princess Royal*	**Rear-Adml. Sir John Orde Bt.**			*Rear-Admiral*
		Captain John Draper	**90**	**740**	*Sir John*
3rd	*Excellent*	Captain Cuthbert Collingwood	74	590	*Orde Bt.*
3rd	*Alexander*	Captain Alexander Ball	74	590	
3rd	*Majestic*	Captain George Blagdon Westcott	74	590	
2nd	*Namur*	Captain Thomas Sotheby	90	788	

ORDER OF SAILING IN TWO SQUADRONS

LARBOARD OR LEE SQUADRON

STARBOARD OR WEATHER SQUADRON

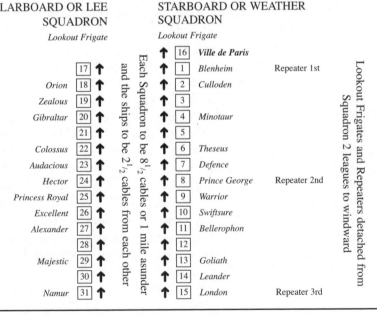

Lookout Frigate   *Lookout Frigate*

↑ 16   *Ville de Paris*
1   *Blenheim*   Repeater 1st
17 ↑
Orion   18 ↑   2   *Culloden*
Zealous   19 ↑   3
Gibraltar   20 ↑   4   *Minotaur*
21 ↑   5
Colossus   22 ↑   6   *Theseus*
Audacious   23 ↑   7   *Defence*
Hector   24 ↑   8   *Prince George*   Repeater 2nd
Princess Royal   25 ↑   9   *Warrior*
Excellent   26 ↑   10   *Swiftsure*
Alexander   27 ↑   11   *Bellerophon*
28 ↑   12
Majestic   29 ↑   13   *Goliath*
30 ↑   14   *Leander*
Namur   31 ↑   15   *London*   Repeater 3rd

Each Squadron and the ships to be 2½ cables from each other

Squadron to be 8½ cables or 1 mile asunder

Lookout Frigates and Repeaters detached from Squadron 2 leagues to windward

On arrival off Cadiz, *London* came under the orders of Sir John Orde. At the end of April Nelson returned to the Fleet, having recovered from the loss of his arm at Tenerife, and was appointed by Lord St. Vincent to a detached command which would culminate in his great victory at the Battle of the Nile. This appointment, however, caused bitter offence to Rear-Admirals Orde and Parker, both of whom were senior to Nelson and felt they should have been chosen for the command. An extremely acrimonious exchange between Orde and St. Vincent ensued which would come to a head two years later.

During April and May, off Cadiz as part of Sir John Orde's Larboard Squadron, the crew of the *London* were to experience the full significance of the 'Mediterranean Discipline'. When an execution had taken place in the past, it had always been the custom for seamen from another ship to come on board and undertake the hanging. Lord St. Vincent, however, considered that the deterrent value of an execution would be the greater if undertaken by the victim's own shipmates alone. The procedure was therefore always the same: boats from every ship in the Fleet, fully manned and armed, would surround the ship in question to ensure no weakening in resolve and the sentence would be implemented by the condemned man's shipmates "alone and no part of the boats' crews of other ships, as usual on similar occasions, is to assist in the punishment".

On 14th May *London* sent a boat to attend the execution of Andrew McCrink, a marine in the *Swiftsure,* and on the 29th to the notorious execution on board the *Marlborough* which was to test the strength of the 'Mediterranean Discipline' to its limit: *Marlborough*, which had a high proportion of seditious Irish seamen, had arrived in the Mediterranean with several men in irons, a plot having been discovered to seize the ship and carry her into a French port. The ringleader of the conspiracy, Peter Anderson, had been tried and sentenced to hang on the morning of the 29th. On the evening of the 28th, Captain Ellison, the *Marlborough's* commander, came aboard the Flagship and advised the Admiral that the extent of the disaffection in his ship was so great that he feared a general uprising if the sentence were to be carried out; he pleaded, moreover, that if it were to go ahead, the hanging should be undertaken by seamen from another ship. Lord St. Vincent refused to move on either point.

The following morning, on the orders of the Commander-in-Chief, the guns of the *Marlborough* were housed and secured and her gun ports closed. A boat from the *London*, and one from every other ship on the station, was armed with a carronade and twelve rounds of shot, manned by a seasoned gunner's mate, four quarter-gunners, a contingent of seamen and marines and commanded by a Lieutenant; the assembly of boats was commanded by Captain Campbell of the *Blenheim* who was ordered to surround the *Marlborough* and, in the event of any uprising, to fire into her at point blank range until it was quelled — if necessary, sinking the ship where she lay.

At 0730 the boats took up their station and Captain Campbell ordered the tampions to be removed from the carronades and the guns to be double-shotted. All hands from the other ships at anchor were ordered on deck "to witness punishment" and their shrouds and yards were crowded with men craning for a better view. At 0800 a signal gun on the Flagship gave the order for the execution to take place and thousands of expectant officers, sailors and marines held their breath as they waited to see if 'Old Jarvie's' authority would prevail. Anderson's body was seen ascending to the yard-arm then, when it was halfway up, to a gasp of horror from the onlookers, it fell back to the deck; the rope had slipped from his executioners' nervous hands but within seconds they had renewed their grip and completed the sentence. The boats remained at their station until the statutory time for the body to hang at the yard-arm had expired and then returned to their ships. On board the *Ville de Paris*, Lord St. Vincent turned on his heel to go below remarking to the officer beside him: "Discipline is preserved, Sir."

CHAPTER 5

The Pursuit of Bruix

Sunday 24th June 1798
H.M.S. London
off Cadiz

B y and large, Captain Purvis was blessed with good youngsters who would repay his patronage with distinction in their later naval careers. A godfearing man, he would impress upon those boys in his charge, at every available opportunity, the importance of divine worship, of close attention to duty and of the paramount requirement for total obedience to orders and superior authority. Ever mindful of his duty to do his best for them, he lost no opportunity to augment their education or foster their professional advantage. Among his family and friends ashore, he spoke with pride of the achievements of officers who had been boys in his care. The regard was mutual and several of them would correspond with him and visit him for the rest of his life.

However, as anyone who has read the Hornblower novels will know, not all Midshipmen were models of diligence. One such in the *London*'s gunroom was Mr. Cornwal Fathwell who bullied the younger boys to the point of despair and whose general behaviour made him a constant thorn in the sides of the ship's officers and petty officers alike. Sharp-witted and knowing, as his type often are, he was expert at side-stepping trouble and had for long avoided being brought to book and punished for his behaviour — the earnest desire of his messmates and victims. The opportunity arose on 24th June when Fathwell was in charge of one of the *London*'s boats with orders to stop and examine the books of a privateer off Cadiz. Boarding the vessel, probably the worse for drink, he treated the ship's captain and officers with arrogance and contempt, demanding wine and helping himself to the Captain's watch and some items of officers' clothing before he left. A complaint was lodged to Captain Purvis who reported the incident to the Commander-in-Chief.

At a Court Martial on board the *Prince* two days later, Fathwell was found guilty and sentenced to be degraded from the rank of Midshipman in the most ignominious manner by having his uniform stripped from his back upon the quarterdeck of the *London* before the entire ship's company. He was, moreover, to forfeit all pay accrued and due to him and be rendered incapable of ever serving as an officer or petty officer in any of His Majesty's ships.

This, however, was not sufficient for Lord St. Vincent who added his own refinement to the punishment in an order to Captain Purvis the following day:

... and you are to cause his head to be shaved and a label to be affixed to his back expressive of the disgraceful crimes he has committed and he is to be employed as a constant scavenger in cleaning the head [the seamen's lavatories] until further orders.

His ordeal was not to last long; the following day Captain Purvis received orders from the Admiral to discharge Fathwell into the *Lion* to do duty in her foretop.

The following month trouble on board Captain Purvis's old command, the *Princess Royal*, came to a head: an Irish lawyer, Thomas Bott (alias Batt), had enlisted in the Navy with the sole purpose of indoctrinating the seamen of the Fleet and encouraging mutiny. He had already recruited considerable support among the *Princess Royal*'s Irish contingent by the time the plot was discovered and he, together with some twenty other ringleaders, was arrested. Bott made a full confession and was hanged aboard the *Princess Royal* on 4th July with Michael Connell and Daniel Sweeney; others were to follow. Lord St. Vincent wrote to Nelson:

The officers throughout the whole fleet were to have been massacred, and if the ships from Ireland, with the London and Hecla, had joined, I was to have been hung, with the other admirals, captains and officers. The plan afterwards was to go up and revolutionize your squadron and then proceed to Ireland,

Mutiny and desertion were not the only crimes which invoked the death penalty: on 26th August David Finness, a seaman of the *Prince,* was hanged for "the unnatural and detestable sin of buggery upon the persons of James Lyons, Thomas Willison and Joseph Perry, three boys belonging to the said ship". Contrary to popular belief, sodomy was rare in ships of the Royal Navy and, when it did occur, it was invariably punished by death.

In the same month, Captain Purvis received the sad news from home that his wife, Mary, had died on 1st July. She was a gentle woman who had been a caring stepmother to her husband's two sons by his previous marriage though she had lost both her own children in infancy. It is probable that she died in attempting to have a third. Apart from the distress of losing a loving wife, John Purvis now had the additional worry of what to do about his sons. He knew that, in the short term, his excellent father-in-law, Daniel Garrett, would make whatever arrangements were necessary for their welfare but, when he got back to England, he would have to address the situation himself. John was now eleven so he could take him on board the *London* with him but Richard was only nine and would have to be placed in the care of a nurse, or with relations, until he was old enough to come to sea.

There was better news in September when reports reached Cadiz of Nelson's great victory at the Battle of the Nile:

The Commander-in-Chief has inexpressible happiness in communicating to the officers, seamen and marines of His Majesty's ships before Cadiz that an action was fought at the mouth of the Nile on the 1st, 2nd and 3rd of August and under the blessing of God, and the intrepid conduct of the officers and crews of the squadron under the orders of Rear Admiral Sir Horatio Nelson, Knight of the Bath, a most signal and glorious victory obtained over that of France . . .

Although great news for the Navy and the nation, Captain Purvis must have received it with a twinge of regret having, yet again, missed a major fleet action through having been in the wrong ship, in the wrong place at the wrong time. For his brother, George, it was a different matter: on 10th December 1796 Nelson had written to him from *Captain:*

Sir — I hereby fully authorize you to settle all Prize Concerns which may be due, or become due, to me, from any vessels taken by the Fleet under the command of Admiral Sir John Jervis; and I request all Prize Agents to consider this letter as full a power as if made in all due form. I am, Sir, your most obedient servant, Horatio Nelson.[1]

George Purvis's integrity and business acumen was well known among senior officers and he consequently held the Prize Agency for all the Flag-Officers, as well as Nelson, who would take a percentage of the Nile spoils. His commission on the whole transaction would be considerable which suited him well as he had, by now, had quite enough of Lord St. Vincent and had already decided to leave his service at the end of the summer campaign. The relationship between the two men had been excellent up until the past year and the Admiral had frequently expressed his appreciation of his secretary's efficiency. In 1791 he had written to him: "I do assure you, that in my judgement, this adventure could not have succeeded with any tolerable degree of economy but for your unremitted attention. . ."[2] He had also urged him to use his Admiral's free postal concession for his private correspondence: " I hope you will have no scruple to correspond with your mother and brother, or indeed any other correspondents, under my cover."[2]

However, his Lordship had recently become increasingly critical of him and dissatisfied with everything he did. George believed that someone had been poisoning the Admiral's mind against him and he thought he knew who it was. Now, with his Nile commission, he could resign with dignity and retire in comfort with his wife and family of whom he had seen very little in recent years.

Having obtained the Admiral's permission to return to England in November, believing it mutually understood that he would not return, George embarked on a Lisbon-bound ship at Gibraltar. However, as he left the Flagship, Lord St. Vincent told him that he must be back in a month. Saying nothing, George left and wrote to the Admiral when his ship reached Lisbon:

Above: Toulon Harbour from Mount Faron. The French aircraft carrier *Clémencau* can be seen in La Petite Rade in roughly the same position as Lord Hood's Fleet was moored in 1793. Directly behind her is the north-west arm of the harbour where the *Princess Royal* was moored to bombard La Seyne.

Above: Napoleone Buonaparte who, as an unknown young Captain of Artillery, established the shore batteries at La Seyne which exchanged fire with the *Princess Royal* on a daily basis.

Left: Admiral Samuel Hood, Viscount Hood, commanded the British Fleet at Toulon. His brother was Admiral Alexander Hood, Lord Bridport.

Above: The night sky is lit up by explosions and the flames of burning French ships as the Allied Fleet prepares to evacuate Toulon.

Left: Captain (later Admiral) Sir William Sidney Smith who was tasked with the destruction of the French ships. With the wealth to indulge his thirst for adventure, he was in Toulon as a Volunteer in the *Swallow*, a small ship he had purchased and fitted-out at his own expense. Smith was aged twenty-nine at the time and, despite his best endeavours, was only able to destroy fourteen ships out of thirty-nine due to the haste of the evacuation.

Right: French memorial on Balaguier: "On this shore in December 1793 the military operations undertaken by the Army of the Convention for the Liberation of Toulon came to a victorious conclusion, the Fort of 'Little Gibraltar' having succumbed under the fire of the French batteries and the assault of the infantry. The Army was commanded by Dugommier and the Artillery Commander Napoleon Bonaparte."

Above: The Tour de la Balaguier from which the British were driven out on the night of 17th December 1793. **Left:** The main gateway.

Below: Inside Fort Napoleon, built in 1831 on the ruins of Fort Mulgrave or 'Petit Gibraltar' as the French knew it. The British Garrison was overwhelmed when it was stormed by 7,000 Republican troops with the loss of some 250 British sailors, soldiers and marines including Midshipman Wilkie and nine seamen from the *Princess Royal*. Over 1,000 French were killed and Buonaparte was seriously wounded.

Above: Lord Hood's Flagship the *Victory* with the British Fleet lying off Bastia in 1794.

Left: A watchtower built by the Genoese in the 16th-century during their occupation of Corsica. Some eighty-five of these encircled the island to guard against Saracen raiders and around sixty still survive.

Below: The Citadel at San Fiorenzo.

Below: Vice-Admiral Sir Thomas Fremantle who, as a Captain commanding the *Inconstant,* was the first to reach the *Ça Ira* and engage her. He later became Commander-in-Chief Mediterranean and died in 1819, aged 54, at Naples.

Above: The French ships *Censeur* and the dismasted *Ça Ira* are engaged by the *Courageux* and *Illustrious* during Admiral Hotham's action off Genoa on 14th March 1795. *Courageux, Illustrious* and *Princess Royal* were all badly damaged during a running battle on both sides with the main French Fleet engaged to port and the *Ça Ira* and *Censeur* to starboard; the two crippled French ships eventually struck to *Princess Royal*.

Though Nelson is generally credited with their capture, these three British ships, together with *Bedford, Captain* and *Inconstant*, played a far greater part in the action and suffered greater casualties. The dismasted *Illustrious* broke her tow, drove ashore and was wrecked a few days later.

Admiral-of-the Fleet Sir Richard Howe
Earl Howe.

Admiral-of-the Fleet Sir John Jervis
Earl of St. Vincent.

Admiral Purvis's younger brother, George, was secretary, successively, to two of the greatest Admirals in the history of the Royal Navy — Lord Howe and Lord St. Vincent. With the latter, he was present at the Battle of Cape St. Vincent in 1797 while his brother was ashore awaiting a ship. In 1796 Lord Nelson appointed George Purvis as his Prize Agent although he later reneged on the agreement.

The three engravings on this page belonged to George Purvis and are reproduced by permission of the present owner, Mrs. Anthea Carmichael.

Vice-Admiral Sir Horatio Nelson
Viscount Nelson.

George Purvis and his wife Renira (née Maitland) and their idyllic *Cottage Orné* built in the grounds of the Blackbrook Estate, Fareham, which George purchased on his retirement from a lucrative career at sea as an Admirals' Secretary and Prize Agent. 'Blackbrook Cottage' remained in the family for about 100 years and in 1927 was bought by the Church Commissioners as the Bishop's Palace for the Diocese of Portsmouth. Renamed 'Bishopswood', it remained the Bishop's Palace for seventy years and is now back in private ownership. It is believed to have the largest thatched roof in Europe. George and Renira's elder daughter, also Renira, married Admiral John Child Purvis's elder son, Vice-Admiral John Brett Purvis.

Top: The *London,* a 98-gun sister ship of the famous *Victory,* which Captain Purvis commanded from 1797 to 1801. He was appointed to her in the final stages of the Spithead Mutiny during which the ship had been the scene of some of the worst violence. Admiral Sir John Colpoys **(centre left)** and Captain Edward Griffith **(centre right)**, a nephew of the Admiral, had been removed from the ship on the insistence of the mutineers.

Left: Richard Parker, one of the principal architects of the Nore Mutiny, who was sentenced to death by a Court Martial and was executed on board the *Sandwich* on 20th June 1797.

My Lord — Early in the month of September your Lordship was pleased to consent to the request I made to return to England as soon as the business of the summer campaign was ended. From the dissatisfaction and keen reproaches so repeatedly uttered by your Lordship on my total inability to fill the office you had so long instructed me with, I seriously did conclude that your Lordship tacitly considered this permission as final and that you would take measures for providing a more capable successor. I believe this was generally understood in the Fleet and Mr Yeo was named to me as the person your Lordship had fitted upon. I was never undeceived in this impression until your Lordship mentioned, at the moment of my departure, that I must return in a month. The dread of being again subjected to that agony of mind under which your Lordship has at times seen me oppressed, induced me to withold from you my determination not to resume on this station the honor of serving your Lordship in quality of Secretary, although I did not assent that I should obey the injunction you imposed.

The duty I owe to my family and (to use your Lordship's words) to my honor, peace of mind and future happiness, impels me to solicit your Lordship to be pleased to accept my resignation on the day I quitted Gibraltar, and to forgive my not then entering into the explanation (from the terror of a total stop being put on my release) which I now embrace the earliest opportunity to communicate.

I have owed many obligations to your Lordship, I am proud to declare that I have requited them by the strictest principles of integrity, a faithful attention to your interests on all occasions and an _endeavour_ to discharge my public duty with punctuality but never to commit my Admiral. I am not at a loss to divine the source of your Lordship's prejudice against me, because I have observed others equally attached, but more deserving, sink under it.

I sincerely wish your Lordship a continuance of that success which has hitherto crowned your indefatigable labour for the public weal; and from an intimate knowledge of your unrivalled talents, I have no doubt of the further great advantages the country will derive therefrom. Be assured, my Lord, I shall ever maintain and profess these sentiments.

With all due respect I have the honor to subscribe myself, my Lord, your Lordship's most faithful and most obedient humble servant, George Purvis.

But Neptune had one further adventure for George before he left the sea: at Lisbon he took passage in the _Colossus_, 74, which was wrecked off the Scilly Isles on 7th December. The islanders took off the passengers and crew in small boats — a protracted business as there were many Nile wounded who, naturally, had to be evacuated first. George eventually got back to England though some of the Nile prize papers he was carrying were lost in the wreck.

The Admiral's new secretary was not, as expected, Mr. Yeo: he was the Purser from the *London*, one Benjamin Tucker, who apparently filled the role to His Lordship's satisfaction and whose son, Jebediah, was to become St.Vincent's first biographer.

Thus, with a new Purser, Richard Booth, the *London* continued her patrols through the Strait of Gibraltar for the rest of the year 1798 with no occurrence of note though in November the island of Minorca was recaptured by a small squadron under the command of Commodore John Duckworth giving Britain, once again, a viable base in the western Mediterranean.

In the Georgian Navy little regard was paid to today's conventions of Christmas cheer and goodwill; it was 'business as usual' on board the *London* as the journal for Christmas Day 1798 records:

Punished Wm. Davis (marine), John Hart (sm), Jas. Veasey (marine), Timothy Thorn and Jas. Paine (sm) with 12 lashes each for drunkeness and insolence. Richard Danvers (sm) for mutinous expressions. Wm. Newcombe 6 lashes for insolence and disobedience.

Back in England Mr. Garrett, true to his son-in-law's expectations, had engaged Ann Porter, a gentlewoman who had fallen on hard times, to look after young Richard. John was now aged eleven and, not wishing to lose one day in the progression of his naval career, Daniel had sent him on board the *Alecto,* a fireship commanded by his son Henry, pending his father's return.

This return was unlikely to be in the foreseeable future; in January 1799 Lord St. Vincent needed every ship he could get his hands on. With the destruction of the French Fleet at the Nile and the capture of Minorca in November, Britain had, once again, got her foot in the door of the Mediterranean. France was wounded and apprehensive.

At Brest, the French Atlantic Fleet of twenty-five ships-of-the-line lay at anchor blockaded by Lord Bridport's Channel Fleet; in Cadiz were seventeen Spanish ships-of-the-line blockaded by Lord Keith's Squadron which included the *London*; the Spanish also had five of-the-line at Ferrol giving Britain's enemies a massive potential force of forty-seven plus frigates and ancillaries. Their obvious course was to consolidate this force and break into the Mediterranean, firstly to release and repatriate Bonaparte's army which was marooned in Egypt and, secondly, to engage the inferior British Fleet and drive it from the Mediterranean.

France's finest Admiral, Eustache de Bruix, who was then serving as the French Minister of Marine, was therefore put in command of the Brest Fleet with orders to break out and join up with the Spanish Fleet at Cadiz having collected the ships at Ferrol on the way. To accomplish this, an elaborate deception was planned, which included the orchestrated 'capture' by the British of a French ship carrying phoney plans, to convince Britain that a Franco-Dutch springboard invasion of Britain, via Ireland, was imminent. The deception was a complete success and Bruix slipped out of Brest on 25th April heading south-west while Lord Bridport headed in the opposite direction believing him bound for Ireland.

Waiting in Bruix's path off Cadiz was Lord Keith's Squadron of sixteen of-the-line including the *London*. Lord St. Vincent, whose health had seriously deteriorated, flew his Flag on a depot ship at Gibraltar. On 3rd May Lord Keith received intelligence that the five Spanish ships of-the-line had left Ferrol and that Bruix's Fleet was approaching the Strait of Gibraltar.

At 0950 Captain Purvis received the order to "prepare to weigh" and at 1015 for "all boats to repair on board their ships". The Squadron weighed at 1100 and stood out to sea to place itself between the Spanish Fleet in Cadiz and the French Fleet approaching from the west. At 1000 the following morning with the French Fleet in sight the ship was cleared for action and the Squadron formed line of battle in close order. Thirty-three enemy sail were counted; the British Squadron numbered sixteen.

There was a fresh and rapidly strengthening north-west wind as Bruix's ships approached on a north-easterly course on the port tack. Lord Keith ordered his ships to lay off on the same tack to receive them. As the onshore wind strengthened to gale force it soon became clear that the Spanish ships in Cadiz would not be able to leave the harbour, even if they wanted to. Then, to the surprise of the British, Admiral Bruix declined Lord Keith's challenge, ordering his Fleet to wear again and stand away to the south-west. By the evening the wind had increased still further and visibility had deteriorated to the point that it was almost impossible to see the French Fleet through the driving spray. It appeared, however, that

Bruix had no wish to enter Cadiz, nor to engage the British Squadron, but was intent on running before the gale to pass through the Strait and enter the Mediterranean as quickly as he could.

The following day, Lord St. Vincent at Gibraltar witnessed the awesome sight of Bruix's Fleet passing the Rock. Although there were thirty British ships of-the-line in the Mediterranean, they were widely dispersed: sixteen were with Lord Keith off Cadiz; four were with Duckworth at Minorca; Nelson had one at Palermo; Troubridge four at Naples; Ball three blockading Malta and Sir Sydney Smith had two at Acre, bolstering the Turkish defence of that port to block Bonaparte's Egyptian army from returning to France overland through Syria. An immediate consolidation was necessary; firstly he had to recall Keith's Squadron from Cadiz but how to get the order to him, with a westerly gale blowing through the Strait, was another matter. Three attempts failed: the first messenger was captured by the Spanish at Algeçiras; the next got to Tarifa where he disappeared; the third crossed to Tangier to try and reach the Squadron from the North African coast and he, too, disappeared. Then Benjamin Tucker, the Admiral's new secretary, volunteered to take a boat with a hand-picked crew of oarsmen and try to pull through the Strait. The boat was almost swamped and had to turn back after a day and a night in the attempt. Eventually, a message was got through to the Squadron by trickery: Sir Isaac Coffin, an American who had served as Commissioner of the Dockyard at Lisbon, managed to obtain a Spanish transit passport by false pretences. Reaching Cadiz, he bribed a fisherman to take a message out to the British Squadron offshore which promptly abandoned the blockade and arrived at Gibraltar on 10th May.

Lord St. Vincent then resumed sea command, hoisting his Flag again in the *Ville de Paris*, with Lord Keith in the *Barfleur* as his second-in-command, and weighed anchor on 12th May to collect Rear-Admiral Duckworth and his four seventy-fours from Minorca.

Captain Purvis in the *London* was then to be involved in what must surely have been the most futile and frustrating exercise of his career to date — a three-month search for Admiral Bruix during which the British Fleet would cross and recross the Western Mediterranean, following up doubtful or out-of-date intelligence as to his whereabouts, never once catching sight of him, let alone engaging his Fleet, and eventually pursuing him all the way back to Brest from whence he came.

With the British blockade of Cadiz lifted, the Spanish Admiral Massaredo felt it was now safe to take his Fleet to sea which he did on 14th May, sailing east and arriving at Cartagena on the 20th. However, violent storms on the 17th and 18th took a heavy toll on his Fleet with two ships colliding and ten out of his seventeen ships of-the-line being partially or wholly dismasted. Bruix, meanwhile, had reached Toulon where he received orders to support the French forces in Italy and thence to proceed to Alexandria to embark Bonaparte's stranded army.

The *London* anchored at Port Mahon, Minorca, on 21st May, Captain Purvis's good seamanship having saved the ship from major damage in the storms which had ravaged Massaredo's Fleet. They sailed the following day in company with twenty sail of-the-line, three frigates, one brig and a hospital ship heading, initially, for Toulon; but on the 26th Lord St. Vincent learning, it is thought, that Massaredo was in Cartagena, altered course to the west to place himself between the Spanish and French Fleets. For the next four days the British Fleet cruised off Cape de Creux [Cap de Creus] and down the Spanish coast as far as Barcelona with no sign of an enemy. Then on the 30th St. Vincent learned that Bruix had left Toulon three days earlier so the Fleet turned round and headed east again. Meanwhile, lest the French should be heading south-east for the Tyrrhenian, the Admiral detached four ships of-the-line under Duckworth, now a Rear-Admiral, to reinforce Nelson at Palermo. This loss of strength was made up for later the same day with the arrival of Rear-Admiral Whitshed in the *Queen Charlotte*, 100, with four other ships of-the-line from the Channel Fleet which now had no need to blockade the empty port of Brest. As Captain Purvis watched the *Queen Charlotte* join the Fleet off Cape de Creux, he had no idea that his son, John, was a Midshipman aboard her, Henry Garrett having obtained a berth for him in the Flagship before she sailed from England.

On 2nd June Lord St. Vincent finally gave in to the illness which had been dogging him for several months and, handing over command to Lord Keith, left the Fleet in the *Ville de Paris* to return, via Minorca, to England. This difficult, dedicated, dynamic man had done more than any other to reform the Royal Navy into a motivated, superbly-effective, battle-winning force. Nelson, imploring him not to leave wrote: "We look up to you as we have always found you, as to our father, under whose fostering care we have been led to fame." But he had had enough; his exertions, as he explained in a letter to the First Lord, having been sapped "to the very foundation by such a rapid decline of health as to bereave me of all powers both of body and mind". But he was to rise again and Captain Purvis had not seen the last of 'Old Jarvie'.

The new Commander-in-Chief, Lord Keith, headed for Toulon arriving off the port on 3rd June to learn that Bruix had left the previous week heading up the Ligurian coast towards Genoa; the British Fleet followed and on the 5th received a report that the French Fleet had been seen at anchor in Vado Bay, near Savona. Bruix had, in fact, been landing troops and stores for the relief of Savona, which was under siege from the Austrians and Russians, but had left on the 1st or 2nd, had lain off Genoa until 6th June when he had headed south-west on a parallel course to Lord Keith who was coming the other way to find him. The two Fleets must have passed just out of sight of each other travelling in opposite directions.

It then became apparent that Lord St. Vincent had not, altogether, relinquished the reins as on the 8th, when the *London* was off Villefranche, Lord Keith received orders from him at Port Mahon, to proceed to Rosas Bay, some seventy-five miles north-east of Barcelona, to intercept Bruix whom Lord St. Vincent believed to be heading for Cartagena to link up with Massaredo. It was therefore another 'about turn' for the British Fleet but, instead of heading straight for Rosas Bay, Keith sailed first for Minorca, and thence back again towards Toulon off which on 19th June his advance division fell in with and captured five French warships — three frigates and two brigs — which were eventually all commissioned into the Royal Navy. This was the only solid achievement of an otherwise sterile summer.

From Toulon it was back east to Villefranche, Genoa, Corsica, back and forth along the Ligurian coast until 4th July without sight of an enemy vessel. Lord Keith then headed back to Minorca where the Fleet anchored off Port Mahon on 9th July. By this time, Bruix, having amalgamated with the Spanish Fleet at Cartagena, had passed back through the Strait of Gibraltar and was about to enter the unguarded harbour at Cadiz from where the joint Fleet sailed for Brest on the 21st — twenty-five French and fifteen Spanish ships of-the-line.

Lord Keith weighed from Port Mahon on the 10th and set off in pursuit having, several times, sent orders to Nelson to send ships to take over the protection of Minorca. Nelson ignored these orders. Before he sailed, Captain Purvis took his son, John, into the *London* with him; the boy's Mediterranean adventure was over and he must now, under his father's guidance, get down to the serious apprenticeship of a sea officer.

By the time the British left Gibraltar on 30th June the Franco-Spanish Fleet was three weeks ahead of them. The Commander-in-Chief urged his Captains to press on regardless carrying all the sail their ships would stand. Steadily the gap narrowed. On 8th August off Cape Finister [Finisterre], intelligence received from a Danish ship led Lord Keith to estimate that they were now about two days behind the enemy. The next day they met a British frigate, the *Stag,* 36, which reported them off Cape Ortegal on a north-easterly course. With a final, desperate push the British Fleet headed across the Bay of Biscay with every knot each Captain could squeeze from his sea-weary ship. On 14th August they were off Brest and Lord Keith sent Sir Edward Pellew in the *Impétueux* to look into the harbour where he reported the entire Franco-Spanish Fleet safely at anchor. They had arrived just the day before.

With armchair wisdom and hindsight, it is difficult not to indulge in some brief speculation as to how the whole course of history might have been changed: What if Lord Bridport had intercepted Bruix when he left Brest in April? Or if Bruix had accepted Lord Keith's challenge off Cadiz in May? Or if Lord Keith had followed Lord St. Vincent's orders more closely and proceeded direct to Rosas Bay in June? Or if the Fleet had managed to squeeze an extra half knot from its ships and bring Bruix and Massaredo to battle before they reached Brest in August?

Though numerically inferior, the morale, training, discipline and seamanship in the British Mediterranean Fleet was at such a high pitch that it would almost certainly have defeated any enemy it

TABLE H. LORD BRIDPORT'S CHANNEL FLEET
2nd SEPTEMBER 1799

Rate	Ship	Commander	Guns			Division
2nd	*Téméraire*	Rear-Adml. Sir John Warren Bt				
		Capt. Thomas Eyles	98	STARBOARD DIVISION	Sir John Warren	
3rd	*Dragon*	Capt. George Campbell	74			
3rd	*Superb*	Capt. John Sutton	74			
2nd	*Neptune*	Capt. James Vashon	98			
	Nassau †	Capt. George Tripp	64			VAN
3rd	*Ajax*	Capt. Hon. Alexander Cochrane	74			
1st	*Royal Sovereign*	Rear-Adml. Sir Alan Gardner Bt.				
		Capt. Bedford	100	LARBOARD DIVISION		
3rd	*Sans Pareil*	Capt. Charles Vinicombe Penrose	80		Sir Alan Gardner	
3rd	*Repulse*	Capt. James Alms	64			
3rd	*Monarch*	Capt. James Robert Mosse	74			
3rd	*Centaur*	Capt. John Markham	74			
3rd	*Achille*	Capt. George Murray	74			
3rd	*Impetueux*	Capt. Sir Edward Pellew Bt.	74			
2nd	*Prince*	Rear-Adml. Sir Charles Cotton Bt.				
		Capt. Samuel Sutton	98	STARBOARD DIVISION	Sir Charles Cotton	
3rd	*Captain*	Capt. Sir Richard Strachan Bt.	74			
3rd	*Russell*	Capt. Herbert Sawyer	74			
2nd	*Glory*	Capt. Thomas Wells	98			
3rd	*Prince Frederick*	Capt. John Stephens Hall	64			
3rd	*Renown*	Capt. George Hopewell Stephens	74		CENTRE	
3rd	*Caesar*	Capt. Sir James Saumarez	80		*Lord*	
1st	*Royal George*	Admiral Lord Bridport			*Bridport*	
		Rear-Adml. Charles Morice Pole			*Commander-*	
		Capt. Ross Donnelly	100		*in-Chief*	
2nd	*Formidable*	Capt. Edward Thornbrough	90	LARBOARD DIVISION		
3rd	*Saturn*	Capt. Thomas Totty	74			
3rd	*Defiance*	Capt. Thomas Revell Shivers	74			
1st	*Ville de Paris*	Capt. Walter Bathurst	110		Rear-Admiral Pole	
3rd	*Agamemnon*	Capt. Robert Devereux Fancourt	64			
3rd	*Robust*	Capt. George Countess	74			
3rd	*Terrible*	Capt. William Wolseley	74			
2nd	*Barfleur*	Capt. Hon. Charles Paget	98			
3rd	*Canada*	Rear-Adml. J. A. Whitshed				
		Capt. Hon. Michael de Courcy	74	STARBOARD DIVISION	Rear-Admiral Whitshed	
3rd	*Magnificent*	Capt. Edward Bowater	74			
3rd	*Raisonable*	Capt. Charles Boyles	64			
2nd	*London*	Capt. John Child Purvis	90			
3rd	*Ruby*	Capt. Hon. Francis Ffarington Gardner	64			
3rd	*Pompée*	Capt. Charles Stirling	80		REAR	
1st	*Queen Charlotte*	Capt. Andrew Todd	100			
2nd	*Atlas*	Vice-Adml. Lord Keith				
		Capt. Jones	98	LARBOARD DIVISION		
3rd	*Ramilles*	Capt. Richard Grindall	74		Lord Keith	
2nd	*St. George*	Capt. Sampson Edwards	98			
3rd	*Venerable*	Capt. Sir William George Fairfax	74			
3rd	*Juste*	Capt. Sir Henry Trollope	80			

† Armed Transport

might have encountered; and with, perhaps, something approaching 100 ships involved, such an engagement might have been the greatest British victory of all time. But that is not what happened.

After the bitter disappointment of this historic chase, Captain Purvis anchored the *London* in Torbay on Friday 16th August where he was placed again under the orders of Lord Bridport in the

Channel Fleet. On 1st September he sailed for a three-week patrol on his old blockading ground off Ushant where he was to watch the enemy Fleet he had so recently chased up from the Mediterranean. On his return to Torbay, the *London* requiring some work on her hull, he was ordered to Spithead to await a place in Portsmouth Dockyard. On 31st October he entered the harbour and started unrigging the ship and on 11th November warped into his allocated dock having removed the remainder of the ship's pig ballast. The work was completed by the end of the month when *London* moved back to Portsmouth Harbour where she remained moored until 16th January 1800 when a pilot took her out to anchorage in Spithead.

On 4th January, the eleventh birthday of his younger son, Richard, Captain Purvis took the boy into the *London* to join his brother and the other youngsters in the gunroom. He had applied for a place for him at the Naval Academy in Portsmouth Dockyard but none had been available. Rather than leave him in the care of the sixty-five year-old Ann Porter until such time as a vacancy might occur, he thought it better to take Richard to sea with him. He wrote to Daniel Garrett explaining his reasons and seeking his father-in-law's endorsement which was readily forthcoming:

I perfectly coincide with you that as you have now masters of every sort to teach every branch of learning to your sons, that Richard being with you will be of service to him in every respect and particularly in that of his time going on in the Service. This will not I apprehend preclude you if you choose it putting him into the Academy when a vacancy offers for him. Under your own eye, both John and Richard will I am sure improve in all those requisites for their situations.[3]

Mr Garrett also made it clear that, while he realised that his son-in-law's distress at the loss of his wife was equal to his own at the loss of his daughter, John would have his blessing, and would suffer no withdrawal of his support and friendship, should he decide to remarry in the future:

. . . for when the war is over I trust I shall see you again happily settled in your sweet cottage with some worthy and good woman as your companion and wife who will make as affectionate a friend to you as did our much lamented and beloved Mary. You are deserving of domestic happiness and we trust and hope that by and by you will again enjoy it.[4]

An ever-steadfast friend, Daniel Garrett also undertook to attend to his son-in-law's investments and financial matters while he was at sea and to keep an eye on his cottage and his servants at Wickham so he should have no worries ashore and could concentrate on the demands of his ship and on winning the war.

Initially uncertain as to whether he would be sent to rejoin Lord Keith or remain in the Channel with Lord Bridport, his orders for the latter eventually came through and he moved the *London* to Torbay to resume his patrols off Ushant as part of the Blockade of Brest. On returning from one such in April, he learned that Lord Bridport had been ordered to haul down his Flag and had been replaced by none other than Lord St. Vincent, now sufficiently recovered in health to take on the shaking-up of the Channel Fleet as he had shaken-up the Mediterranean Fleet four years earlier. Now aged sixty-five, he had recently been challenged to a duel by Vice-Admiral Sir John Orde, still burning with resentment over the slight he had received two years earlier; it had taken the direct intervention of the King to put a stop to this absurd affair of honour.

There were no surprises for Purvis who knew exactly what to expect from the new Commander-in-Chief but those Captains who had never served under him were in for some unpleasant shocks. Firstly, there was the nature of the blockade itself:

In today's vernacular, St. Vincent's blockade strategy might be described as one of 'zero tolerance'. It was not simply a question of keeping the mighty Franco-Spanish Fleet bottled up in Brest, it was necessary to prevent its resupply with every item of stores and equipment required to keep it in a seaworthy condition. Such items would normally be conveyed by coastal vessels to avoid the protracted and expensive business of overland transport. Under Lord Bridport, the blockading squadrons stood well out to sea and much of this merchant traffic was slipping in to the harbour by keeping close to the coast. Now, frigates and cutters were ordered to patrol close inshore, in the very harbour mouth, just out of range of the enemy shore batteries; not one single vessel, of whatever size, was to be allowed to enter or leave Brest. An inshore squadron of ships-of-the-line patrolled the treacherous area of the 'Black Rocks' between Ushant and the harbour mouth and the main force, also, had to move much closer in to keep the inshore squadron in sight

and in position to respond immediately to their signals in the event
of an attempted break out. The coast off Ushant abounded with
treacherous reefs and dangerous currents making this close
blockade extremely hard work for the ships' crews and requiring
constant vigilance and impeccable pilotage from the officers. The
new orders, and their instigator, were not welcomed by the old, tired
hands of the Channel Fleet who had been used to a much easier life
under the previous Commander-in-Chief. It had been simple, and
common, in those days for a Captain to plead necessary repairs to
his ship to get into port where he could stay for as long as he could
string out the work. Not any more; Captains were forbidden to take
their ships to Spithead and, if they required spars or rigging to make
good storm damage, it must be indented for immediately the ship
moored in Cawsand Bay: ". . . that I may know where to attach the
blame if she is not at sea in a reasonable time, which never ought to
exceed a week." Lord St. Vincent's belief was that a warship's place
was at sea; officers were forbidden to sleep ashore; no boats were
allowed to be afloat after sunset and Captains were called upon to
explain the slightest delay in provisioning or repairs. 'Old Jarvie'
made himself deeply unpopular with the old guard and became,
behind his back, the object of much lampooning and abuse.

Early in May the blockade was dispersed by a violent storm, the
worst in living memory, in which several ships of the Fleet were
dismasted or damaged and three sloops-of-war were lost with all
hands. Lord St. Vincent ordered his ships to act independently and
run for cover but if any of their crews thought this heralded a brief
period of respite they were to be disappointed; they were ordered
back to sea to resume the blockade the moment the storm had
abated. The *London* was ordered to provision for five months at sea
and aware that the Commander-in-Chief would brook no delays,
Captain Purvis's concern can be understood:

London, Cawsand Bay, 14th May 1800. To: Agent Victualler, Plymouth.
Sir, His Majesty's Ship under my command having been at this anchorage since
the 9th instant and the demands having been sent immediately on her arrival, I am
sorry to be obliged to express my surprize that neither beer nor water has been yet
received on board as my orders from the Earl of St Vincent are to get ready for
sea with all possible dispatch.

And to his Purser, Richard Booth:

As I conceive from the length of time the ship has been at this anchorage the
provisions, beer, water and all species of necessaries ought to have been on board
and a report made from you to me of such being the case, I desire you will
immediately make me acquainted with the cause of the delay that I may
endeavour to remove it.

The following day, eight days after his arrival, he was able to report
to Rear-Admiral Hon. George Berkeley that he was ready for the
marathon summer patrol off Ushant which Lord St. Vincent had
planned for the Channel Fleet:

Sir — In obedience to your directions, I beg leave to inform you His Majesty's
Ship under my command has completed her provisions for five months in
compliance to the orders I was under, her stores to Channel service so far as the
nature of the supply in the dockyard would admit and being paid she is now in
readiness for sea.

His ship's company may have been paid but Captain Purvis had not
as he had pointed out to the Principal Officers and Commissioners
of His Majesty's Navy on 8th May:

Gentlemen, Having within a few days completed my third year in command of
this ship, I trust you will not deem me troublesome by stating that my pay for the
second year is not yet received by my agent and amongst various reasons he has
given me for its being witheld he informs me a Mr [Chusor] had drawn a Bill on
your Board for £123.11.6. in favour of Mr Gaudolphi for stores purchased by him
at Leghorn on 16 February 1796. I beg to state to you that I had nothing to do
with such purchase in any respect whatever; when stores were necessary,
demands were directed to be presented to the Commander-in-Chief for his
inspection and approval and by his order they were had from such persons as he
thought proper to appoint and receipts given accordingly by the officer in whose
department they properly belonged. I must therefore request you have the
goodness to direct that the imprest or the hindrance may be removed that I may
receive the pay which has so long been due to me.

One of the favourite stories told of the mischief of 'Old Jarvie' is
how, one day in squally weather during the blockade of Cadiz, he
signalled for all the Chaplains of the Fleet to repair on board the

Flagship. This entailed a long pull from their ships in choppy seas until they arrived aboard the *Ville de Paris*, sick, soaking wet and in low spirits. Lord St. Vincent greeted them on the quarterdeck and suggested that they should go below where he felt they might like to hold a little conclave with 'The Bishop' as he called his own Chaplain. He had a generally low opinion of the clergymen serving with the Channel Fleet having written to the Archbishop of Canterbury on the subject and having reported to the First Lord that: ". . . we have some roué parsons who really should not hold their situations." When Captain Purvis passed on a request from the *London*'s Chaplain for two weeks leave in the middle of the summer blockade, he cannot, therefore, have been expecting a cordial response from the Commander-in-Chief:

I have received your letter of this date enclosing one from the Revd. Cudworth Bruch, chaplain of His Majesty's Ship under your command, requesting to be indulged with a fortnight's leave and notwithstanding I am persuaded the chaplains in this fleet should perform their duty more conscientiously than they do (and Lord Spencer is of the same opinion) I will transmit his letter and recommend that it might be complied with.

Though the 'Mediterranean Discipline' was slowly taking hold and morale in the Channel Fleet steadily improving, there was still a seditious element in several of the ships. In the *Terrible,* according to Lord St. Vincent, were "two hundred Irish of the very worst description", and "the licentiousness on board the *Pompée* and *Montague* is enough to ruin any fleet". He also considered that the *London* still had "a deal of mischief in her", over which Captain Purvis kept a constant watching brief. On 30th July he wrote to the Commander-in-Chief:

I beg leave to inform your Lordship that the man (a quartermaster whose name is in the margin [Daniel Dorman]) I have long had every reason to deem the most disaffected person aboard His Majesty's Ship under my command and in consequence have had a watchful attention paid to his conduct; but he has been too guarded to allow himself to be brought to punishment until last night when he was heard by the Master-at-Arms singing a song replete with expressions of a treasonable nature and tending to stir up mutiny in the minds of those about him. I have him in confinement with the promise of a court martial but as I cannot, I fear, sufficiently establish the charge, there being only one witness, I must request your Lordship will be pleased to remove him from the ship and I will take the liberty of giving him a proper correction at the gangway just before he leaves here. Whoever your Lordship may think proper to place him with will find him in every respect (except that which he is now charged with) a very useful, able, perfect seaman.

to which Lord St. Vincent replied the following day:

I enclose an order for the discharge of Daniel Dorman into His Majesty's Ship *Alcmène* but I trust you will not suffer him to go from the *London* without receiving what he deserves; and I desire you will acquaint Captain Digby of his disposition that he may be on his guard against it.

After the thrashing he no doubt received from a burly boatswain's mate as he approached the brow of the *London,* it is unlikely that Daniel Dorman sang songs "replete with expressions of a treasonable nature" on board his new ship.

The 1800 summer blockade of Brest was to last for 121 days during which the Commander-in-Chief neither relinquished his station nor relaxed his demands for a moment. For much of the time the *London* was in Rear-Admiral Berkeley's inshore squadron in the area of the Black Rocks and the strain of constant operations in such notoriously dangerous waters clearly had its effect on Berkeley, who, Lord St. Vincent told the First Lord:

... does not like the Black Rocks where I was obliged to pin him for though when under sail with an easterly wind he was strictly enjoined to be close in with them, at daylight every morning, I generally found him without me; probably not imagining that I was upon deck at 3 o'clock a.m.

Captain Purvis, however, did not have to endure the full course of this campaign as, early in August, a squadron of five of-the-line and six frigates was detached, under the command of Rear-Admiral Sir John Warren, to launch a joint-service attack on the Spanish port of Ferrol where six of Admiral Masseredo's ships were reported to be ready for sea. After provisioning in Cawsand Bay, *London* sailed on 11th August anchoring off the Isle of Honat [Île d'Houat], a small island off Belle Isle [Belle-Île] on the 16th. Here the British had established a large encampment and the following day the boats were employed embarking field pieces, howitzers and artillerymen for the attack. It was not, however, the artillerymen who worried Captain Purvis. He wrote to Sir Edward Pellew:

In the party of 23 artillerymen just embarked on board His Majesty's Ship under my command there are two women and possibly more may be on their way to the ship with the remaining party. I am therefore to request you will be pleased to direct me whether they are to remain on board and, in case they are, in what manner they are to be victualled, particularly in the event of the men being landed and the women left on board. P.S. Should it be thought proper to victual the women, I must beg of you to send me an order for that purpose.

The request for such an order, in such a seemingly minor matter, was not unusual. A Captain who failed to obtain authorisation for the slightest increase in his scale was likely to have the difference debited to him personally. "Survey" was the constant cry; every worn out rope, every rotten piece of cheese, even a mentally-disturbed officer suffering hallucinations had to be 'surveyed' by an appropriately-appointed person or persons before it, or he, could be discarded, thrown overboard or sent ashore to hospital as the case might be; and the request for, and verdict of, every 'survey' had to be recorded officially in the ship's books so there could be no misunderstanding at a later date.

At 1600 on 16th August the *London* anchored in a small bay between Cape Prior and Ferrol. Having landed the artillerymen she carried, together with their guns and equipment, Captain Purvis sent the boats to move the troops from the transports to the shore. Anchored with *London* in the bay were Admiral Warren's Flagship, the *Renown*, together with *Impetueux, Ajax, Courageux, Gibraltar*, four frigates, one sloop-of-war, one gun-brig, fourteen cutters, one schooner, seven troop ships and sixty-three transports. The troops landed numbered some 9,000.

CHAPTER 6

Royal George

Wednesday 27th August 1800
H.M.S. London
off Ferrol

T here is a song sung by English children which commemorates the undistinguished leadership of Prince Frederick Augustus, Duke of York and Albany, the second son of George III, in Flanders in 1793, at the time Captain Purvis was commanding the *Princess Royal* at Toulon:

> *The grand old Duke of York,*
> *He had ten thousand men,*
> *He marched them up to the top of a hill*
> *Then he marched them down again.*

A similar memorial must surely have been earned by Lieutenant-General Sir James Pulteney in command of the land forces in the Ferrol expedition. Having disembarked his 9,000 men from the massive armada of ninety-seven ships anchored in the bay, he abandoned the attack and re-embarked them all the following day.

   The 26th had started with promise as Captain Purvis recorded:

There was little or no opposition made by the enemy and by 12 o'clock the whole of the troops were landed amounting to about 9,000. The enemy in the fort discharged their guns and on then being fired at by the Impetueux and a gun brig, they all ran away.

The next morning the British troops and a detachment of seamen drove the enemy back and took possession of the high ground commanding the town and harbour. It is probable that the force could then have taken Ferrol, and the six Spanish ships of-the-line, without difficulty. However, the General, possibly misled by false intelligence as to the strength of the enemy, decided to abort the operation and, later in the day, re-embarked his men on board the ships in the bay which had that morning been joined by *Argo, Magicienne, Indefatigable* and *Diamond* making a grand total of 101 sail.

But the expedition was not to be entirely without glory: the Squadron headed south and on the 29th anchored in Vigo Bay where Captain Purvis sent two of his boats, fully manned and armed, to join a force of twenty boats, commanded by Lieutenant Henry Burke, tasked with cutting out the French privateer *La Guêpe*, 18, from beneath the batteries of Vigo Bay. In one of the *London*'s boats was fifteen year-old Midshipman John Scott, a special protégé of Captain Purvis.

The ship was boarded and, after fifteen minutes of furious fighting, captured. Three British seamen and one marine had been killed and one seaman lost; three Lieutenants, twelve seamen and five marines were wounded. John Scott took a prominent part in the fighting for which he later received a commendation; William Griffiths of the *London* was one of the seamen killed in the action and the enemy suffered twenty-five killed and forty wounded.

At 0500 on the 30th, Captain Purvis saw his boats returning with their prize in tow. He then sent the launch with a prize crew of one petty officer and sixteen men to take control of her and to bring the French prisoners, numbering 112, back to the *London*. The following day he received a letter from Sir John Warren:

I request you will communicate to the officers, seamen and marines belonging to His Majesty's Ship under your command who were employed with the boats on the 29th Inst. in engaging and capturing La Guêpe, French privateer, that I am highly pleased with the very great bravery displayed by them in the above service and I beg you will return them my thanks for their meritorious conduct which I shall take the earliest opportunity to represent to the Commander-in-Chief.

A week later the Squadron was still at anchor in Vigo Bay unable to put to sea against a strong westerly wind which in the early hours of 7th September increased to gale force with squally showers. Captain Purvis ordered the *London*'s cable to be lengthened and at 0300 learned that the *Stag*, 32, had parted her cable and driven ashore. He immediately ordered the launch and large cutter to be hoisted out, loaded with the kedge anchor and a nine-inch hawser and sent to Captain Winthrop's assistance; but the frigate was doomed and all the boats' crews could do was to save as much of her stores as they could. Presently the stricken ship was seen to be on fire fore and aft and later blew up. Captain Purvis hoisted in his boats and ordered the *London*'s yards turned in to the wind.

A little later a distress signal was received from the *Tartarus*, bomb, and Captain Purvis, again, ordered the launch to be swung out and loaded with anchor and cable. Then, the next day, having taken into the *London* the crew of the wrecked *Stag*, the *Julius Caesar*, a large transport, broke loose and drove athwart the *London*'s cable carrying away her own mizzen mast and both the *London*'s bumpkins. Captain Purvis got his carpenters to make a new mizzen for the *Julius Caesar* which was ready and sent over to her the next day. On the 10th the wind changed and the Squadron ran out of Vigo Bay to the comparative safety of the open sea.

While at anchor off Vigo, a Midshipman who was thought to have deserted in Cawsand Bay had rejoined the ship and Captain Purvis wrote to the Admiralty to have the 'R' removed from his record:

Mr William Garde Hill, Midshipman, having been made run on books of His Majesty's Ship under my command on 9th August 1800 but having voluntarily joined the ship at sea on 7th Inst. I have reason to think he did not intend to desert the service and therefore request you will please to cause his R. to be taken off.

After cruising off the Portuguese coast for the next three weeks, the *London* returned to Cawsand Bay on 10th October where Captain Purvis received a letter from Sir John Warren passing on Lord St. Vincent's approval of the part played by his ship at Ferrol:

The Commander-in-Chief having expressed to me his entire approbation of your conduct and the officers, seamen and marines of His Majesty's Ship under your command upon every occasion that presented during the late expedition, has desired me to return his thanks for the zeal which was manifested and the exertions made by them upon that service . . .

But 'Old Jarvie' had not mellowed. The following day:

Lord St Vincent desires the utmost despatch in provisioning the ship, getting her to sea and joining him off Brest.

Anxious to comply with the Commander-in-Chief's wishes and to avoid any delays caused by his sailors embarking upon a drunken run ashore in Plymouth, Captain Purvis placed a marine sentry at the dockyard gates with strict orders not to allow any of the Londons through; but this was not allowing for the marine sentry himself becoming drunk:

London, Cawsand Bay, 14th October 1800. To: Maj-Gen John Campbell Sir — Corporal John Staples of the marines serving aboard His Majesty's Ship under my command having got drunk when on duty at the Dock Gates and in consequence allowed the seamen to pass out of the Yard contrary to very particular orders he had received, I am to request you will please to exchange him for another Corporal from Headquarters.

On the same day, a Plymouth Sound pilot came on board and advised Captain Purvis that his ship was anchored on foul ground and that it was essential he should move his position. While manoeuvring his ship, a difficult undertaking involving the employment of warps and kedge anchors, with an unfavourable wind impeding the operation, a lighter drew alongside with water he had ordered. Preoccupied with the movement and safety of his ship, Purvis sent the lighter away telling its Master to deliver the water to another ship in the Fleet and to return to the *London* the next day. The following correspondence illustrates the extraordinary extent to which Lord St. Vincent concerned himself with the minutiae of his Fleet's day-to-day business and also what a demanding and tenacious taskmaster he could be in matters of seemingly minor import:

Lord St. Vincent to Captain Purvis, 28th October 1800

Sir — As I am under the necessity of representing to the Lords Commissioners of the Admiralty when the water which is sent off for the supply of His Majesty's Ship under your command is not immediately taken on board, I desire you will state to me in writing for their Lordships' information the reason of 25 tons not being taken on board the ship you command in Cawsand Bay on the 14th Inst. and 65 on the following day all of which had been previously demanded.

Captain Purvis to Lord St. Vincent, 28th October 1800

My Lord — In obedience to your Lordship's directions of this day to state the reason the water was not received on board His Majesty's Ship under my command on the 14th and 15th Inst. whilst in Cawsand Bay, I beg to state that there was none came alongside on the 14th but on the evening of that day the pilot came on board and represented that the ship was anchored in foul ground and he deemed it very necessary she should be moved as soon as possible and that he would be on board in the morning to shift her berth; when the ship was fast moving the two lighters came on board and as there was a fresh breeze of wind which required working into the bay, the lighters were directed either to go to some other ship or return when the London came to an anchor; but the masters of those lighters chose to return with the water into the harbour.

Lord St. Vincent to Captain Purvis, 8th November 1800

Having transmitted to the Agent Victualler at Plymouth your answer to my letter on the subject of the water not being taken on board the London when last in Cawsand Bay, I have recd. the enclosed reply thereto . . .

Captain Purvis to Lord St. Vincent, 10th November 1800

My Lord — I have just had the honor to receive your Lordship's letter of the 8th Inst. enclosing a letter from the Agent Victualler at Plymouth, another from Mr Tonkin and a receipt for water from the Purser's Steward of His Majesty's Ship under my command dated 14th October. I beg leave to state to your Lordship that on examining the Log Book I find the water alluded to was recd. on the 15th pm which accords with the date of the receipt which before escaped my observation, having only attended to the Sea Log, but in respect of the succeeding day, it was not possible to have cleared any lighter of water without neglecting business of much greater importance the ship shifting her berth, the sheet and small bower cables being to shift and the pilot a considerable time in mooring the ship the wind being unfavourable for that purpose and thereby rendering it necessary to run out warps to place her properly. I enclose to your Lordship the letters of Messrs. Miller and Tonkin and the Purser's Steward's receipt.

On 6th November, between the two phases of this extraordinary correspondence, Captain Purvis was called upon to explain why one of his officers, sent into Plymouth in the ship's launch for water, had left the boat while it was alongside the wharf in contravention of the Commander-in-Chief's Standing Instructions:

Captain Purvis to Lord St. Vincent, 6th November 1800

My Lord — In obedience to the orders I have just received respecting the Lieutenant who went out of the launch of His Majesty's Ship under my command to the wharf on the 6th Inst., I beg to state to your Lordship that on the above mentioned day Lieutenant William Archbold was sent with the launch for water and it appears that on his arriving at the wharf and finding there was no guard there, he got out of the launch whilst the water was filling to look after the two men who were placed at the cocks, that he was not one instant from the edge of the wharf and that none of the boat's crew was out of the boat the whole time, except the above mentioned two men who attended the cocks.

By this time Lord St. Vincent, his health having deteriorated to the point where he could not countenance the prospect of another winter at sea, had taken up his headquarters at Torre Abbey in the centre of what is, today, the town of Torquay. From here he continued to command the Channel Fleet, observing its performance from the shore and was pleased to report to the First Lord that: "the whole fleet can be got under sail and well out of the Bay in an hour and a half from the time of making the signal to unmoor." This was a level of competence never previously attained by any Channel Fleet and, when the wind was fair, its place was at sea off Brest.

The story is told how on one occasion, when the Fleet was at anchor in Torbay, 'Old Jarvie' had indulged his love of entertaining by inviting his Flag Officers and Captains to a grand ball at Torre Abbey. Delighted at the prospect of a night ashore and a break from their unceasing and exhausting routine, the officers arrived at the Abbey to be met at the door by the Commander-in-Chief who told them that an easterly wind was coming and that they must return to their ships immediately and get ready for sea.

Through November, December and January 1801 Captain Purvis patrolled among the Black Rocks, an area known in the Channel Fleet as 'New Siberia', his seamanship taxed to the limit in the violent winter storms which on two occasions drove the Fleet back to Torbay. Meanwhile, there was trouble brewing in the Baltic.

Resentful of Britain's interference with their supply of naval and military matériel to republican France, and egged on by Bonaparte and the Tsar of Russia, Sweden and Denmark had renewed the League of Armed Neutrality, an alliance with Russia and Prussia under which they sought to enjoy unrestricted trade with Britain's enemies. British merchantmen lying in Russian ports were impounded pending Britain's agreement to their demands which, if complied with, would negate the whole effect of the blockade which the Royal Navy had for so long been enforcing. Clearly the Baltic powers needed to be disciplined. Lord St. Vincent, an expert in such matters, advocated "a great stroke at Copenhagen", as being the most convenient and cost-effective form of admonition.

A Fleet was therefore assembled for an expedition to the shallow waters of the Baltic and the *London* "on account of her easy draught of water", was selected as the Flagship for the force. Its brief was an initial show of strength which would, it was hoped, bring the Baltic powers into line but, if this failed, the Fleet must be prepared for a punitive strike. Sir Hyde Parker, a sound administrator and diplomat, was therefore given overall command with Nelson as his second-in-command in case some serious fighting should be necessary.

There was another reason for appointing Sir Hyde Parker: aged sixty-one, overweight, underworked, complacent and recently married to Admiral Onslow's eighteen year-old daughter, he was the very antithesis of Lord St. Vincent's concept of the ideal Flag-Officer. There can be little doubt that 'Old Jarvie' derived much malicious amusement in dragging the old man from his young bride and packing him off to the Baltic to do some proper work.

It was therefore necessary for Captain Otway, commanding the *Royal George* and carrying the Flag of Sir Hyde Parker, to swap ships with Captain Purvis. The transfer was carried out at sea with Ushant Lighthouse bearing south-south-west six or seven miles distant, on Tuesday 10th February 1801. The boats of both ships were employed throughout the day in transferring Captain Purvis's furniture and accoutrements, which were modest, to the *Royal George* and Captain Otway's and Admiral Parker's furniture and accoutrements, which were considerable, to the *London*. As was the practice, each Captain took his key personnel with him; Captain Purvis took his Master, five Lieutenants, his boys, including his sons, John and Richard, and several petty officers.

Sir Hyde Parker's force went on to fight the Battle of Copenhagen during which Nelson, yet again, disobeyed orders — this time by looking through his telescope with his blind eye and pretending not to see Sir Hyde Parker's signal from the *London* to discontinue the action. It is as well that he did; it saved the British fleet from disaster and resulted in a resounding victory and the resumption of British influence among the Baltic powers.

For Captain Purvis there was no such glory; in his new command, the *Royal George,* he resumed his old station among the 'Black Rocks' soon to discover that his ship was in very poor condition; many of her sails and much of her rigging was worn out and in urgent need of replacement and the cutwater (the leading edge of the ship's bow) was damaged and admitting a serious amount of water. On 27th March he anchored in Cawsand Bay and took stock of the situation.

Ordered to provision for a five-month period and enjoined, as usual, to get his ship to sea in the shortest possible time, he rushed to provision her, to undertake emergency repairs on the cutwater, which really required major attention in the dockyard, and to obtain replacements for the worst of the worn-out sails and rigging.

In the previous month Lord St. Vincent had left the Channel Fleet to take up the appointment of First Lord of the Admiralty in London. He had been succeeded by Lord Cornwallis to whom Captain Purvis was able to report on 31st March:

... not a moment has been lost in getting His Majesty's Ship under my command ready to sail for, tho' there is a considerable defect in the cutwater, I have just sufficiently secured it to enable me to proceed to sea. A large quantity of sails and rigging has been condemned and others now coming on board so that this, I trust, is the last day I shall have any communication with the shore, except paying the ship tomorrow, after which I shall immediately sail.

He sailed on Friday 3rd April and was at sea off Ushant for five months returning to Cawsand Bay on 3rd September. During this time the supplies of fresh water in the *Royal George* fell to dangerously low levels and the ingress of salt water from the damaged cutwater rose to dangerously high levels. The ship was regularly making four inches of water every hour and her pumps were in operation round the clock.

On arrival back at Cawsand Bay he immediately arranged for the cutwater to be surveyed by the dockyard and reported to Sir Andrew Mitchell:

Sir — I have this moment been informed by the builders that the event of the survey of the leak of His Majesty's Ship under my command is that it cannot be got at where the ship now lies.

He was therefore ordered into Hamoaze, a creek to the north of Dock (the old name for the naval area of Plymouth; today called Devonport), to have the ship's defects made good and on 13th September warped alongside the *Ripon*, hulk, and began removing the guns. Here Captain Purvis learned of the death of his mother, aged eighty-one, and travelled to Colchester to attend her funeral at St. Giles's where he met up, and exchanged news, with his two brothers, Richard and George.

Richard had been ashore for some time and was living at Beccles, in Suffolk, wondering what to do with his three younger sons. He was duly grateful to John, for the excellent start he had given his eldest boy in the Navy and the good care he had taken of him as a Midshipman in the *London*. Young Oadham was now in the West Indies, he said, and seemed set for a promising career in the service.

George, with the considerable prize commission he had earned during his years at sea, had bought the Blackbrook Estate, just outside Fareham. There was an existing mansion house on the estate, Blackbrook House, but it was too austere for George and his wife Renira's taste so they had built, in the grounds, their own, idyllic, *cottage orné* with a thatched roof supported by a colonade of rustic pillars. Here, three days before Christmas, Renira had given birth to another daughter whom they had christened Georgina.

George had been appointed a Magistrate for the County of Southampton, was thinking about taking a commission in the local militia and was, by and large, leading a far happier life than he had under Lord St. Vincent's heel. There had been, however, a curious and disturbing development: during the summer he had learned that Nelson had arbitrarily reneged upon their Prize Agreement and had, apparently against the wishes of the other eligible Flag-Officers, appointed another Prize Agent, Alexander Davison, for his victory at the Nile. Davison was a man of humble origins who had amassed great wealth in the administration of lucrative government contracts and would later be tried, convicted and imprisoned on seven charges of corruption and conspiracy. He was, at the time, unknown to the other Flag-Officers who had no reason to have confidence in either his competence or integrity. Admiral Sir John Orde, no friend of Nelson or St. Vincent, had sprung immediately to the defence of George Purvis's interests:

Sir John Orde to Lord Nelson, 6th July 1801

. . . I will therefore now mention my regret at your having found it necessary to put the Agency of the Flag share of the Nile Prize Money in other hands than those of our approved and very worthy Agent, Mr Purvis, as the change has already occasioned some difficulties to the parties concerned and may eventually, from some little error, be a means of preventing him getting a commission on it unless your Lordship interferes in his behalf, though his doing so, is I believe desired by a great majority (perhaps the whole) of the Flag Officers with whom I conceive the appointment of their Agent rests.[1]

Lord Nelson to Sir John Orde 7th July 1801

. . . respecting the Agency for the Nile, I did what I thought proper and what I own, I thought no person, much less my brother Admiral, would start an objection to. Mr Purvis for many months, I am sure, is perfectly happy I am right and that he was wrong on such a particular occasion to have said a word. One sole Agent was my wish and nothing was intended or could hurt Mr Purvis's feelings.[1]

Sir John Orde to Lord Nelson 13th July 1801

. . . I did not mention Purvis to your Lordship in view of discussing his general claims to your Lordship's favors, or the propriety of his conduct in any transactions between you. I did so in justice to the character of a very honorable, honest Agent and in support of the consistency and propriety of my own conduct in not abandoning such a man when I conceive my right to continue him in the exercise of his former employment is equal to your Lordship's power to deprive him of it . . .

The full weight of Admiral Orde's resentment for Nelson's preferment over his more senior colleagues then became apparent:

. . . I should not wonder if subordinate officers detached from a Fleet, when fortunate enough to make prizes, wished to appoint a sole Agent to dispose of them (although I never remember hearing of such an instance) and I am ready to allow they might on soliciting expect an acquaintance with their views by the parties concerned, if <u>perfectly disengaged</u> in that line but I must own I feel distress and astonishment to find your Lordship expecting such a sacrifice on the part of your brother Admirals with respect to the Nile Prize Money, in favour of a man unknown to most of them and little acquainted with the employment when it was unsolicited on your part and so be effected at the expense of a man who had every claim to a continuance of their support and confidence. Much more am I astonished to find your Lordship not only expecting such abandonment of a faithful servant but seemingly dissatisfied with your brother officers for stating any objection to your persevering in the appointment of a man as their Agent who they may feel uninterested about.[1]

George Purvis to Sir John Orde, 20th July 1801
. . . I would earlier have replied to your obliging letter of the 12th to have returned my hearty and sincere thanks for the steady and persevering part you have taken in what regards my interest in the Nile Prize Money, and the very handsome terms you have used of me in your letter to the Lord Nelson; for your satisfaction and my own vindication, I must solemnly aver to you that his Lordship's assertion to you that I am (or ever have been) perfectly satisfied that he was right and that I was wrong in what regards this business, is notoriously false and, but for the mark of <u>Private</u> on your letter, I would find means to confute him: — after declaring that he was under obligations to me, and that he hoped he might have an opportunity of requiting them, my feelings must indeed have been blunt had they not been affected by receiving from him the only injury he had it in his power to inflict, or rather presumed to have, for it never was vested in him. On the other side I send you a copy of this great man's Power, in his own hand-writing.[1]

It is as well for our nation that Nelson was apt to act impulsively without respect for authority or established procedures. In his own words: "I have fought contrary to my orders and perhaps I shall be hanged. Never mind; let them." There can be no gainsaying that many of his, and thus our, greatest triumphs were as a result of such renegade behaviour. Yet his treatment of George Purvis does seem to have been lacking in both consideration and honour.

The *Royal George,* with her cutwater repaired, was to undertake one further patrol off Ushant during which, on 12th October 1801, the King announced that Britain was at peace with France and hostilities at sea were to cease. Captain Purvis anchored in Torbay on 3rd November and was to remain there until 8th January 1802 when he sailed for Cawsand Bay and then back again to Torbay on the 15th. The *Royal George* was to remain here for almost three months, the Channel Fleet being held in readiness while the terms of the peace were negotiated. Meanwhile, the usual run of ship's business continued including a Court Martial for Lieutenant John Fairbairn "having repeatedly behaved with great contempt to the First Lieutenant when in the execution of his duty, particularly this morning when getting the yards and topmast up".

It was happier news for Monsieur Honore Bouden: in December 1799, Captain Purvis had applied to the Admiralty for permission to take a French prisoner-of-war into the *London* to teach the French language to his boys. Their Lordships had acceded to his request provided he chose "a person from whose principles no mischief will be likely to happen". The resultant choice, Monsieur Bouden, had served him well for two years in both the *London* and *Royal George* but now that the war was over and: "having received intimation that he will be well received in his own country, and being very desirous of returning there," Captain Purvis applied for, and obtained, permission to discharge him from the Service.

The peace was ratified on 27th March 1802 with the Treaty of Amiens, a feeble affair which consolidated Bonaparte's outstanding success on land and did little to reward Britain for the Royal Navy's outstanding success at sea. Britain handed back all her overseas conquests except for Ceylon and Trinidad; France gave up Naples and the Papal States and agreed to withdraw from Egypt although, unknown at the time to the negotiators at Amiens, the French had already surrendered to a recently-landed British army. It was clear from the outset that France had no intention of abandoning her bid for world supremacy, or of respecting the spirit of the Amiens Peace, and Britain responded by remaining in Malta instead of restoring it to a reformed assembly of the Knights of St. John; Minorca having been handed back to Spain, the Royal Navy badly needed a Mediterranean base.

What Bonaparte badly needed was a lull in hostilities in which to rebuild his fleet and to fine-tune the civil reforms he had introduced. These 'Napoleonic Codes' had transformed every aspect of legal, social and economic practice in France and her satellites and parts of them remain the basis of French, and European, law to this day. Bonaparte would have been gratified had he known that what he had failed to impose upon Britain by force of arms would be imposed by political evolution two centuries later but, in March 1802, he had far from given up the attempt and only the most ingenuous believed that the peace would last for long.

In April Captain Purvis was ordered to take the *Royal George* to Plymouth to be paid off. On the 16th the pilot moved the ship back into Hamoaze and work started on stripping and clearing her out for paying off. First, for reasons of safety, her powder was unloaded to be followed by sails, rigging, spars, masts, cables, anchors, guns, shot and hundreds of empty casks. Surveying masters from the dockyard came aboard to survey every item of slops, stores and equipment and mark them off the ship's books accordingly; purser's, gunner's, boatswain's and surgeon's accounts had to be reconciled and closed by the appropriate authority.

Finally, Captain Purvis had the ship washed and cleaned thoroughly before handing her over to the dockyard. Then on the morning of Saturday 24th April, in pleasant weather with moderate breezes, Rear-Admiral Dacres came on board with the pay clerks to pay the ship off. Captain Purvis recorded the final entry in his log:

N.B. The Ship's Company behaved extremely well, very orderly and quiet; which was the case with respect to the crews of most of the ships on their being paid off. Signed: John Child Purvis, Captain.

That their behaviour remained orderly and quiet when they hit the bars and fleshpots of Union Street that evening, their pockets full of back pay, is improbable.

Once again, Captain Purvis was ashore on half-pay with no ship. The following month he learned of the death of his elder brother, Captain Richard Purvis, aged fifty-nine, leaving a widow, four sons and one daughter. The eldest son, Oadham, was already well established in the Navy; and about to go forward for his

Lieutenant's exam, thanks to the interest of his two uncles; John had carried him as a Midshipman in the *London* and George had arranged his berth in the *Ville de Paris*. George's creative pen had also recorded 'service' for him in the last three ships in which he had served — the *Boyne*, the *Lively* and the *Victory*. The other boys were aged sixteen, thirteen and ten and would require career guidance for which their widowed mother might well turn to her naval brothers-in-law to provide. In the meantime, however, John Purvis had the placement of his own sons to worry about. His brother-in-law, Henry Garrett, now a Post-Captain, was commanding the *Endymion,* a 40-gun frigate, and readily agreed to take young John on board until he could secure a better berth for him. One such presented itself a few weeks later and John joined the *Cambrian,* 40, Flagship of Admiral Sir Andrew Mitchell, bound for the North American Station. Later in the year Sir Andrew moved his Flag to the *Leander,* 50, and took John with him.

At the same time, Captain Purvis was notified of a vacancy at the Naval Academy, in Portsmouth Dockyard, for his younger son, Richard, who was already showing signs of academic prowess and who, his father felt, would benefit from the better and more formal tuition he would receive at the Academy. Captain Purvis, who had made little in the way of prize money in the course of his long and hard-slogging career to date, could not have afforded the fees at the Naval Academy, which were much the same as those for Eton, but had managed to secure one of the fifteen places which the King had insisted should be reserved for the sons of sea officers to be educated at public expense.

However, after two years at sea, Richard hated the confined environment of the Academy and, within his first year, had written to his father begging him to consider the possibility of an alternative career. He realised that his father could not afford to buy him a commission in an infantry or cavalry regiment and he himself was unwilling to embark upon the further study which would be necessary for the artillery or engineers. The most suitable prospect seemed to be the military service of the Honourable East India Company where a cadetship could be obtained, without premium, by interview alone. It was a strange request from a boy whose future in the Navy was reasonably well secured by his father's interest and who had already served three years of a demanding apprenticeship. Captain Purvis tried hard to change his mind but, realising that the boy was determined, eventually agreed to, at least, examine the possibility. He wrote to Richard from Brentford on 15th May 1803:

That I have been mindful of your interest you can have no doubt, and I trust you will be as much so in respect to the advice I gave you before I left Hants. I will again repeat my earnest desire that you will pay the strictest attention to your business at the Academy for should we not succeed in the pursuit of our new plan, we may at least have the pleasing reflection that no time was lost in the former one . . .[2]

The following day war was declared with France. Captain Purvis now had to find himself another ship while, at the same time, making arrangements for Richard's new career. Having, himself, no contacts with the East India Company, there was little advice or help he could give the boy. Daniel Garrett offered to pull whatever strings he could but, in the meantime, suggested that John should get in touch with his cousin, Charles Purvis, whose wife was the daughter of a former Director of the Company. Charles Purvis was the current head of the senior branch of the family, proprietor of the Darsham estate and High Sheriff and Deputy Lieutenant of Suffolk. In recent years, however, he had let out Darsham House and moved to Bath, the fashionable spa town which, next to London, was the hub of society in Georgian England. Captain Purvis therefore wrote to his cousin who promptly invited him to spend part of the summer with him and his family in Bath.

At Charles Purvis's beautiful mansion, No.2 Lansdowne Crescent, and in the elegant drawing rooms of Bath, the rugged sea captain made a great hit with the ladies who were delighted to be in the company of one of the brave sailors of the Royal Navy — the only thing that stood between their civilised milieu and the imminently-threatened invasion by the barbaric soldiery of republican France. His cousin later wrote to him:

Our party, my dear John, regretted your departure amazingly and the girls were quite disconsolate; what you have done to them I can not conceive; I only know they have ever since sworn by their agreeable Captain — but you, young fellow, seem not aware of the mischief you make . . .[3]

Charles Purvis also promised that, if young Richard was determined to go to India, he would use his influence to get him appointed to the Bengal establishment which, of the three presidency armies in India, was generally thought to offer the best prospects to a young officer. Meanwhile, Captain Purvis learned, his widowed sister-in-law at Beccles had also approached Charles Purvis for his assistance in getting her second son, John Leman Purvis, into the Bengal Army; so, when he got a ship, Captain Purvis would not be called upon to find a berth for another nephew; instead, he intimated to his cousin, Charles, that he would keep a place for a boy of his choosing in return for his assistance with Richard.

In the summer of 1803 the Channel Fleet blockading Brest was under the command of the highly-respected Admiral Hon. William Cornwallis — 'Billie Blue' within the Service — with two extremely able Rear-Admirals, Cuthbert Collingwood and Edward Pellew, commanding detached squadrons blockading Rochefort and Ferrol respectively. During August, while staying with his cousin in Bath, Captain Purvis received the orders he had been hoping for: he was to repair to Plymouth and take passage to the Fleet off Ushant, where he would relieve Captain Brace in command of H.M.S. *Dreadnought* under the orders of Admiral Cornwallis.

CHAPTER 7

Dreadnought

Thursday 8th September 1803
H.M.S. Dreadnought
off Ushant

The most notorious of the many corrupt 18th-century dockyard practices was the 'Devil Bolt'. The main frames of wooden warships were clamped together by enormous copper bolts some two inches in diameter and two or three feet in length. Upon the integrity of these bolts depended the safety of the ship. The 'Devil Bolt' had a copper head and tail, a couple of inches long, with the space between them filled with a wooden plug. Thus, on inspection, the bolt appeared to have been fitted; in practice, dishonest dockyard officials had pocketed the considerable price of the copper which had been saved. Several warships were known to have foundered, and thousands of seamen drowned, as a result of this unscrupulous deception; and this was only one of hundreds of similarly-fraudulent practices which were reducing the sea-worthiness of British ships and endangering the lives of their crews.

It is not surprising, therefore, that Lord St. Vincent, with his passionate concern for the welfare of British seamen, should, as First Lord of the Admiralty, target corruption in the dockyards as energetically as he had targeted sedition in the Mediterranean and Channel Fleets. It was a worthy and necessary crusade but was undertaken, perhaps, at an unwise point in time.

During the brief lull in hostilities, Bonaparte had made full use of the freedom of the Channel which France temporarily enjoyed. While in Britain shipbuilding had ground to a halt due to industrial action and political wrangling over Lord St. Vincent's reforms, the French navy had been refurbished, augmented and trained. Flushed with his military success on the continent, Bonaparte was now determined to conquer the only power which stood in the way of his domination of Europe and, ultimately, the world. A vast invasion fleet of over 2,000 landing craft and support vessels had been assembled in the Channel ports and the civil population of England was in perpetual alarm. Charles Purvis wrote to his cousin:

We have nothing but the threats of Bonaparte; thank God this Country was never so unanimous and there are certainly very many people, who calculating even for the Horrible Carnage that must ensue, that wish he would attempt to put his threats in execution and ease their minds from the irritation they now suffer.[1]

and from Daniel Garrett:

We are told by the Ministers etc. that we are to expect Bonaparte in ten or twelve days — let him come from the shores of France — I hope and trust he will never put his foot in England nor in France again.[2]

Captain Purvis took command of the *Dreadnought* off Ushant on Thursday 8th September 1803. Having read his Commission to the crew, he opened the orders which awaited him from Admiral Cornwallis in the *Ville de Paris*. He was to deliver some letters and papers to Rear-Admiral Collingwood, whose Inshore Squadron was off Brest, and then return to Cornwallis, off Ushant, for further orders. In the meantime, he had a problem with his First Lieutenant and wrote to the Commander-in-Chief:

Lieutenant James Oades Lys belonging to His Majesty's Ship under my command having represented to me by letter of yesterday's date that he was surveyed at the hospital at Plymouth before the Governor Physicians etc. about 3 weeks ago for deafness and mental derangement, that they pronounced him incurable and therefore could not admit him into the hospital, I beg leave to enclose his letter and to state to you, I understand from Captain Brace he has not done any duty these last four months and very little before and, as he is senior Lieutenant and subject to occasional madness, I request you will be pleased to direct his being removed from the ship.

Admiral Cornwallis, who was determined to enforce the blockade in 'St. Vincent' rather than 'Bridport' style, ordered Captain Purvis to stop and search any neutral vessel he encountered and, assuming he had no cause to detain it, to enter in the ship's papers that "she had been so examined by you and apprized of the blockade". *Dreadnought* sighted the Inshore Squadron off Brest on the 15th and, there being much to attend to on board his new command, Purvis sent one of his Lieutenants over to the Flagship with the orders instead of going himself and renewing his longstanding friendship with Admiral Collingwood. As Captains, they had served together in the Mediterranean in the nineties — Collingwood commanding the *Excellent* and Purvis the *Princess Royal* and, later, the *London*. It was unusual to send a ship of-the-line with despatches, a task usually undertaken by brigs or packets, as Admiral Collingwood noted in his reply:

Though I should have had great pleasure in seeing you, I am very glad you did not give yourself the trouble to come on a business which your Lieut has performed admirably. We begin to look out for you as we used to do for "Little Nimrod" that had many a trip with orders. I think when Bonaparte is informed that our packet boats carry ninety guns he will not look to the sea for his glory. I have sent you a couple of the Black Rock Trout, taken yesterday — fishery we have there; they are part of some my friend De Courcy sent me.[3]

Having returned to Lord Cornwallis, the *Dreadnought* was again sent to Admiral Collingwood with orders and from there to gather intelligence from the ports of L'Orient and Rochefort:

Having delivered the packet you will herewith receive to Rear-Admiral Collingwood, inshore off of Brest, you are immediately to proceed along the French coast, looking in to L'Orient and by observation, as well as intelligence, you may be able to obtain, learn what force is in that port and particularly whether the French line-of-battle ship said to have been refitting is there. You are then to go on and gain what information you can of the force at Rochefort and upon finding the three-deck ship fitting at that port still there, you are to continue upon that station for the purpose of watching her and to intercept her should she attempt to put to sea. You are also to do your utmost to prevent any part of the enemy's cruizers from getting out or into that port, or any of their prizes being carried there. Should the French three-deck ship above mentioned have sailed from Rochefort before you get there, you are in that case to join me without loss of time off Ushant or wherever else you may learn I am with the squadron, with such information as you may have been enabled to obtain which, during your absence from the squadron, you are to communicate to me by every opportunity. P.S. You will be careful to protect and assist the trade of HM's subjects.

Captain Purvis looked into L'Orient then sailed down the Biscay coast to Rochefort from where he was able to report to the Admiral on 28th September:

In L'Orient, a line-of-battle ship, full-rigged and top gallant yards across but no sails bent except the fore and mizzen topsails. There were also in that port a frigate and an armed brig the two latter in a state of refitting. They had all French colours up. In the port of Rochefort near the Isle d'Aix is a three-deck ship and a large frigate both apparently ready for sea. I was informed yesterday by an American ship that there was another 3-deck ship expected from Rochefort to the same anchorage to take in her guns, but she is not within the reach of our view.

The *Dreadnought* was then ordered to continue cruising on the same station until 15th October when Captain Purvis should rejoin Admiral Cornwallis off Ushant "or wherever else you may learn I am at the time". When he rejoined the Squadron a letter from Daniel Garrett awaited him: there was speculation in the newspapers that a naval promotion was imminent. Promotion from Captain to Rear-Admiral was, in those days, purely by seniority and as John Purvis was by now a senior Captain, near the top of the list, his advancement could be expected at the next general promotion. Daniel Garrett expected his son-in-law to be an Admiral in a few days but was less sanguine about the prospects of his son, John, being made a Lieutenant, though he had long-since passed his Lieutenant's exam and, thanks to his father and his uncle George, acquired the necessary qualifying seatime:

You must push him on with Lord St Vincent as, without his Lordship's orders, Captain Oughton says he will not perhaps be made a Lieutenant.[4]

The *Dreadnought* patrolled the Biscay coast from Ushant to Ferrol through the storms of October and November 1803 with the prospect of more severe weather as the winter approached. A victim of penny-pinching government constraints, several of the ship's sails and much of her running rigging was worn out and unfit for Channel service. Captain Purvis wrote to the Navy Board requesting an increase in the number of staysails he was allowed when his ship next got into port:

His Majesty's Ship under my command having been in situations on a lee shore where the greatest dependance must necessarily be placed on such sails as are best calculated to stand the most violent gales, and as the nature of the present war requires ships of her class to be frequently placed in deep bays such as we are now in, and as the winter season is now coming on, I take the liberty of requesting you will be pleased so far to depart from what may be considered as an old establishment, as to give directions that the ship may be allowed when we next arrive at Plymouth two main staysails and three fore staysails . . . I am induced more particularly to make this application because it often happens that sails of such description are nearly worn out when the ship leaves port, tho' perhaps not quite so bad as to be condemned which most likely will be the case when we go into port where our stay will not admit of an answer to any letter I may then write on the subject.

In addition to worn out sails, the ship was:

. . . so extremely crank as sometimes in blowing weather to prevent my carrying sufficient sail to keep properly up with the Commander-in-Chief as well as the unfair pressure with which the masts are at those times charged.

Forty-five tons of additional iron ballast was requested when the ship returned to Plymouth which appears to have cured that particular problem.

Young Richard's preparations for India were meanwhile going ahead under the supervision of Daniel Garrett with some assistance from George Purvis. George was now gazetted as a Captain in the Fareham Militia which was training intensively, to be ready for Bonaparte's arrival. Captain Purvis, constantly at sea, could do nothing to assist his son during this important period of his life. He wrote to him from the *Dreadnought* off Ushant on 2nd November:

You may be assured, my dear boy, it is one of the first wishes of my heart that, whatever line of life you make choice of, that success and every possible good should follow. I wish I could be with you at this particular time for many reasons; but that cannot be. Our good friends the Garretts will, I am sure, stand in my stead and give you every assistance and advice you may stand in need of.

On 24th November the *Dreadnought* was ordered to exchange her foreyard with that of the *Prince of Wales* which had sprung. In towing the massive foreyard alongside, the tow broke and the yard drifted away to windward. Captain Purvis sent boats in pursuit but it was a very dark, stormy night and he soon had to recall the boats and abandon hope of recovering the yard. The following day he explained to the Admiral his presence in Cawsand Bay:

I continued sailing during the night keeping sight of the Admiral's lights until the main topsail, main staysail and mizzen staysail blew away in the violent squalls we experienced. I made the Lizard lights at 10 o'clock this morning when, considering the crippled state of the ship, I thought it best for His Majesty's service to bear up for this place which I hope will meet your approbation and I beg to assure you I will lose no time in completing the ship with water, provisions, etc. and joining you.

In addition to the appalling weather, Captain Purvis was singularly unfortunate with his officers in the *Dreadnought*: when he first took command in September he had had to dispose of a deaf First Lieutenant who was prone to periodic fits of insanity; the following month he had had to request the court martial of Lieutenant Thomas Sandsbury for "having been repeatedly in a state of intoxication when having charge of the watch," and on 7th December his Master, John Gridley, "discontinued every part of his duty (even to the keeping of the ship's reckoning)". This, with the very precise navigation and pilotage required in the treacherous waters off Ushant, was an even more serious impediment than a mad, or a drunk, Lieutenant. Captain Purvis requested a replacement Master but by 30th December none had been received and Gridley still declined to undertake any duty. The situation was exacerbated when on 4th January 1804, with the *Dreadnought* about to sail on another patrol, Purvis was ordered to discharge his French pilot into the *Terrible* whose need of him, apparently, was greater.

Through January, February and March, Captain Purvis patrolled off Ushant beset by some of the most violent Channel storms in memory, his potential fighting strength weakened by the removal of forty of his marines and his ship's company 109 below strength. Time and again the Squadron was blown off station and individual ships had to run for cover or limp into the nearest anchorage to repair storm damage.

On 29th January *Dreadnought* anchored for five days in Torbay where a letter from Daniel Garrett was waiting:

I have been daily in expectation of seeing in the News Papers of your arrival at Plymouth or in Torbay — thinking that it was impossible for you and the other Ships to keep the Sea in the midst of such storms and hurricanes — and I hope soon to hear that you are well and have escaped all the dangers which must have surrounded you. We on Xmas Day drank your health — and so we shall again by and by.[6]

The main purpose of Mr. Garrett's letter was to advise his son-in-law that Richard had been appointed to the Bengal Native Infantry subject to an interview in London the following week. This he duly attended and passed, after some confusion regarding his birth certificate which Uncle George was called upon to regularise.

Captain Purvis was at sea off Ushant from 4th February until 30th March 1804 and was therefore unable to see Richard off when he sailed for India in the East Indiaman *Sir William Bensley* on 10th February. He had not seen his son for the past eighteen months and would not see him again for almost fifteen years. While the *Dreadnought* lay at anchor in Torbay awaiting a favourable wind, he wrote his last letter to Richard before the boy left England. It impressed upon him the need to live within his income and contained some 'Good Advice', which would be repeated with unfailing regularity during the course of their fifteen-year correspondence. The letter so perfectly illustrates the importance which John Purvis placed upon honourable, god-fearing behaviour and strict attendance to duty that it is reproduced here in full:

My dear Richard, — I received your letter of the 16th on my arrival at this place yesterday, and as the Wind will not admit of your Sailing, I think it probable this will catch you before you go. Mr. Garrett has indeed, my dear Richard, taken uncommon pains and trouble on your account, and as I am well acquainted with his disposition and goodness of heart, I can venture to assure you, that you cannot gratify him in anything so much as scrupulously attending to the good advice he has and will continue to give you as long as you remain within his reach. I have occasionally given you advice since your having decided on the plan of going to India, but as my Mind has been so much employ'd on the business of the Ship and the continual interruptions in consequence of the uncommon bad Weather we have had; I have not been so collected as I would wish to inforce on your mind the very great consequence it is to you to preserve through life a fair and unspoted Character, too much cannot possibly be said on so interesting a subject, and as Mr. Garrett will probably commit some of his thoughts to paper for your future guidance; I intreat you to pay every possible attention to them, preserve them, and read them over frequently and always keep in your mind the pleasure and satisfaction I shall derive from hearing as good accounts of you as I have of your Brother; I have been very much gratified from reports frequently brought me of his good conduct, Gentlemanlike behaviour and great attention to his duty, he has met with many friends in a distant country, who are always showing him civilities, tho' totally unknown to me; Remember Richard the strong admonitions I have so frequently and forcibly given you in common with the other youngsters on board the London and Royal George, I think they can never be forgot unless the Heart should become so corrupted as not to retain a virtuous sentiment; this my dear Richard I trust will never be your case; God forbid it should; I only wish you clearly to understand how much I am interested in your doing well and always acting uprightly honourably Religiously and honest; never suffer yourself to be led out of the proper path, by any specious deceitful Characters, which you may [chance] to fall in with; civility is due to all, but do not hastily form friendships with those you scarcely [are] acquainted with, you will have the advantage of being recommended to some of the Principal Gentlemen in the Settlements, to them you should look for advice, and their reports of you will give me I hope all the satisfaction I can wish. I come now, my dear Richard, to another matter which I desire you pay the greatest attention to, this is your expenses; the fitting you out is more than I can well afford and therefore the most exact economy on your part is absolutely necessary, the Sum to be paid will reduce my income considerably and I had nothing to spare before; you must make your pay support you in India as others do; your two Uncles as well as myself had no assistance from our Father, and yet pass'd on without ever disgracing our family in any respect whatever; If I could assist you in the early part of your service I would, but this heavy expense of the outfitting will prevent me. Be assured my dear Richard of my best love, and that it may please God to forward your happiness and take you under his protection is the sincere wish of your affectionate Father, Jhn. Chd. Purvis. [7]

Daniel Garrett wrote to Captain Purvis in February to confirm that Richard had sailed and to bemoan the fact that the promotion had still not been announced. As a staunch Tory, he had little sympathy with Lord St. Vincent's political principles and compatriots:

I was in great hopes that ere this I should have congratulated you on being an Admiral — what can the great man mean in postponing such a necessary and proper boon to gentlemen who have so dearly earned and deserved such promotion. He is not backward in promoting his own creatures and turning out others . . . I suppose you will not stay long in Torbay — the first fair wind will take you back to Brest. You have a great deal of fagging and no Prize Money — nothing but wear and tear![8]

And back to Brest he went for another month of fagging until the end of April when the welcome and long-awaited communication from Mr. William Marsden at the Admiralty Office was received:

Sir — His Majesty having been pleased to order a promotion of Flag Officers of his Fleet and my Lords Commissioners of the Admiralty having in pursuance thereof signed a commission appointing you Rear-Admiral of the Blue Squadron, I have the honour to acquaint you herewith.

But the rank in itself was not enough. As John Purvis had pointed out to his son, he had received little in the way of prize-money during his career and had difficulty enough making ends meet on a Captain's pay. Now, the last thing he wanted was to be put ashore as a half-pay Rear-Admiral; he needed a job. On 3rd May, off Ushant, he acknowledged Mr. Marsden's letter:

Sir — I have received your letter of the 23rd Ult. giving me an account of my being promoted to the rank of a Rear Admiral of the Blue and I request you will be pleased to make known . . . my earnest desire of being employed.

The *Dreadnought* returned to Plymouth on 12th May 1804 and Rear-Admiral Purvis went ashore where, in spite of his plea to the Admiralty, he was to remain unemployed for two years. Although Britain was locked in a bitter struggle with France, the recent promotions had created a glut of Flag-Officers with not enough jobs to go round.

On 2nd August Admiral Purvis was married for the third time. His bride was Elizabeth Dickson, only daughter and heiress of Admiral Sir Archibald Dickson, Bart, an old brother officer who had recently died. As Captains, Dickson and Purvis had commanded the *Egmont* and the *Princess Royal* in Lord Hood's Mediterranean Fleet at Toulon in 1793. At thirty-six Elizabeth Dickson was twenty-one years younger than her groom and had previously been married to her cousin, Captain William Dickson of the 22nd Regiment of Foot, who had died at San Domingo [Haiti] in 1795.

Elizabeth was a well-educated and cultured woman with a sociable nature and considerable poise and self-confidence; as such, she was well-qualified to undertake the social duties of a Flag-Officer's wife and, moreover, had received £15,000 in 3% Bank Annuities under the terms of her father's Will. On the death or remarriage of her stepmother, she would inherit the balance of her late father's estate including a mansion house at Hardingham in Norfolk. Now, even if John Purvis never got the chance to hoist his Flag, with a Rear-Admiral's half-pay and his wife's income, the couple could live in reasonable comfort for the rest of their lives.

In September they travelled to Suffolk to visit Mrs. Lucy Purvis, the widow of John's elder brother Richard. Lucy was a daughter of the Revd. John Leman, Rector of nearby Wenhaston, the family having been prominent in the Suffolk clergy for many generations. Lucy was in mourning for her eldest son, 'Oadham' who, having obtained his promotion to Lieutenant, had died in the West Indies in January. She told John, who had done so much to help him, that he had left his ship which was returning to England, and remained in the West Indies in the hope of improving his prospects of promotion. At least, Admiral Purvis later wrote to Richard: "He left a good character which was some consolation to those who regarded him."[9] Lucy's second son, John Leman, was now a Lieutenant in the Bengal Native Infantry and her third son, George Thomas, was preparing to follow him to India.

The following month Sir John Orde obtained satisfaction for the slight he had received from Nelson's preferment six years earlier. William Pitt, who had returned to office in May, decided that Britain might just as well be at war with Spain as to suffer the effects of her continued abettment of Bonaparte's regime. Sir John Orde, commanding the Squadron off Cadiz, was therefore ordered to intercept the annual Spanish Treasure Fleet loaded with gold, silver, copper and tin. Its capture on 3rd October brought massive prize-money to all involved and Orde became considerably richer, for a great deal less effort, than he would have done in command at the Nile. Nelson was furious: "Now he is to wallow in wealth while I am left a beggar," he wrote. George Purvis must be forgiven a wry chuckle when the news reached England.

Spain, consequently and understandably, declared war on Britain in December and a Franco-Spanish Treaty followed in January 1805 by which time Napoleon Bonaparte had been crowned as Emperor of France. Thus far, he had had no way to launch his invasion of Britain due to the Royal Navy's command of the Channel but now, with the Spanish Fleet added to his own, he might be able to undertake it. Its success would depend on being able to lure the British Fleet out of the Channel for long enough for the Franco-Spanish Fleets to create and control a corridor through which the invasion armada could cross unmolested. A feint at British interests in the West Indies was considered an appropriate bait which was duly taken by Nelson who then chased a French force across the Atlantic only to find that they had turned about and returned to Europe.

Throughout the first nine months of 1805 an involved cat-and-mouse game was played between two very able strategists — the Emperor Napoleon and Lord Barham who had succeeded Lord St. Vincent as First Lord on the return of Pitt's government. The game reached its climax on 21st October with Nelson's historic victory over a superior Franco-Spanish Fleet at the Battle of Trafalgar during which Admiral Horatio Nelson was killed by a sniper's bullet in the hour of his, and the Nation's, greatest triumph; but Napoleon had abandoned his plans for invading Britain well before this. By the end of August he had accepted the fact that he could never induce the Royal Navy to drop its guard for long enough to enable his forces to cross the Channel; the invasion camps on the French coast had been broken up and the troops dispersed early in September.

Ashore and unemployed in Wickham, Admiral Purvis had missed out on yet another major fleet action. Had he not received his promotion he would probably have been at Trafalgar — his last command, the *Dreadnought,* had been there as part of Admiral Collingwood's Lee Column and had taken a prominent part in the battle suffering seven killed, twenty-six wounded and considerable damage to her spars and rigging. His friend, Cuthbert Collingwood, had enjoyed better fortune; he had commanded a ship of-the-line at 'The Glorious First of June' and at the Battle of St. Vincent and, now, as Nelson's second-in-command, at Trafalgar after which he had been ennobled and appointed Nelson's successor as Commander-in-Chief Mediterranean.

Earlier in the year Admiral Purvis had learned of the death of his nephew 'Leman' on service with the Bengal Native Infantry in Rangoon. This was the second son that his sister-in-law, Lucy, had lost in the space of a year. The third son, George, had left for India in April and had taken with him a letter for Richard from his father. The Admiral had not heard from his younger son since his departure for India — an omission which did not please him, particularly as, shortly after his arrival in Bengal, Richard had drawn £100 on his father's account without any note of explanation:

I have written you many letters since you sailed . . . but the last I received from you was from Cawsand Bay and for no purpose whatever but that of recommending a Bumboat Woman. I think a little reflection will show you this neglect on your part must be very displeasing to me.[9]

However, his disappointment with Richard was countered by his pride in John who was in the *Driver,* sloop, in the West Indies and had been promoted to Lieutenant in May aged just eighteen. In November he was deeply saddened by the death of his former father-in-law, and stalwart friend, Daniel Garrett, who had provided such unflagging support during Richard's preparations for India; but from Richard, himself, he had still heard nothing and by 28th April his patience was wearing thin:

It is now more than two years since I received a letter from you . . . you wrote to Mr. Garrett and Mr. Maidman from Madrass telling them you intended to address me on your arrival at Calcutta, when you did get there, you drew two Bills on me without even a letter of advice and in a few months afterwards you drew another Bill with as little ceremony; how you can reconcile all this to your own feelings,

I cannot form any judgement, since it is so different from my conduct when I was as far removed from my Father, and also from that of your Brother towards me;[10]

Better news was not long in coming; Lord Collingwood, in his new appointment as Commander-in-Chief Mediterranean, was exhausted and inadequately supported. He had written to the Admiralty requesting that Rear-Admiral Purvis should be sent out as his second-in-command. Early in June a letter from the *Ocean,* off Cadiz, arrived at Wickham:

My dear Purvis, — I was so glad to hear from you and thank you most sincerely for your kind congratulations and good wishes for me. I am here almost worn to a shadow sometimes with fatigue and otherwise with anxiety. I have no soul with me as flag officer and Admiral Knight at Gibraltar is rather worse than having nobody there. Some time since I mentioned my desire to have another flag officer sent to me to Mr. Grey — and proposed you as one who I should prefer — and if he accedes to it I shall be very happy in having so excellent a second. I beg my kind regards to Mrs. Purvis and to your brother and am, my dear Sir, your faithful servant, Collingwood.[11]

to be followed a few days later by the long-awaited order from the Admiralty:

By the Commissioners for executing the office of the Lord High Admiral of the United Kingdom of Great Britain and Ireland, etc. You are hereby required and directed to repair without loss of time to Portsmouth and hoisting your Flag on board His Majesty's Ship Chiffone at Spithead remain there until you receive further orders.

The most important chapter in the life of John Child Purvis was about to begin.

PART 2

Admiral

CHAPTER 8

The Long Blockade

Saturday 14th June 1806
H.M.S. La Chiffone
Spithead

A t 0700 on Saturday 14th June 1806 H.M.S. *La Chiffone* weighed anchor from Spithead and dropped down with the ebb towards St. Helens in a light westerly breeze. At her masthead flew the Flag of Rear-Admiral of the White John Child Purvis and on her quarterdeck the Admiral stood conversing with his three V.I.P. military passengers, Generals Sir John Moore, Fraser and Sherbrooke who had come aboard with their suites only half an hour previously.

The ship was bound for Gibraltar at the head of a convoy of thirteen merchant sail. At Gibraltar, by orders of the Admiralty, Admiral Purvis was to place himself under the command of Lord Collingwood and shift his Flag into whatever ship was appropriate at Gibraltar "or as Lord Collingwood may appoint for the purpose". *La Chiffone*, with the three Generals, was then to proceed to Malta.

As an Admiral, Purvis had nothing to do with the handling or day-to-day management of the ship; this was the job of her Captain, John Wainwright. The Admiral was, of course, in overall command of the convoy and would, as a matter of courtesy, be consulted and kept informed by Captain Wainwright on any matters of import but, unless the convoy was attacked by an enemy force, which was unlikely, he was effectively a V.I.P. passenger himself.

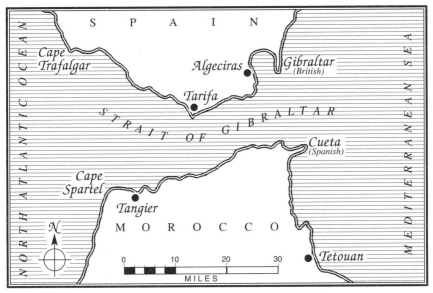

The doorway of the Mediterranean

It had been a moment of considerable pride for him when he had come on board at Spithead twelve days earlier and seen his Rear-Admiral's Flag hoisted for the first time. Having been piped aboard and welcomed by the Captain at the head of his assembled officers and crew, he had received an 11-gun salute from the *Duke William* which was moored nearby.

Apart from some heavy weather and a five-hour chase off Cape Finisterre of an unidentified vessel which eventually hove to and hoisted Danish colours, the passage to Gibraltar was uneventful. During the two-week voyage Admiral Purvis had many interesting discussions with his military guests about the situation in Europe. In December, Bonaparte had decisively defeated the Austrians and Russians at Austerlitz resulting in the unconditional surrender of the former and the retreat of the latter back to its own borders. Sir John Moore was of the opinion that in the Emperor Napoleon Britain faced not only a statesman of dangerous and undisclosed ambition but a military commander of unique ability. His opinion was to be confirmed by personal experience two years later.

On the morning of Friday 27th June Lord Collingwood's Squadron was sighted some ten leagues off Cape Spartel and

Captain Wainwright hove to to windward of the Flagship, *Ocean*, and launched the barge to take Admiral Purvis over to report to the Commander-in-Chief. Lord Collingwood directed him to transfer his Flag to the *Minotaur,* 74, in which he was to lead the Larboard Division of the Fleet when in order of sailing. The following day Admiral Purvis bade farewell to the three Generals and, together with his secretary, George Hayward, his Flag Lieutenant and his retinue, transferred to the *Minotaur* in which he hoisted his Flag.

One of the first actions taken by the Commander-in-Chief to relieve some of the pressure he was under was to transfer much of his day-to-day administrative work to his second-in-command. This included dealing with applications for routine surveys on stores and equipment allegedly unfit for service which, in a system which demanded a proper account of every last biscuit and shackle, was a substantial volume of work in itself. There followed a spate of applications for surveys some of which, one suspects, may have been temporarily withheld to spare a Commander-in-Chief who was known to be already overworked; pipes of sour wine; casks of rotten meat; tattered sails and worn-out running rigging; boatswain's, gunner's and surgeon's stores and a bullock which was received dead and "on trial was found not to bleed and was therefore adjudged unfit for men to eat". For each application a suitably qualified officer, petty officer or team had to be appointed, their reports appraised and an appropriate decision made, promulgated and recorded. For personnel, however, Lord Collingwood retained the responsibility and applications for surveys on officers and men for invaliding were to be directed, as previously, to him.

Weekly sick returns and weekly returns of the consumption and remains of water and provisions were, likewise, to be made to Rear-Admiral Purvis who also assumed the responsibility for urging economy and castigating waste:

As the fleet will suffer on many occasions from the limited supplies expected from England, unless there is an individual and general regard paid to the great husbandry of the stores, captains of ships are to pay the greatest attention thereto.

Strictest attention is to be paid to the expenditure of water while at the same time the ships' companies are to be allowed to drink as much as they want at the scuttle casks under the charge of a sentry and the directions of the Officer of the Watch.

Discipline was another area where Lord Collingwood felt able to delegate authority and the convening of Courts Martial was passed over to Admiral Purvis who also found himself acting as President of most of them. The offences ranged from serious breaches of international law to such bizarre charges as breaking wind in the gunroom mess: on the one hand George Miller Bligh, commander of H.M. Sloop *Pylades,* was accused of violating Portuguese neutrality by the capture of a Spanish brig off the coast of Portugal; on the other, Lieutenant William Hugh Somerville of the *Renommée* was accused of making a nuisance of himself to the officers of the gunroom mess "by easing himself and other filthy practices . . . and that his conduct had been in several other instances unbecoming the character of a gentleman". All such charges had to receive the due and proper process of naval law.

Some trials were brief and straightforward such as the case of James Crapps, a seaman of the *Prince,* who was accused of robbing Colonel Lemesle, a French prisoner-of-war confined in his ship. Rear-Admiral Purvis, the President, and the eight Captains who comprised the Court — Pender, Fremantle, Hardy, Lechmere, Hallowell, Mansfield, Pilfold and Thomas — assembled on board the *Prince* at 0800 on 22nd July. The evidence was presented, the charge irrefutably proven, a verdict of guilty agreed and a sentence of 100 lashes passed all within an hour.

More complicated and of longer duration was the Court Martial of the same Captain Hardy, commander of the *Zealous,* some two months later. He was accused of repeated breaches of the Second Article of War, unofficerlike conduct in the treatment of his officers, oppression and a negligent performance of his duties. Again under Admiral Purvis's Presidency, the Court comprised Captains Pender, Hallowell, Lord Beauclerk, Thomas, Fremantle, Mansfield, Codrington and Pilfold (the last four all having commanded ships at Trafalgar). The Court convened at 0800 on 17th September and sat for over twelve hours on the first, second and third days. It was told how Captain Hardy was habitually drunk and was prone to accuse others of the same offence; he had confined the Master-at-Arms for drunkeness "when he was perfectly sober but Captain Hardy was himself drunk", and had abused and displaced Jeremiah Malone, signalman, with the same accusation.

The proceedings of the Court were impeded when one of the principal witnesses, Acting Lieutenant William Carr, refused to answer a question which was put to him "and seem'd to endeavour to withhold the truth". He was ordered out of Court. On the fourth day, despite Carr's reticence, Captain Hardy was found guilty of several of the charges preferred against him and was sentenced to be dismissed His Majesty's Naval Service. Acting Lieutenant Carr was severely reprimanded by the Court.

The question of Portuguese neutrality was particularly sensitive. Portugal, though neutral, was Britain's only friend in Europe and the supply of the Mediterranean Fleet was entirely dependent upon the goodwill of that nation. The Portuguese government, while anxious to assist Britain as best it could, was mindful of its vulnerability within Napoleon's imperial scheme and necessarily anxious that such aid as it provided should remain covert. For the same reason, Portugal felt bound to protest loudly and publicly at any violation of her neutrality by British ships enforcing the blockade of France and Spain when they seized, stopped or delayed enemy or neutral ships within Portuguese territorial waters. On Lord Collingwood's directions, Admiral Purvis made sure that his Captains were fully aware of the issues involved:

You are hereby required and strictly enjoined carefully to abstain from every act which may be derogatory from the respect due to, or injurious to, the rights of, Portugal. That no interruptions be given to the ships and commerce of a nation between whom and His Majesty there subsists the most perfect amity . . . on your meeting with Portuguese ships and vessels they are to be treated with that kindness and regard which is due to a nation with which there subsists the most cordial friendship by aiding and assisting them in whatever they may need aid or assistance and by every act which may manifest a sincere friendship.

On 22nd September Admiral Purvis shifted his Flag from the *Minotaur* to the *Queen,* which, one month later, put in to Gibraltar for work to be undertaken on her copper bottom. During her two-week stay alongside the new mole, two gunboats, each manned by twenty-five seamen and commanded by a Lieutenant, were commissioned from the *Queen* to patrol the approaches and to escort any merchantmen standing in to Gibraltar Bay. On the 24th one of the gunboats, commanded by Lieutenant Foote, was seen to be captured by a Spanish gunboat in the middle of the Gut and carried into Tarifa. Application was immediately made to Captain Monat, the Agent for Prisoners-of-War at Gibraltar, "to use every means in his power to get the officers and men back as soon as possible". They were returned on 4th November and the following day a 19-gun salute was fired "in commemoration of the Powder Plot".

The *Queen* left Gibraltar at 0600 on 8th November and on 9th December Admiral Purvis shifted his Flag again, this time to the *Atlas,* an old 98-gun second-rate which had been reduced to a 74-gun third-rate in 1802. He was to remain at sea in her continuously, without even dropping an anchor, for the next one year and seven months.

On 14th January 1807 Lieutenant John Brett Purvis joined the ship as fifth Lieutenant. He had been aboard the *Terrible,* commanded by Captain Lord Henry Paulet, since the previous October pending a vacancy for a Lieutenant in his father's Flagship. The next stage would be to bring him to the attention of the Commander-in-Chief and Admiral Purvis wrote to Lord Collingwood requesting that when a vacancy should arise in the *Ocean*, his son John might be considered for the post.

For the first half of the year 1807 Admiral Purvis remained as Lord Collingwood's second-in-command attending, in the main, to the more mundane requirements of keeping a fleet at sea. There were endless surveys, sometimes of sufficient importance to invoke the enjoinder that the surveyor, or surveyors, should "take this survey with such care and equity that if required you may be able to make oath to the impartiality of your proceedings". Then there were orders from the Admiralty with which it was needful to ensure that the Captains of the Squadron complied; such as the misappropriation of government paint:

Being aware of the practice now prevalent of Captains indenting for paint for the guns and carriages of their ships and then appropriating the paint for other purposes and applying to the guns and carriages paint delivered from the dockyard, some descriptions of which are comprised of materials that, instead of preventing, tend to accelerate the decay of the carriages and the said Board having at the same time requested that orders may be given for prohibiting the commanders of His Majesty's Ships from painting the guns and carriages of any other than the established colours viz. red, white and chocolate. You are hereby required and directed to take particular care that the guns and carriages belonging to the ships and vessels under your command be painted in the established colours above mentioned and in no other; and that the paint delivered from the ordnance be not applied to any other purpose than that for which it was intended.

Of greater importance, perhaps, was the need to keep the Squadron provisioned and the greatest difficulty here lay in the acquisition of fresh beef. With ten to twelve ships manned by upwards of 6,000 men the requirement was enormous. Live bullocks were purchased wherever they could be obtained and slaughtered aboard individual ships. Portugal was the principal source of supply but, to avoid the attention of French agents, and thus conceal any transactions which might anger the already-threatening French Emperor, the Portuguese government was reluctant to provision British ships from Lagos, the most convenient port for the Cadiz Squadron.

Mr. Michael Petaro, the agent in Lisbon, was "authorised to express the unalterable and friendly disposition of His Royal Highness towards his faithful ally and his desire of complying with any demands of provisions made by the commanders of His Majesty's squadrons as far as may be consistent with his neutrality and the circumstances of the times". Petaro pointed out that in Lisbon, a large and mercantile city, such transactions would not be noticed as they would be in a small town like Lagos. From Lisbon, he saw no difficulty in undertaking the supply of fifty live oxen a week provided the commanders of the ships which came to collect them "disguised the main purpose of their visit". He suggested that ships coming for oxen should, ostensibly, be coming to collect mail and that their commanders should carry a written order to the Agent for Packets to this effect. Each ship that Admiral Purvis sent to Lisbon for bullocks was therefore briefed on this subterfuge and directed in much the same form as was Captain Mitford of the supply ship *Duchess of Bedford*:

On your arrival there deliver to Mr. Petaro the letter herewith given you who will cause as many bullocks to be procured as can conveniently (without crowding) be placed in the ship. In the performance of this service there requires some address and good management lest the emissaries of the enemy take means to prevent future supplies for which reason you will receive an order to apply to the Agent for Packets at Lisbon for such mail as may be there intended for this quarter, that it may appear your business at Lisbon was for that service only and therefore you will make that application before you go to Mr Petaro.

The other source of fresh beef was Morocco. In the previous year the Moroccan Emperor had supplied the French with 2,000 head of live cattle and James Green, the British Consul in Tangier, had been trying to obtain the same undertaking for Britain. It was not, however, to be granted without a counter concession as Green reported: it was customary for the Emperor's navy "if such it can be called, consisting of five rotten sloops-of-war and two half-galleys the latter of which can hardly float", to cruise in the Western Mediterranean between May and September. The ships were now in urgent need of cordage and boatswain's stores and all applications made by the Emperor had been side-stepped diplomatically by the consuls of those nations who had no particular need of Morocco's services and no wish to become involved in the refurbishment of its navy. Now, Green reported, he had obtained an undertaking for the supply of 1,000 bullocks at $44.50 a head provided the transactions were conducted in the utmost secrecy and the British government agreed to provide the stores and equipment for the Emperor's ships.

Lord Castlereagh, the Minister of War, agreed with the proviso that the indulgence "be not brought into precedence . . . he is to consider the indulgence as an act of friendship from His Majesty in consideration of the amicable disposition which he had evinced towards Great Britain". From thereon Admiral Purvis lost no opportunity of collecting bullocks from Tangier. His two logistic workhorses were the armed defence ships *Lord Eldon* and *Duchess of Bedford* both of which made regular trips to Lisbon and Tangier for beef. When these two were otherwise employed, he would reluctantly have to send a warship; a frigate such as the *Euryalus,* commanded by Captain Hon. George Dundas, could carry three dozen head in the humane conditions upon which the Admiral insisted. The bullocks it brought back were then distributed among the Squadron — *Atlas* 4; *Glory* 4; *Terrible* 4; *Illustrious* 3; *Excellent* 4; *Magnificent* 4; *Revenge* 4; *Courageux* 3; *Zealous* 5 and *Niger* 1.

Sometimes bullocks would be collected from the port of Tetouan and the commanders of the ships involved were under strict instructions not to rock the boat by "any sort of disturbance between the ship's company and the inhabitants". Admiral Purvis had already received complaints about British sailors running riot ashore in Tetouan and nothing could be allowed to prejudice the goodwill of the Moroccans and the supply of the precious beef so vital to the British Fleet.

Wine was another commodity requiring local purchase and the Admiralty was far from happy with the prices being charged by Mr. Petaro at Lisbon which varied between 3s/10d and 3s/11d per gallon. Their Lordships were therefore delighted when the Commander-in-Chief arranged the purchase of 30,000 gallons of cheap Spanish Marsala to be shipped to Deptford, plus a further 250 pipes for the Cadiz Squadron (it was perhaps prudent not to enquire too deeply into its source). Then, when Lord Collingwood advised them that he had authorised a trial purchase of wine from Malta at 10d per gallon, their approbation was unbounded.

Fresh vegetables, though readily available from Spanish bumboats which regularly plied for trade among the ships of the Squadron, were considered an unnecessary indulgence. Anti-scorbutics such as onions and lemons were issued but other fresh produce was only authorised in very special circumstances: when Captain William Pierrepont of the *Zealous* reported that eighty-eight of his men were down with scurvy, and when a survey panel of surgeons had confirmed his claim and recommended "a liberal supply of vegetables", Admiral Purvis authorised a purchase from the bumboats of an appropriate supply of vegetables but "as will serve for the sick only".

A concession might also be made when a ship had been at sea for a long period but never without the customary cautions and formalities. When Captain Samuel Pym of the *Atlas* requested this indulgence after his ship had been at sea for thirteen months, his crew existing on a diet of dry biscuits, pulses, salt pork and fresh beef, Admiral Purvis replied:

In consequence of your representation to me by letter of this day's date that the crew of His Majesty's Ship under your command had been nearly 13 months at sea and during the whole of that time they had rec'd but a very few trifling supplies of vegetables, and that a market boat was then alongside with a quantity of such sort as were useful and would keep and were to be sold at a very low price, I do hereby authorise you to order the purser of the ship to purchase such part thereof at the cheapest rate as are perfectly good, directing him to draw on the Commissioners of His Majesty's Victualling Board for the amount and furnishing proper vouchers for the same.

The irregularity of such dealings with enemy tradesmen is more easily understandable when one considers the almost-friendly disposition which existed between Britain and Spain at a higher level. When Don Francisco de Orta y Arcos, Governor of the Spanish enclave of Cueta on the North African coast, applied to Britain to be allowed to return to Spain with his family and baggage on account of ill health, Admiral Purvis ordered all cruisers, both ships of war and privateers, "to permit the said Governor . . . to pass free and unmolested with his family and baggage". Even more unusual was an application from the Marquis del Solorna on behalf of the Countess of [Tarnes] whose husband, the Count, was Inspector of Troops in the Havannah. The Countess had heard that her husband had "failed in his employment and also according to advice has given her much grief not having been able from that province to communicate to her the particulars of his misfortune". The Marquis requested that any papers addressed to the lady which might be found on board any Spanish ship from the Havannah captured by the British, should be extracted and forwarded to her. The Spanish were clearly not pursuing the interests of Bonaparte's empire with the same fervour as the French.

Another of Admiral Purvis's duties was the appraisal and dissemination of intelligence no matter how unlikely. A letter from James Pringle, the Consul-General in Madeira, reported the presence of a French general and his suite, in plain clothes, on Gran Canaria. His aide had been observed taking despatches to the French Commissary on Tenerife and the General had followed a few days later with a weighted box which he kept beside him on deck throughout the voyage ready to throw overboard should a British ship approach. He was thought to be General Brune and was disguised as the master of a Dutch merchantman.

Then there was a report from the Admiralty that the French were sending out officers in Portuguese ships to the Brazils. They were to be introduced into the Spanish settlements in South America with the purpose of indoctrinating, organising and disciplining the Spanish forces there. All Portuguese ships bound for the Brazils were therefore to be stopped and searched and any Frenchmen made prisoners. However, with an eye to the delicate diplomatic position of Portugal, the reason for such searches must be concealed from the Portuguese.

French spies lurked around every corner: a certain Major Burke, claiming to be in possession of important intelligence for the British government, was suspected of being one such on account of his foreign manners and accent. Admiral Purvis had him to dinner and afterwards wrote to Sir Hew Dalrymple: "I do not think him either an Englishman or Irish although he professed to come from the latter country and accounts for him speaking in the manner he does by a long residence in Spanish America." The Admiral put him on the next ship to Portsmouth with orders that he should be handed over to the Port Admiral immediately upon arrival. A covering letter warned Admiral Montagu of the circumstances which in view of "his dialect being not exactly what might be expected from a British officer," seemed to require "some little degree of caution".

But by June 1807 a situation of far greater gravity had developed in the Mediterranean. Since Austria's capitulation, Russia and Turkey remained as Britain's only viable allies with influence in the Eastern Mediterranean. Charles Arbuthnot, the British Minister in Turkey, had been warning for some time that The Sublime Porte (the Ottoman court in Constantinople) was beginning to fall for the blandishments of Napoleon and had been pleading with Lord Collingwood to send a detachment for the protection of British trade and interests in Turkey. In November 1806 Rear-Admiral Sir Thomas Louis had been despatched to the Dardanelles with three of-the-line reinforced in January by Vice-Admiral Sir John Duckworth with a further five. Threats and diplomacy had failed and Duckworth's Squadron, with the British community embarked, was badly mauled as it passed back through the Dardanelles.

With fears that if Turkey turned against Britain, Egypt also might join with France, Major-General Fraser (one of the passengers in *La*

Chiffone) with 5,000 troops was despatched to Alexandria which was captured but a subsequent attack on Rosetta [Rashid] failed with a heavy loss of British lives including General Fraser himself. It was clearly necessary for Lord Collingwood to move his station eastward up the Mediterranean where he would be in closer control of the deteriorating situation. The Admiralty also suggested that where Duckworth had failed in negotiations with the Turks, Collingwood, assisted by Sir Arthur Paget, a diplomat appointed to replace Arbuthnot, might succeed.

He therefore sailed from Cadiz on 27th June 1807 leaving Rear-Admiral Purvis in command of the blockade.

Lord Collingwood and Sir Arthur Paget, both accomplished diplomats, had no more success than had Admiral Duckworth in pursuading the Sublime Porte where its best interests lay. After a month of evasive replies to his overtures and endless eastern prevarication, Collingwood's patience was exhausted and he sailed for Sicily leaving Paget with two ships to try for a last ditch settlement. It was of no avail.

On 1st July a Russian fleet of ten of-the-line and two frigates under Admiral Dimitri Seniavine had defeated a Turkish fleet having previously captured two islands strategically situated in the approaches to the Dardanelles. Seniavine had served in the British Navy, in which he still had many friends, and had thus far been a trusted ally in the war against Napoleon. But one week later the Treaty of Tilsit was signed in which Tsar Alexander I, greedy for the spoils which a ride on the Napoleonic bandwagon might bring him, allied Russia with France against Great Britain. How fickle were her erstwhile friends when tempted with the lands of their neighbours.

Britain, not for the first or last time, now stood alone. Napoleon, with his 'Continental System', had effectively imposed a total blockade on British trade with the continent which included the vessels of neutral countries carrying British goods. With Spanish gunboats and French privateers active in the Strait of Gibraltar and along the North African coast, it was now necessary for neutral, as well as British, merchantmen to be escorted through the Strait. Admiral Purvis therefore ordered all neutral ships carrying British goods to come to the Squadron where they would be formed into escorted convoys: "They must not on any account attempt to pass the Gut without protection," he told his Captains.

Portugal was now Britain's only legitimate doorway into Europe and it was not a situation which Napoleon was prepared to accept for much longer. In September his threats to the Portuguese became more ominous: he would no longer tolerate an English ambassador in Europe, he told them, and would declare war on any nation which was still receiving one in two months time. The following month a French Imperial army of 24,000 under General Junot entered Spain en route for Portugal to implement this threat.

With Junot marching upon Lisbon, Admiral Purvis despatched Captain Musher in H.M. Sloop *Redwing* to the Tagus on 18th November with orders to take off Lord Strangford and Mr. Gambier, the British diplomats. In the event of their having already been evacuated:

> . . . you are then to collect all such intelligence respecting the Portuguese and Russians as may be in your power and return to this rendezvous as expeditiously as possible. On your approaching the Portuguese batteries you are to hoist a Flag of Truce and make known the business you are employed on taking special care not to expose the sloop you command to the risk of being disabled by shot from the batteries for want of having the Flag of Truce flying. You are to deliver the two letters herewith given you according to their address but in the event of Lord Strangford having taken his departure for England and Mr. Gambier remaining there, I think it necessary for His Majesty's Service that you should act as Mr. Gambier may recommend stating to him, however, at the same time, that the Redwing is very much wanted here.

The *Redwing* certainly was very much wanted; the Cadiz Squadron was suffering from an acute shortage of sloops and smaller craft. With Lord Collingwood at the other end of the Mediterranean, Admiral Purvis was under orders to open all his correspondence, action it as appropriate and then send the originals with a note of the action he had taken to the Commander-in-Chief. This tied up at least two small ships carrying despatches to and from the Eastern Mediterranean, the commanders of which were always enjoined to: "Keep a sufficient weight attached to the despatches at all times and to throw them overboard and sink them in case of danger or capture." Nor was it ever certain where Lord Collingwood could actually be found at any given time; Captain Handfield of the sloop *Delight,* charged with the delivery of despatches, was ordered to proceed first to Sicily, then to Malta and: "If Lord Collingwood is not at either place, you are to open the secret, sealed rendezvous I herewith give you for your further guidance."

Sloops, brigs and gunboats were also required for carrying Admiralty despatches to England; for carrying the despatches of Sir Hew Dalrymple, Governor of Gibraltar; for the escort of merchant convoys through the Gut; for looking out for and escorting the packet from England into Gibraltar Bay and for lookout duties on the headlands to ensure the Squadron was not surprised by an enemy fleet. Typical of this last duty were the Admiral's orders to Captain Hornby of the sloop *Minorca* to take station from five to fifteen leagues south-south-west of Cape St. Mary:

. . . for the purposes of giving me notice of the approach of the enemy's squadron which may be coming to this quarter and of annoying and intercepting their trade, particularly some of their small vessels which are now on their passage from South America and others which are about to sail from Huelva and Cadiz outward bound for their colonies. It is proper to inform you that the enemy's vessels above mentioned are generally rigged with one mast and appear very like their larger class of fishing boats for which some of them have been mistaken. . . . On obtaining any intelligence of importance which can be depended on, you are to communicate it to me on this rendezvous with all possible dispatch. You are to continue on this service until 1st August next when you are to rejoin me at this rendezvous, unless you should receive intelligence or have occasion to communicate with me sooner, or should fall in with the packet from England in which case you are to accompany her to the Squadron.

It was essential for regular contact to be maintained between the Squadron and its detached lookouts. Captain Raith of the sloop *Scout* was ordered:

Whilst cruizing on your station off Capes Trafalgar and Spartel, to approach the Squadron off Cadiz at least once every 5 days, sufficiently near to distinguish signals, showing your sloop's number and waiting for a reply. And when circumstances consistent with your orders make it necessary for you to go to Gibraltar, you are always before you leave to enquire whether the water transports are loaded and waiting for convoy to the Fleet and then, if no other escort is there, to bring them out under your protection.

With a shortage of small ships, it was often necessary for Admiral Purvis to allocate one of his precious ships of-the-line to tasks which should more properly have been undertaken by frigates or sloops. In the summer of 1807 his battle force consisted, nominally, of the *Intrepid*, 64, eight seventy-fours — *Courageux, Excellent, Illustrious, Magnificent, Revenge, Saturn, Terrible* and *Zealous* plus the *Glory,* 90, an old second-rate which was approaching the end of her service and his own Flagship the *Atlas*. These were the ships with which he would be required to engage any enemy fleet which broke out of Cadiz or approached from the west, from Brest or Ferrol, or from the east, from Toulon or Cartagena. In reality, he was lucky to have half this number available for action at any given time. Constant demands were made upon his force to provide escorts for troop convoys between Gibraltar and Sicily and merchant convoys with valuable cargoes; then the Squadron had to be supplied to remain at sea and if no frigates were available these tasks had to be undertaken by battleships. In August Lord Beauclerk in *Saturn* had to be sent back to England for a dockyard refit and in September Captain Hon. Philip Wodehouse in *Intrepid* had to transport General Fox and his family back to England, the General having "expressed a strong desire to be conveyed home in her".

By the time Captain Musher in the *Redwing* reached Lisbon, a squadron from England under Sir Sidney Smith had arrived at the Tagus to take off the British diplomatic personnel and to oversee the evacuation of the Portuguese royal family to Brazil. He had with him the *Foudroyant,* 80, and two seventy-fours, the *Conqueror* and the *Plantaganet,* which he had been ordered to detach to reinforce Admiral Purvis at Cadiz. However, on reaching the Tagus, Rear-Admiral Smith discovered the Russian Admiral Seniavine with nine ships of-the-line, and one frigate, who had crept into Lisbon en route from the Mediterranean to the Baltic, anxious to avoid a confrontation with his friends and former allies in the Royal Navy (he later resigned from the Russian navy rather than engage in hostilities against Britain). Sir Sidney therefore decided to retain the ships destined for the Cadiz Squadron to ensure an effective blockade of the Russian Squadron in the Tagus. Admiral Purvis thus got the *Redwing* back but lost his expected reinforcement of three ships of-the-line.

In the meantime, there were more demands upon his precious frigates. Moves were afoot for troops from Sicily under Sir John Moore to sail for the Tagus and to be ready to take the Portuguese island of Madeira to prevent its occupation by the French. On 19th November Admiral Purvis issued 'Most Secret' orders to Captain Hon. George Dundas of the frigate *Euryalus* to be in readiness:

. . . to proceed with such transports with troops as are now expected at Gibraltar from Sicily with Lieutenant-General Sir John Moore. You are on arrival of the Lieutenant-General at Gibraltar to communicate with him and if he should require more than one frigate in addition to what he may have brought with him for the security of the convoy, you are to direct Captain Hillyar of the Niger to put himself under your orders for that purpose. You are to act in concert with the Lieutenant-General till you arrive off the Tagus when Rear-Admiral Sir Sidney Smith will take charge of the transports and you, together with such other ships and vessels as are under Lord Collingwood's command are immediately to return without loss of time to me off this rendezvous. And whereas it may possibly be intended that Lieutenant-General Sir John Moore should proceed to or detach a part of his force against the island of Madeira and the remainder to be sent to England you are (in the event of your being the senior naval officer) to attach yourself to that part thereof which may be intended for Madeira and give that for England in charge of Captain Hillyar of the Niger directing him to proceed to Spithead and acquaint the Secretary of the Admiralty of his arrival. Should it be so arranged that you proceed to Madeira you are to conform yourself to the confidential instructions with which the Lieutenant-General is entrusted and act in co-operation with him, or the officer he may attach in command, with the strictest cordiality and confidence.

The Portuguese royal family and many of its adherents left Lisbon with the bulk of the Portuguese navy on 29th November and was seen safely on its way into exile in Brazil by Sir Sidney Smith's Squadron. The following day Junot entered Lisbon and, supported by Seniavine's Russian ships, closed the Tagus gateway to Britain. The following month a squadron under the command of Sir Samuel Hood supported an unopposed landing and occupation of Madeira.

While these great events were being enacted, Admiral Purvis continued in his role as doorman of the Mediterranean, juggling his ships to meet the demands of British trade, the military command, Lord Collingwood's detachment in the east and the maintenance and supply of his own Squadron. Water was a particular problem; not only were the casks badly coopered which resulted in much waste from leakage but the whole process of loading water at Gibraltar was painfully slow due to a shortage of boats. The dockyard, it appears, was reluctant to lend the Squadron boats for this purpose for fear that they would be damaged. Admiral Purvis despatched Captain Lord Henry Paulet in the *Terrible* to speed up the process. His orders were specific:

> ... your Lordship will please to apply to Commissioner Middleton for one of the dockyard launches for the sole purpose of loading the transports and that you will direct a proper officer and a set of trusty men to be employed on that service, and that the officer be made accountable for her safety and that she be always returned carefully in the evenings to the place assigned for her within the Mole and as there frequently is a considerable swell where the boats take in the water, you will direct that no boats whatever be allowed to go there without being provided with a grapnail *[sic]* and rope to haul off by when it becomes necessary.

Nor did the demands of a difficult command at a critical point in history exempt him from the trifles of housekeeping within his Squadron. In December the Transport Board requested an enquiry into the treatment of ulcers in the *Excellent*. The Board pointed out that between 29th July and 20th October there had been twenty-seven reported cases in that ship "which induces us to suspect that the practice of the surgeon is not judicious".

Chapter 9

Vivan los Ingleses!

1st January 1808
H.M.S. Atlas
off Cadiz

At the start of the year 1808 Admiral Purvis had been at sea for one year and two months, the last six months of which he had been in command of the Cadiz Squadron. His Flagship had been provisioned at sea and had not once dropped an anchor nor been driven through the Gut by westerly gales.

On 14th January one of his lookouts reported to him that the enemy's ships in Cadiz were apparently ready for sea and had moved out into the fairway with the evident "intention of taking the first opportunity of escaping". He also received intelligence that the enemy squadrons in Cartagena and Toulon were expected to make an early attempt to sail and join up with those in Cadiz. The Admiral considered it necessary to have a line-of-battle ship off the Lighthouse of St. Sebastian and despatched Captain Sir John Gore in the *Revenge* with instructions to "be very attentive to all their movements and make known to me by signals all such as you may deem necessary for my information".

At the same time he was also advised that a convoy of troop transports from England had been dispersed in a gale; he therefore had to detach *Scout* and *Sabrina* to search for stragglers and escort them safely into Gibraltar. Then, a report that the enemy was using every possible means to get supplied from Algeçiras and Ceuta necessitated the detachment of another three ships to patrol the eastern end of the Strait; if westerly gales prevented them from keeping station, they were to anchor in Tetouan Bay until the weather moderated: "On no account get blown up the Mediterranean," he ordered them, "frequently stand well in to Gibraltar and show your number paying strictest attention to signals."

Meanwhile, the French, who had already insinuated some 54,000 men into Spain, had assembled a substantial body of troops and provisions with the intention of occupying Ceuta from where they would be in a stronger position to discourage the Emperor of Morocco from his friendship towards Britain. Lieutenant-General Sir Hew Dalrymple, Governor of Gibraltar, planned to get there first with a *coup de main* under the command of Major-General Brent Spencer. Intrinsic to the success of his plan was naval support from as many of Admiral Purvis's small ships as could be spared. In reality, none could be spared but, in response to Sir Hew's urgent pleas, he took *Scout, Redwing* and *Minorca* off their stations and detached them with all the brigs and gunboats he could muster to the Ceuta expedition. He also considered it advisable that a naval officer of ability and experience should be on hand to give directions and to liaise with the General and therefore sent Captain Charles Boyles, his friend and trusted second-in-command, to Gibraltar with the *Windsor Castle*.

With the *Scout* and *Redwing* detached, the west end of the Gut was left exposed to the depredations of the enemy's privateers and gunboats and there were no frigates left to fill the gaps; *Hyena* was off Cartagena and *Grasshopper* was carrying despatches to the Commander-in-Chief. Thus severely stretched, Admiral Purvis learned that the French warships in Cadiz had now come to single anchor indicating that they were preparing an imminent break out. He therefore positioned his depleted force off the harbour approaches where he would be ready to receive them.

The enemy, however, was coming from another quarter. With Admiral Purvis poised off Cadiz without a frigate, sloop, brig or gunboat to watch the western approaches, five French ships of-the-line under Rear-Admiral Allemand slipped in to the Mediterranean keeping close to the North African coast and taking advantage of poor visibility during a westerly gale; they had escaped from Rochefort when the British Squadron under Rear-Admiral Sir Richard Strachan, which was supposed to be blockading the port, had left its station to seek an overdue convoy of transports with provisions. When Sir Richard returned to find his prisoners gone, he set sail for Gibraltar believing them, most probably, bound for the Mediterranean. Among his ships was the frigate *Cambrian* commanded by Captain Hon. Charles Paget, brother of Sir Arthur Paget whose diplomatic mission to the Sublime Porte had ended in failure. Sent ahead to make contact with the Cadiz Squadron and unaware of the dispersal of the Squadron's ships and the imminent threat from the French in Cadiz, Paget wrote to his brother:

There's no doubt but that a French squadron may at any time get into the Mediterranean unperceived by ours off Cadiz, if ours is always where we found it. I am confident for instance that Sir Richard might with the greatest ease by keeping the Barbary Shore well on board have passed up completely unknown to Admiral Purvis. When they did see us, we put them for two or three hours in a fidget and occasioned a General Chace.[1]

This was hardly the case: despite his shortage of ships, Admiral Purvis had positioned the *Bulwark* as lookout well to the south and just within signal range of the Flagship. The strangers were sighted and reported at sunrise and, although the Captain of the *Bulwark* believed them to be friendly, there was sufficient doubt for the Admiral to order a General Chase at 0927. Private signals were exchanged with the *Caesar* and the strangers' identity established forty-three minutes later at 1010. Had they been enemy ships, the Cadiz Squadron would undoubtedly have intercepted and destroyed them.

Believing the French ships to be heading for Toulon to join up with Ganteaume's Squadron, Admiral Purvis felt that Strachan's ships should proceed into the Mediterranean to reinforce Lord Collingwood or Admiral Thornborough. He preferred that Sir Richard should do this on his advice rather than on his order as Captain Paget, who appears to have been habitually critical and contemptuous of his superiors, related:

Sir Richard is a good deal annoyed at going into the Mediterranean but he was
obliged (he told me) as Admiral Purvis, that glorious hero, had intimated to him
that if he, Sir Richard, did not follow his *advice* in going he should take upon
himself to *order* him. Of the two Sir Richard preferred taking the advice, meaning
if he found on getting to Gibraltar or elsewhere that the report was without
foundation to return immediately to England. This he could not do had Admiral
Purvis furnished him with an order to proceed and join Lord Colley or old
Thornborough.[2]

The report was not without foundation; Allemand reached Toulon
on 6th February and Vice-Admiral Ganteaume's reinforced fleet of
ten ships of-the-line, three frigates, two sloops and seven armed
transports put to sea the following day. Sir Richard Strachan joined
Vice-Admiral Thornborough at Palermo giving him a total force of
eleven of-the-line. (Thornborough's Flagship the *Royal Sovereign*
was commanded by Henry Garrett.) For the next two months this
French Fleet cruised in the Mediterranean, for most of the time
shadowed by British frigates. Against its ten of-the-line Admiral
Thornborough had eleven, Lord Collingwood five and Rear-
Admiral George Martin at Palermo a further three; but at no point
did a British squadron manage to find and engage the French Fleet
which returned to the safety of Toulon on 10th April. While
Ganteaume was roaming unchallenged in the Mediterranean,
Rosilly in Cadiz, aware that Admiral Purvis was waiting for him
outside the harbour, thought better of coming out and ordered his
Captains to stand down from their state of immediate readiness.

Meanwhile, on 16th February an event had occurred which was to
change the whole balance of the conflict: without any declaration of
war, French forces had seized the Spanish frontier fortresses of
Pamplona, San Sebastian, Figueras and Barcelona thereby opening
the whole Spanish frontier to the ingress of French troops. Five
weeks later an army under Marshal Murat entered Madrid. It now
remained to be seen whether Spain would accept French
domination or had the spirit to resist.

Early in April the awaited vacancy for a Lieutenant in Lord
Collingwood's Flagship came up and young John, not yet twenty-
one, left the *Atlas* for the *Ocean*. Here he would be under the eye of
the Commander-in-Chief and Admiral Purvis was content that

therein lay his best possible chance for early promotion. He was, however, less happy about the progress of his younger son, Richard, in India. In September he had received a letter from him, which had taken fifteen months in transit, advising him that he was in debt and asking for his father's assistance. The Admiral, convinced that his son must have been gambling, had replied with some severity:

... I am indeed more disappointed than I can find words to express ... I think it very disgraceful to be in debt ... I have no money to spare; what little I have I have saved in the course of a long and fatiguing service; I derived no riches from my parents and they never paid a quarter as much for me in my whole life as I have already done for you ... I again repeat, I suspect it is a gaming debt which has given you this trouble and if so you will never be happy till you have determined to leave it off and never again risk the inquietude I judge you feel.[3]

Nevertheless, he authorised his son to draw on him for £100 which sum was not to be exceeded. Richard had told him that it was necessary for him to maintain an establishment of twenty servants; his father's advice was simple:

Whenever a person involves himself in debt, the most honorable plan he can possibly adopt is to lessen his expenses immediately by discharging every unnecessary part of his establishment and not from a false pride continue the destructive habits which have brought him into so mortifying a dilemma.[4]

It was a further eight months before Richard received this letter — more than two years since he had appealed for help — by which time he had preempted his father's advice and had reduced his debts to the point where he had no need of the £100. The Admiral insisted, just the same, that he should have it.

It soon became apparent that the Spanish people were not going to put up with French domination nor to accept Joseph Bonaparte who had been nominated by his brother as King of Spain in place of the effectively-deposed Charles IV. The notorious *Dos de Mayo* on 2nd May, a violent but disorganised revolt in Madrid which was brutally and bloodily put down by the French, was followed by uprisings throughout Spain.

Off Cadiz in the early hours of Sunday 15th May the lights of a strange fleet were sighted to the south-west which at dawn was identified as a convoy of troop transports under the command of Major-General Spencer. At 1500 the General moved into the *Atlas* with his suite and immediately began discussions with Admiral Purvis as to how their force could best be used to aid the Spanish patriots.

The following morning the gunboat *Revenge* was sent in to Cadiz under Flag of Truce with the British commanders' proposal which was conditional upon the prior handing over of the French warships in the harbour. The Spanish responded by ignoring the proposal and moving the French ships, and their own, to the Carracas, an anchorage deep within the harbour out of reach of the British Squadron's guns. A letter to the Marquis del Solorna, Governor of Cadiz, enquiring as to how the British force could best help the Spanish people was acknowledged together with a request that no further communications of the kind should be addressed to him. Shortly thereafter a signal was received from the *Bulwark* reporting that the Marquis had been murdered by the people of Cadiz. On 23rd May Admiral Purvis sent the troop transports, escorted by the *Minorca, Alceste, Grasshopper* and *Imogene* to anchor at the entrance to the harbour where they would be ready to disembark at short notice if required.

On the 27th, following an uprising of the citizens of Seville, the Andalusian Junta approached Sir Hew Dalrymple with the first official appeal for British assistance. Such assistance, however, was sought in the form of money, arms and ammunition and, despite repeated overtures from Admiral Purvis and General Spencer, nothing would induce the Spanish to allow the landing of British troops at Cadiz nor to accept the help of the Royal Navy in reducing and capturing the French warships in the harbour. It was therefore decided that the British troop convoy should return to Gibraltar and General Spencer moved to the *Alceste* which was to escort it. A few hours after the convoy had sailed, the *Revenge* again appeared from Cadiz signalling frantically to the Flagship that she had a Spanish Admiral and General on board who wished to speak to the British Admiral. The troop convoy was recalled and General Spencer moved back into the *Atlas*.

The Spanish delegates turned out to be Rear-Admiral McDonald and Don Pedro Cruez, Judge of the Royal Court of Judicature of

Seville. For two days they conferred with the British commanders on board the *Atlas* being ferried back and forth into Cadiz in the *Revenge* to put the proposals and counter-proposals under discussion to their colleagues ashore. By midnight on 1st June some sort of loose concordat had been reached: the British naval Squadron could anchor inshore off Cadiz but was on no account to interfere with the French ships which the Spanish Navy had the resources to reduce without British assistance. General Spencer's troops were not required on shore but should be held in readiness to land further up the coast to intercept any approach of French forces.

At noon on Monday 6th June 1808, Admiral Purvis anchored his Squadron in twenty-four fathoms some seven miles off Cadiz. He himself had been at sea, without even dropping an anchor, for one year and seven months during which time not a single square-rigged vessel had been permitted to pass in to or out of the Port of Cadiz. It had surely been a blockade as successful as any ever undertaken by the Royal Navy.

At 1445 on 9th June the British Squadron observed the Spanish commence action against the French ships in Cadiz. The Spanish Admiral fired a gun as a summons for the French to surrender; the French returned the fire. Spanish gunboats and shore batteries bombarded the enemy ships until 1930. Later in the evening Admiral Purvis sent in a boat with medical aid for the Spanish. The action continued sporadically for a few days until, at 0800 on the 14th, the French surrendered; each ship fired a gun and hauled down its colours. Admiral Rosily's ships had been trapped in Cadiz since the Battle of Trafalgar nearly three years earlier and it was an ignominious end to his command. At 1000 Spanish colours were hoisted on the French ships and their crews were taken off as prisoners-of-war. A *feu de joie* was then fired starting with the shore batteries and finishing with the recently-surrendered enemy ships.

Richard Purvis, much later, read of the capitulation in the Indian newspapers and wrote to his stepmother:

The newspapers in this country said nothing of my father's having received the French Fleet as prizes; but that it had surrendered to the Spaniards. I wish the former had been the case as the Prize Money would no doubt have been acceptable to the Admiral.[5]

There now existed a strange situation in which, although Britain and
Spain were still officially at war, each nation was ready to embrace
the other as a partner in common hatred of the French. A delegation
of Asturian patriots arriving in England to solicit Britain's help
invoked a huge wave of sympathy, and relief, at home; yet in the
war zone a degree of reserve was still necessary; large numbers of
Spanish civilians, particularly from the higher social orders who
had most to fear from the forces of revolutionary France, expected
asylum in the British Fleet. Admiral Purvis wrote to General
Spencer:

I have written to Sir John Gore to desire he will be very cautious in receiving
persons of any description to remain in the fleet. It is to be recollected that they
are our enemies and from everything that we have seen of them they have no
claim to such marks of attention from us particularly when the receiving of them
in such numbers (as is but reasonable to expect will offer) must be attended with
such great inconvenience to the ships. Whatever messages may be sent to
individuals in Cadiz, I think you will agree with me in scrupulously avoiding
holding out to them anything like a promise of what cannot on our part be
granted.

Three Spanish gentlemen from Cadiz considered that they had
intelligence of sufficient importance to the British Government to
ensure their passage. Admiral Purvis sent them to England in the
Minorca which was taking despatches home but with a strict
enjoinder to Captain Hornby "not to allow them to go on shore
without directions of the Admiral at the port you arrive at to whom
you are to make known their having intelligence to communicate to
Government". Most asylum seekers were sympathetically, but
firmly, turned away.

   At 1500 on 11th June Lord Collingwood returned in the *Ocean* in
company with the *Repulse*. Admiral Purvis had commanded the
Cadiz Squadron for one year. His hopes for his son John, in bringing
him to the notice of the Commander-in-Chief, had been pleasingly
realised: the previous month Lord Collingwood had given him
command of the *Delight*, "a very fine brig lately taken from the
enemy" mounting eighteen 12-pounder long guns and with a crew
of 110 men; in August he was to receive his promotion to
Commander. Now his father's hopes for him were that he should do

well in his first command, make Post quickly and, with good
fortune, get the sort of assignments which would give him the
chance of earning some prize-money.

Though the Admiral's first concern was, naturally enough, the
career of his own son, he also maintained a strong interest in the
progress of all the young officers who had started their careers as
boys under his care: two of the Lieutenants in his Flagship,
Wormeley and Leeke, had been boys in the *London* as had Moresby,
now serving in the *Kent,* and Mapleton, First Lieutenant of the
Imperieuse, who was believed to have made between £7,000 and
£8,000 in prize-money. The popular Surgeon of the *Atlas,* Mr.
Little, had also served with Admiral Purvis, by his own request,
since *London* days.

If a captured ship and her contents were sold, prize-money was
paid on the sum realised. If, however, as was often the case, she was
suitable to be taken into His Majesty's service, the survey and
assessment for prize-money was not lightly undertaken: a survey
panel would be appointed consisting of suitably-qualified dockyard
officers and tradesmen from the Fleet. A typical survey panel,
headed by a naval officer, might comprise a Master Attendant and
Master Shipwright from the dockyard, and two Masters, two
Boatswains and two Sailmakers, taken from different ships to guard
against any form of collusion. If ordnance was involved there would
be two Gunners; provisions or medical stores and equipment would
require the inclusion of a Purser or a Surgeon. Every part of the
prize and her contents was then measured, itemised and realistically
valued with the surveyors aware that they might be required to
swear on oath as to the impartiality of their assessment.

Only then could prize-money be claimed. The total sum was
divided into eight parts: the Flag received one part; the Captain two;
the commissioned officers one; the warrant officers one; the petty
officers one and the seamen and marines the remaining two parts. A
cartoon of the time suggested that wounds and injuries should be
apportioned by the same rules and in 1808 a more equitable
apportionment was introduced with the Flag taking one-third of the
Captain's two parts and the crew receiving four.

Nevertheless, fortunes were still to be made by successful
Captains and their Flag-Officers and Admiral Purvis was already

starting to receive significant sums of money for prizes taken by ships in his Squadron. A good cruise with the chance of prizes was the hope of every young Captain and the most valuable perquisite in every Admiral's gift; and this is what Admiral Purvis now hoped for for his son John.

Richard, in India, had also received his own command — a mud fort on a searingly-hot and dusty plain in the middle of nowhere with no prospect of prize-money, promotion, or any increment to the miserably-inadequate salary he received as a Lieutenant in the Honorable East India Company's service. By his own efforts he had got himself out of debt and restored an amicable relationship with his father but, learning of the success of his brother John, he was beginning to have doubts about the wisdom of his decision to break loose from his father's patronage.

Although, as we have seen, a degree of unity had existed between Britain and Spain since May, hostilities did not officially cease until 4th July shortly after which the Cadiz Squadron received orders from the Admiralty that all Spanish prisoners-of-war were to be freed. General Spencer with his troops having sailed north-west to the Portuguese border without encountering the expected French force, returned to Cadiz and moved his headquarters once again into the *Atlas*.

Ashore in Spain the French were not having it all their own way. bands of *guerrilleros* (the first guerrilla fighters) roamed the country harrying the French supply lines and slaughtering Frenchmen at a rate which has been estimated at 300 a day; on 20th July a French army of three divisions under General Dupont, whose objective had been Cadiz, surrendered at Bailén to the Spanish General Castaños and at 0800 on the 22nd the Cadiz Squadron fired a 15-gun salute in honour of this achievement. The victory was to bolster Spain's confidence in its ability to challenge the French but also, as Admiral Purvis would learn to his cost, to increase their belief in the invulnerability of the port of Cadiz.

General Castaños entered Madrid on 23rd August to a tumultuous welcome and, according to intelligence received from Samuel Whittingham of the 13th Light Dragoons, attached to the Spanish Army, cries of "Vivan los Ingleses" greeted the sight of any British uniform. But the Spanish lacked central command and control and their efforts, though not lacking in gallantry, were scrappy, unco-ordinated and, ultimately, ineffective. Their provincial governments were corrupt and debilitated by self-interest as Major (later Sir) William Cox, 61st Regiment, reported of the Junta at Seville, the nominal authority for affairs in Cadiz:

The fact is their attention has been for some time past so much occupied by vain and frivolous disputes, and by views of private interest and advantage, that they seem to have neglected entirely every concern of real importance and almost to have lost sight of the general interests of the country.

Denied any chance to take an active part in the defence of Cadiz, Lord Collingwood, Admiral Purvis and the Cadiz Squadron sailed for Gibraltar on 26th August. On the 30th *Ocean, Terrible, Northumberland, Excellent* and the *Lord Eldon* sailed to the eastward leaving *Atlas, Repulse, Bulwark, Fame* and the *Duchess of Bedford* at Gibraltar to deal with any contingencies which might present at Cadiz or in the Strait.

The *Atlas*, requiring some recaulking of her topsides and some work on her foremast, warped in to the mole on 5th September where her foremast was removed. Later in the month Admiral Purvis left the ship and visited Cadiz with Lord Collingwood in the *Repulse*. Collingwood was already held in high esteem by the Spanish for his generous and humane treatment in repatriating the Spanish wounded after Trafalgar. Now, his ready compliance with their demands for money, weapons and powder was to consolidate his reputation. He was outraged, however, when he learned that a supply of powder he had scraped together from the ships in his Squadron had been fired off by the Spanish in celebration of a local Saint's Day; the next request for powder met with the retort: "I can spare none for saints; only for sinners."

On 20th September Admirals Collingwood and Purvis went ashore from *Repulse* to dine with General Morla, the Governor of Cadiz. They were besieged by an enormous crowd chanting "Vivan los Ingleses, Viva King George, Viva Collingwood". Their way through the city had to be cleared by a troop of cavalry and after dinner they were taken to the opera which was *en fête* for their visit. On their appearance in the Governor's box, the audience rose to its feet and shouted, clapped and stamped their feet for fifteen minutes. The applause for the performance was completely overshadowed by the applause which preceded and followed it for the honoured British guests. *The Times* of 29th September reported: "Nothing could exceed the warmth with which the people received our officers as they passed. Every demonstration of respect, esteem and gratitude, was manifested, and ardent acclamations attended them wherever they were seen."

But the flattery and attention they received every time they went ashore was not winning the war against Napoleon and the fiesta had to end: Lord Collingwood returned to the blockade of Toulon and Admiral Purvis to the *Atlas* in Gibraltar.

Over the next two months he was involved in the wide range of duties which were the lot of a 'jobbing Admiral' of the time: on one day he would be arranging for the distribution among the Spanish freedom fighters of 8,000 pikes, recently arrived on board the *Ruby*; the next, organising a passage to Malta in the *Redwing* for three Moroccan dignitaries on the first stage of a pilgrimage to Mecca; then issuing orders for the safe repatriation in the Sardinian brigantine *Isabella* of 213 doctors and medical staff from General Dupont's defeated army; then instructing his scouts to watch out for a renegade Irish priest believed to be a French agent looking for an opportunity to escape from Spain; ordering Captain Durham in the *Renown* to place his ship at the disposal of H.R.H. Prince Leopold of Sicily and his suite; arranging safe passage for Messrs. Kemensky and Prasmorsky, emissaries of Baron Stroganoff in Madrid, who were said to be carrying despatches of consequence to Great Britain; every day there was something different.

Although the Gut was a quieter place since the peace with Spain, French privateers were still active in the area and the Moors were unpredictable. The existence of a treaty between Britain and the Dey of Algiers meant little to the piratical captains of Algerine cruisers who specialised in picking off the lame ducks or stragglers in British merchant convoys. On 2nd October the Admiral detailed Captain Hon. Charles Elphinstone Fleeming in the *Bulwark* to provide additional escort cover for a convoy bound for the Tagus; he was to remain with it as far as the latitude of Cape St. Mary near the Portuguese port of Faro:

In the event of your falling in with any of the said Algerines, which have for some time past been seen cruizing near this place, you are to represent to the Commander how completely he is violating the existing Treaty between the two nations by hovering about this port and that you have directions to desire he will discontinue such offensive conduct but in doing this you are cautiously to avoid any violent measures; and in case they should persist in keeping in sight of this port notwithstanding the above-mentioned Treaty and your admonition, you are to take the name of the ship and the commander thereof for my information.

It was said of Captain Fleeming that his name "was a terror to every ship's company he commanded and was cursed from stem to stern in the British Navy".[6] It is to be hoped that he had a similar effect upon the Algerines.

Even more important was the need not to upset the Moroccans who, despite the fact that their cruisers were only seaworthy thanks to Britain's help, were not averse to now using them to snatch the odd prize when the opportunity arose. James Green in Tangier wrote to Admiral Purvis for assistance in arranging the release of a barque which had been so seized; the Admiral replied: "My intention is to send the *Voluntaire* to Tangier . . . but I shall desire Captain Bullen not to use any violent language to the Moors." Similarly, Lieutenant Frew, commanding the gunboat *Revenge,* when ordered to hunt down a particularly troublesome French privateer, was warned not to be deceived by a false commission which her Master was said to carry and on no account to attack her inside Moroccan territorial waters.

With Spain no longer an enemy, the local intelligence flow increased; much of it was spurious but there were some items which were advantageous to Britain such as a report of a large number of Swiss and German soldiers in and around Malaga who, it was believed, would be receptive to an approach to enlist in the British service. Admiral Purvis sent Captain Bullen in the *Voluntaire* to round them up.

But while local intelligence improved, there was a lamentable lack of information on what was happening in the Peninsula as a whole. The Spanish communications network was as disorganised and unreliable as the rest of its armed forces and the British Minister in Seville, John Frere, was infuriatingly uncommunicative seeming to expect local commanders to reach important tactical decisions without knowledge of the overall military situation. Occasional, and excellent, situation reports were received from British officers, such as Samuel Whittingham and William Cox, attached to the Spanish and Portuguese forces, but they took their time in coming and their content was frequently out of date by the time it reached the naval commanders in the Mediterranean. Lord Collingwood in the east was continually pressing Admiral Purvis in the west for news which he was seldom able to provide.

Knowledge of what had, in fact, been happening in the autumn of 1808 would hardly have cheered the Admirals: back in July Major-General Sir Arthur Wellesley (the future Duke of Wellington) had landed at Corunna in advance of a British Expeditionary Force of 9,500 men. He had found the Spanish in a state of total disorder and ignorance with no knowledge of the strength and positions of their own forces let alone those of the enemy. They had been quite adamant, however, that they needed no help from the British so Wellesley had, instead, landed his troops in Portugal, at Mondego Bay, some eighty miles north of Lisbon, where he had been joined by Major-General Spencer's force of 5,000 from Gibraltar.

On 21st August Wellesley had defeated Junot's Army at the Battle of Vimeiro but had then been superceded by Sir Hew Dalrymple from Gibraltar who, despite Wellesley's pleas, declined to pursue and destroy the French. He had then negotiated the notoriously feeble Convention of Cintra by which the French Army was repatriated by the British Fleet with all their weapons and equipment. This, though resulting in a public outcry in Britain and the recall of Sir Hew Dalrymple to face a public enquiry, had at least cleared the French out of Portugal for the time being.

Then in September the British Expeditionary Force, now under the command of General Sir John Moore, had advanced into Spain. General Castaños had already re-entered Madrid and the French had drawn back to the Ebro where 'King' Joseph Bonaparte established his temporary court having fled the capital ahead of Castaños. Napoleon in Paris was furious at this reverse in his fortunes: he declared that his army in the Peninsula seemed to be commanded by "post office inspectors" and he would take the field himself at the head of the *Grande Armée* of 150,000 to smash the divided Anglo-

Spanish forces once and for all. So, while Admiral Purvis swung at anchor in Gibraltar Bay, thirsting for news of what was going on ashore, the endless blue columns of Napoleon's elite troops were marching into Spain in readiness for the *coup de grâce*.

On 14th December Admiral Purvis received intelligence that a massive French army was poised to strike at Madrid; in fact, it had already done so and the city had capitulated ten days earlier. If Madrid fell, he reasoned, it was only a matter of time before the French drove south for Cordoba, Seville and then Cadiz where the humiliated remnants of Rosily's Trafalgar Fleet lay at anchor together with the bulk of the Spanish Navy. If these ships fell into French hands it could prove to be a war-winning acquisition for the enemy; they must be protected from capture at any cost.

But most of the ships were in an appalling state, quite unfit to put to sea, and the Spanish lacked the men, the supplies and, it seemed, the motivation to do anything about it; and with Madrid again in enemy hands would they still believe in their ability to defend the vitally important harbour and arsenal of Cadiz with their own inadequate and disorganised forces? And would they still regard the British with a degree of mistrust and refuse all offers of help?

There was no time to consult the Commander-in-Chief; it could take two weeks to rush a despatch to him and wait for a reply and there was clearly not a moment to be lost; memories of Toulon were still vivid in his mind; on that occasion, lack of forethought and preparation had resulted in more than half the captive ships being retaken by the enemy and used again against Britain. It must not happen again.

Admiral Purvis in the *Atlas* together with *Voluntaire* and *Sabrina* sailed for Cadiz on 14th December where they anchored the following day. Salutes were exchanged and Mr. Duff, the British Consul, came on board to brief the Admiral on the present situation; it was as he had feared: the Spanish had done nothing to prepare either their own or the captured French ships for evacuation. The only evidence of a seaworthy force was one line-of-battle ship and one frigate at anchor off Fort Puntales.

On the 17th he had his barge launched and went up the harbour to look at the French and Spanish ships moored in the Carracas; here his worst fears were realised. Several of the ships were nothing but prison hulks, being full of French prisoners-of-war, and were unlikely ever to be fit to put to sea again. The rest were in a dreadful state of neglect with missing and damaged spars and rigging and riding high in the water suggesting that guns and cable, and possibly even ballast, had been removed. None of the ships appeared to be fully manned; they had skeleton crews, presumably for maintenance but, judging from their condition and the odd sailor that the Admiral saw slouching around the upper decks, all attempts at maintaining these rotting, forgotten hulks had long since been abandoned.

But the French, Purvis knew, would certainly not be wanting in the energy the Spaniards apparently lacked to restore these ships to operational fighting units. It was absolutely imperative that they were made seaworthy and moved from their present position before the French arrived in Cadiz.

Returning to his Flagship, he considered his approach to the Spanish authorities. They were so proud and sensitive to any implied criticism that he knew it would have to be made in very diplomatic terms. Unfortunately, Mr. Duff had advised him, General Morla, the Governor of Cadiz whom he had met, and who had entertained him and Lord Collingwood so handsomely earlier in the year, had been succeeded by a new Governor, Virnes.

He wrote to him the following day.

CHAPTER 10

Mañana, Mañana!

**18th December 1808, H.M.S. *Atlas*, Cadiz
Rear-Admiral Purvis
to His Excellency Governor Virnes of Cadiz**

Excellent Sir,

*Labouring as I do under the disadvantage of not understanding
the Spanish language, I am induced to address Your Excellency in
this way which otherwise might possibly have been unnecessary.*
  *Your Excellency must be well convinced how truly animated the
government and people of England are in the cause of Spain
against our common enemy and that they are equally full of
confidence as to the successful issue of the contest; but as I
conceive there can exist no inconvenience in being prepared
against any reverses which may chance to happen, I take the
liberty of requesting Your Excellency will have the goodness to
inform me whether any plan has been formed for the security of
the ships up the harbour from the grasp of the French should they
unfortunately, by some unaccountable means, get possession of the
arsenal. I trust Your Excellency will give me credit for every good
intention in making this application for although I have no doubt
the subject has been already well considered and arranged by
those who are completely competent to the business, yet
circumstanced as I am it would afford me the greatest satisfaction*

to be admitted confidentially into the measures which are to be resorted to should it eventually become necessary.

The new work which is now raising on the road coming into the town must strike everyone with the idea that government thinking it wise to guard against all contingencies had directed it to be done and I should suppose with submission that the taking precautions for the safety of the ships could not possibly occasion more alarm in the minds of the people than the new work I have alluded to.

I feel it necessary to make my apologies to Your Excellency for the liberty I am taking in thus soliciting a confidential communication with respect to that part of the arrangements which relate to the ships but I am inclined to think it will be received by Your Excellency in the favorable manner which my mind tells me it deserves.

I have the honor to be with sentiments of esteem and regard Your Excellency's most obedient and most humble servant,

John Child Purvis

19th December 1808, Cadiz
Don Josef Virnes, Governor of Cadiz,
to Rear-Admiral Purvis

Excellent Sir,

Satisfied with the reasons which induce Your Excellency to request a confidential knowledge of the measures which are to be adopted for the salvation of the ships of His Catholic Majesty in the unexpected event of the enemy approaching the Carracas, I feel it my duty to answer you with the same confidence and goodwill and to assure you that that object is the peculiar duty of the Commandant General of the Marine who no doubt prepares means which will ensure the success of his undertakings. With regard to myself it only remains to assist in the execution of his wishes, and in case the enemy should in consequence of unforeseen disasters, advance to the borders of my government, which is from the Bridge of Suazo, the ships could neither do me damage or lend me assistance; and as I see many reasons of more importance than that of military aid, to encourage a free communication touching our plans, I should hasten to explain, and examine them with Your Excellency, and to adopt the measures you might think necessary. — But I being only Minister (in order to save the time which must necessarily elapse before I can receive instructions from the Supreme Government of Seville), beg to refer you to the Prince Monforte, Governor-General of the Province and resident at Port St. Mary's, with whom I make no doubt Your Excellency will be agreed on all points; and I have to assure Your Excellency that I should attend to your wishes if it in any way depended upon me, or if I was authorised to interfere in this business.

Your Excellency will have no doubt of the sincerity with which I address you nor of my firm adherence to the cause of my King and Country and the wish which I feel to promote the views of the friendly and generous British Nation — permit me to repeat my assurances of regard and affection for Your Excellency with which I remain, Your most obedient humble servant,

Josef Virnes

20th December 1808, H.M.S. *Atlas*, Cadiz
Rear-Admiral Purvis to His Highness the Prince Monforte,
Governor-General of Andalusia.

Most Excellent Sir,

On Sunday last I took the liberty of addressing the Governor of Cadiz on the subject of His Catholic Majesty's ships now near the arsenal and having had a reference from His Excellency to Your Highness, I presume to request you will be pleased to favour me with a confidential communication as to the plan which has been adopted for the effectual security of those ships against the French should any unforeseen and unexpected chances of war enable the enemy to get possession of the Carracas.

I beg Your Highness to accept my apologies for making this application but, circumstanced as I am you will immediately perceive that I can have no motive in doing so but that I may be furnished with the means of rendering assistance in the event of so unexpected a disaster, and thereby frustrate the views of the French on so important an occasion in which the Spanish and English Nations are equally interested.

I beg Your Highness will be assured of the great regard, respect and esteem with which I have the honor to be,

Your Highness's most obedient and humble servant,

John Child Purvis

21st December 1808, El Puerto Santa Maria
Principe de Monforte, Governor-General of Andalusia,
to Rear-Admiral Purvis

Most Excellent Sir,

I have received the letter of yesterday's date which Your Excellency did me the honor of writing, and in which you informed me of having written to the Governor of Cadiz and of the reference which he had made to me for the solution of all the questions which Your Excellency had proposed.

Your Excellency may well ask a confidential communication of the reasons which have caused the Spanish ships to have been taken into the arsenal of the Carracas, and of the plans which are to be adopted for their security against the French in case that from any accident or disaster they may gain possession of the arsenal.

I rest well assured of the upright and honorable motives which induce Your Excellency to request this communication, they can only be made in order that you may be the better able to lend every assistance and protection to the Spanish Nation, whose interests are the same with those of Great Britain, in the unexpected event of the enemy being victorious. But however much I may wish it, I assure you that I cannot satisfy you as to the steps which are to be taken and can only repeat what the Governor of Cadiz has already said that the Commandant of the Marine has the direction of the ships and that it is his exclusive duty to keep them out of the power of the enemy. — But I shall without delay remit your letter to the Supreme and Central Government of the Kingdom and its answer shall be immediately communicated to Your Excellency.

In the meantime I have the honor to offer myself to Your Excellency's disposition and that your life may be long will be the prayer of your most obedient, humble servant,

Principe de Monforte

23rd December 1808, H.M.S. *Atlas*, Cadiz
Rear-Admiral Purvis to the Commandant-General,
His Catholic Majesty's Marine

Sir,

Notwithstanding the confidence I so fully entertain of the bravery and determined spirit of the Spanish Nation in the noble cause it has so justly undertaken, I cannot help feeling an anxious wish to be made confidentially acquainted with the plans which no doubt have been formed for the complete security of His Catholic Majesty's ships now near the arsenal against the possibility of their falling into the hands of the enemy should the fate of war by any unforeseen disasters enable him to get possession of the Carracas; this has induced me to apply to His Highness the Prince of Monforte, Governor-General of the Province, and His Highness in his reply (which I have just received) refers me to Your Excellency for the information I have requested.

I beg Your Excellency to be assured of my having no view in this solicitation but that of rendering every necessary aid in preserving those ships from all possible risk and I am well assured, I need not add, that in the effecting of which the Spanish and English Nations are equally interested.

It was my intention to have had the honor of presenting Your Excellency with this letter myself but having much business on my hands at this particular time, I have committed it to the care of my Captain who will deliver it into your hands.

I have the honor to be with great regard and esteem,
Your Excellency's most obedient and most humble servant,

John Child Purvis

27th December 1808, Isle of Leon, Cadiz
Pedro de Cardeñas, Commandant-General,
His Catholic Majesty's Marine,
to Rear-Admiral Purvis

Most Excellent Sir,

By the Captain of the Atlas I received your much valued letter in which you honor me with your confidence and desire in return to be informed of the plan formed for the complete security of the ships of His Catholic Majesty which are lying near the arsenal in order that they may be rescued from the power of the enemy should he by the chance of war, or any other unforeseen disaster, gain possession of the Carracas.

I have to inform Your Excellency that in consequence of their importance their defence is carried to the most distant point and in a great measure is connected with the movement of our armies under the conduct of their respective Generals.

The Superior Government, from the reasons already expressed, are considering the danger to be neither sudden nor alarming but very remote, have not given me any instructions as to the plan to be observed in the event which Your Excellency mentions nor do they think at this moment any particular precautions necessary. Nevertheless, they are now by desire of the Governor of Cadiz fortifying the approaches to the arsenal and in order to make it still more difficult of access, are making cuts which will all conduce to its greater security.

With respect to the questions which Your Excellency has proposed through the medium of the afore mentioned Captain, I shall do myself the honor of answering them the moment I can with necessary exactness collect the wished for information.

I remain fully convinced that nothing but the interest of the two Nations prompts you to express your present solicitude and be assured that I shall always feel very happy and desire to be employed in the execution of Your Excellency's wishes.

I have the honor to be Your Excellency's most obedient, faithful servant,

Pedro de Cardeñas

29th December 1808, El Puerto Santa Maria
Prince de Monforte, Governor-General of Andalusia,
to Rear-Admiral Purvis

Excellent Sir,

*I transmitted to the Central Junta, the Supreme Government of the
Kingdom, your letter of the 20th of this month which I informed
Your Excellency I intended doing. — In answer to it I have
received a letter bearing date the 26th of the same month, in
which I am informed by Don Cornel, Secretary of State and of the
War Department, that the Supreme Junta have resolved that all the
ships of the Spanish Navy which may be found in a condition to
put to sea shall be armed and rigged and that in the event of the
approach of the enemy, they may take a position in the canal out
of gun shot and that the others which are not in a state to be
seaworthy will serve as floating batteries to flank the canals all of
which, according to promise, I remit for Your Excellency's
information.*

  *I beg to renew my professions of regard for Your Excellency and
have the honor to be, Your obedient, faithful, servant,*

Principe de Monforte

CHAPTER 11

Cadiz

Tuesday 10th January 1809
H.M.S. Atlas
Cadiz Harbour

The City of Cadiz was founded by Phoenician traders in the year 1100 BC and is believed to be the oldest continuously-inhabited city in the western world. Surrendered to the Romans at the end of the 2nd Punic War, sacked by the Visigoths in the 5th century, occupied by the Moors for 500 years until 1262 AD when it was retaken by King Alfonso X of Castile, its residents have included Hannibal, Julius Caesar and Christopher Columbus who sailed from here on two of his famous voyages to the New World endowing the city with the start of its great entrepreneurial tradition.

The city's time of greatest prestige was the 18th century when it was established as the home port for the Spanish treasure fleets and thus became the trading centre for Spanish wealth from the Americas. Its gilded buildings and affluent citizens betokened its status. Known as 'Gadir' by the Phoenicians and 'Gades' by the Romans, its Spanish name, 'Cadiz', became implanted in the mind of every English schoolboy as the scene of the 'Singeing of the King of Spain's Beard' where, on 19th April 1587, Drake entered the harbour and destroyed some 10,000 tons of Spanish shipping destined for the invasion armada of Britain.

From then on, most British sailors would, at some point in their
career, have found themselves off Cadiz and would have become
familiar with its aspect — the towering Lighthouse of St. Sebastian,
the menacing fortifications of the harbour mouth and, behind them,
the ornate watch towers and the bulk of the magnificent cathedral.
John Child Purvis had started his career off Cadiz as a boy of
fourteen in the *Arrogant* and here he was again as a Rear-Admiral
in command of the British Squadron as he approached the end of his
active service at sea.

The city itself lay at the tip of a long peninsula forming the north-
western end of the Isle of Leon which itself was separated from the
mainland by the channels of Carracas to the east and Sancti Petri to
the south-east. On the other side of these channels was a low lying,
boggy area interspersed by saltpans and a network of narrow,
unnavigable canals. A single bridge, the Suaso Bridge, crossed the
Carracas Channel to connect the Isle with the mainland. On the
north side of the bay were a number of forts to defend the harbour
against the entry of a hostile fleet. The most important, and most
powerful, of these was the Castillo de Santa Catalina. The channel
leading to the inner anchorages of Puntales Road and Carracas
Creek were protected by Fort Puntales on the island side and Fort
Matagorda directly opposite on the mainland.

Of equal, if perhaps not greater, initial concern to Admiral Purvis
than the state of the Spanish ships was the number of French
prisoners-of-war being held in custody in the port. At Bailén the
previous July, General Castaños's promise of safe conduct back to
France for the defeated French army of General Dupont had been
repudiated by the civilian Junta of Seville. Those French prisoners
who had not been brutally slaughtered on the spot had been sent to
Cadiz to join the French sailors from Rosily's surrendered warships.
The result was that Cadiz was bursting at the seams with a volatile
and highly dangerous prison population.

Admiral Purvis made enquiries soon after his arrival: the French
civilian inhabitants of the city, about 500, had been sent to Fort St.
Sebastian, next to the Lighthouse, from where they were not
allowed to move. The large marine barracks on the Isle of Leon was
full of French seamen, as was the military prison at the Carracas

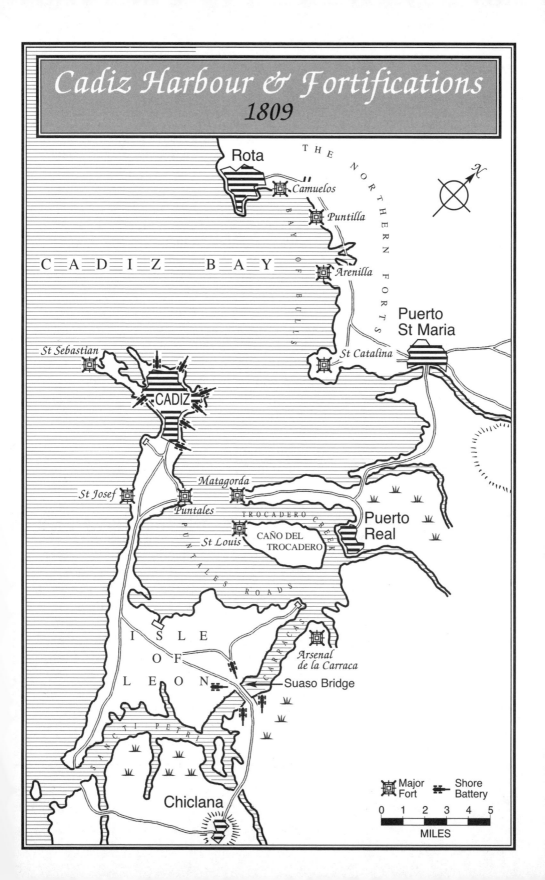

Cadiz Harbour & Fortifications
1809

Rota

THE NORTHERN FORTS

Camuelos

Puntilla

C A D I Z   B A Y

BAY OF BULLS

Arenilla

Puerto St Maria

St Catalina

St Sebastian

CADIZ

Matagorda

St Josef

Puntales

TROCADERO CREEK

St Louis

CAÑO DEL TROCADERO

Puerto Real

PUNTALES ROADS

ISLE OF LEON

CARRACA

Arsenal de la Carraca

Suaso Bridge

SANCTI PETRI

Chiclana

Major Fort

Shore Battery

0 1 2 3 4 5

MILES

Arsenal and, as he had already seen for himself, several of the
Spanish ships up the Carracas were being used as prison hulks in
which French seamen and soldiers were being kept in appalling
conditions which would never have been allowed by any British
commander. Six Spanish ships of-the-line and one frigate were
being so used and all these ships were in such an advanced state of
decay that Admiral Purvis doubted if they could ever be returned to
seaworthy condition — even assuming somewhere else could be
found for the prisoners to enable work to start on them.

He reported to the Admiralty that he estimated the total number of
prisoners to be in the region of 13,000 whereas the Spanish
Volunteers who garrisoned the city numbered about 4,000. If an
organised insurrection should take place, such a body of trained
soldiers and sailors could overwhelm the Spanish forces and take
the city, ships and all. Moreover, from what he had seen of them so
far, the Admiral had no reason to place much confidence in the
proficiency and vigilance of the Spanish guards. The situation was
being daily exacerbated by the arrival of still more prisoners from
the interior.

His first priority was confirmed: he must do everything in his
power to press for the refurbishment of the Spanish ships for until
such time as they were seaworthy he could not ensure their safety
from the French, nor would the Spanish have any warships to
reinforce the British defence of the city and, of equal importance, to
start transporting some of the prisoners-of-war to another place. The
Spanish Government was not unaware of the danger the prisoners
represented: on 10th January the Admiral received an assurance, via
the British Minister in Seville, that it was their intention to start
transporting the prisoners to Majorca and Minorca in their large
ships as soon as they were ready for sea.

Having at last managed to establish some sort of dialogue with
Don Josef Virnes, the Military and Political Governor of Cadiz,
Purvis received intelligence that a letter addressed to Virnes from
General Morla had been intercepted by the patriots. It had been
found to be full of defeatist sentiments and had advised Virnes to
meet the offers which would be made to him by the French and to
be on his guard against the treachery of the British. The furious
patriots instantly dismissed Virnes and appointed in his place

Major-General Don Felix Jones. The Admiral lost no time in visiting the new Governor and impressing upon him the vital need to speed up the work on the Spanish ships.

With General Jones's permission, he made a tour of the Spanish dockyard and inspected the rope houses and some of the store houses. He found about 1,000 men employed in the various departments and no great sign of industry although some effort was being made to commission the *Leandro* and the frigate *Iphegenia*. However, there was no cable whatever in the dockyard as all they had was in use mooring the prison ships. "Their progress is very slow," he reported to Lord Collingwood, "and I am quite at a loss to account for it unless the orders which I have been assured were given for their immediate equipment have not been marked by that energy which to me the case appears so materially to require."

In addition to his worries with the Spanish, there was trouble on board two ships in his own Squadron: he had received several letters from the Masters of merchant ships in the area complaining that the boats of the *Bulwark* had been pressing their seamen indiscriminately and, in one case, had even taken away an indentured apprentice. He sent for the *Bulwark*'s Captain, the despotic Charles Elphinstone Fleeming, who told him that his ship was in a state of near mutiny. The Admiral asked him for a list of the worst troublemakers whom he then removed from the ship, thirty-five in all, and distributed among the other ships in the Squadron — the eight hardest cases being put into the *Loire* which was returning to England with a convoy. He followed the same procedure later in the month when "a turbulent spirit bordering on mutiny" was reported in the *Ocean*. Both ships then quietened down.

The assistance of the Cadiz Squadron was also sought by Major-General Drummond, who had succeeded General Dalrymple as Governor of Gibraltar, for the removal of shore guns from Algeçiras and various other works on the adjacent coast. Admiral Purvis sent an appropriate party to Gibraltar together with an advance warning to Commissioner Lobb at the dockyard that demands for supplies for the Spanish ships, particularly cables, might be imminent. In the meantime he sent Captain Fleeming in the *Bulwark* to Gibraltar to be ready to arrange the acquisition of suitable transports and the loading of the cables into them.

On 17th January the British learned to their astonishment that the Spanish were about to send the *Algeçiras*, their only serviceable line-of-battle ship, to England as personal transport for one Don Pedro Cavallos and his wife and family; it seemed that the comfort of a single dignitary was of greater importance than reducing the dangerous prison population; Admiral Purvis again made representations to the Junta begging them that greater priority should be given to the fitting out of their ships and was relieved to learn that Vice-Admiral Don Ignacio Maria de Alava had now been appointed to personally superintend their preparation. Alava had been at Trafalgar in his Flagship the *Santa Ana* which had suffered grievously at the hands of Lord Collingwood in the *Royal Sovereign* to whom she had eventually surrendered with all three masts down and 500 of her crew dead or dying. He was, at least, an experienced seaman and one who Admiral Purvis felt would recognise what had to be done and would get on with it. He called on him immediately and assured the Spanish Admiral that he could count on British support for whatever materials were needed and also with manpower to assist in the rigging if he would allow British seamen aboard the Spanish ships. When Alava had surveyed the situation for himself and seen that the job would be impossible to complete with the resources at his disposal he replied "your assistance will be joyfully received as it is at this moment much wanted and the seamen may come whenever Your Excellency should determine". Two parties, each of ninety seamen under the command of a Lieutenant, were immediately sent from the *Atlas* and the *Invincible* to two of the Spanish line-of-battle ships, the *Pluton* and the *Glorioso*, and a message was sent to Commissioner Lobb to despatch the cables and supplies to the Cadiz Squadron by the next armed convoy sailing from Gibraltar. At last the work could start in earnest.

If Admiral Purvis imagined that the industry of the British seamen would be matched by a similar effort from those of Spain he was soon to be disillusioned. The parties of seamen promised by the Spanish authorities never showed up and there were no more than twenty Spanish sailors in each of the ships to be refitted; and these, Lieutenant Wormeley in charge of the *Pluton*'s work party reported to the Admiral, would not lift a hand to help and simply lounged about the ship watching the British do the work. Nevertheless, transports from Gibraltar started to arrive in Cadiz with rigging, spars, cables and boatswain's stores; the parties of British seamen reported daily and worked with a will and the Spanish ships steadily started to take shape.

On 28th January a Guernsey trading cutter, the *Phenix*, arrived in Cadiz fifteen days out from Corunna. As soon as she had dropped anchor a gig was launched and her Master came over to the Flagship with a request to see the Admiral urgently. He reported that his ship carried many Spanish refugees he had taken on board at Corunna to where Sir John Moore's army had retreated with the French some three leagues behind them. The British, he said, were in possession of a commanding position from which they could defend themselves until transports arrived from Vigo to evacuate them. The *Phenix* had met these transports, under convoy of the *Endymion*, within one day's sail of Corunna. There were also ten British sail of-the-line in the area, the Master reported.

Within days the Admiral received further news from Captain Donelly in the *Invincible* and then Captain Bolton in the *Tissard* and the full story of General Sir John Moore's famous fighting retreat to Corunna and the skilful, if ignominious, evacuation of his Army became known: "It is with the greatest regret," he wrote immediately to Vice-Admiral Berkeley, "I am obliged to represent the very distressing accounts we have from the North of Spain and particularly of the loss of that excellent officer Sir John Moore and the wound of Sir David Baird with the fate of many more of our brave countrymen."

Meanwhile, the 9th, 27th and 29th Regiments of Foot, under the command of Major-General MacKenzie, lay at anchor in Cadiz in eleven transports, guarded by the *Semiramis*, forbidden to land in the city by the Spanish authorities. They could land at Puerto Santa Maria on the north side of the bay, the Junta had said, but under no circumstances would foreign troops be allowed in Cadiz. Seeing no advantage in having his men ashore in a position far from where they might ultimately be required, General MacKenzie decided not to embark; but the Junta's refusal to allow them to land was a further embarrassment, and sign of mistrust between the allies, and the British Minister ordered that the real reason for the troops remaining in the transports should not be made generally known: "their arrival in the harbour should appear to be only preparative to some other movement."

The prisoner-of-war situation was deteriorating daily with new drafts continually arriving and Admiral Purvis feared that, as the weather started to get warmer, the security risk would be compounded by the certainty of contagious disease breaking out in the hulks. He regularly pressed the Spanish authorities for a note of their intentions but would never receive a straight or satisfactory answer: "None of their movements," he reported to the Admiralty, "are marked by that energy which the times so essentially require."

At last an edict emerged from the Junta that vessels should be hired to start conveying some of the prisoners to the Balearics. Alava asked Admiral Purvis if he could provide these, seemingly unaware of the irony of such a request when all the British Squadron's transports were tied up housing troops which the Spanish would not allow to land. Nevertheless, the British Admiral agreed to direct all available supply ships from Gibraltar to Cadiz for the purpose. There was another consideration: what would the people of Majorca and Minorca have to say about a massive and rebellious prison population being dumped upon them? Would they have the facilities to house them, the money to feed them and the men to guard them? Admiral Thornbrough at Port Mahon thought not: "The Minorcans have not a dollar of public money," he told Purvis, and Majorca was probably likewise. There would be considerable public outcry at the prospect of the prisoners' arrival and it was more than probable that the islanders would refuse to accept them.

Admiral Purvis put this point, in writing, to the Spanish authorities from whom he received a typically evasive reply: Question: "Is there a certainty that the French prisoners will be received at Majorca and Minorca when the transports arrive with them?" Answer: "The Junta have written to Majorca and Minorca announcing the arrival of the prisoners." A later, personal, approach to Admiral Alava on this point met with the rejoinder: "I should likewise wish to satisfy Your Excellency about the doubts you express whether or not the prisoners will be admitted into the Balearics and about the want of means to protect them; but as these cares are not entrusted to me, but to that Government which I obey, I cannot do it."

By the middle of February there were 300 British seamen working on the ships up the Carracas and real progress was being made. Once the Spanish realised that the British had no sinister motive for their assistance, and they themselves were not required to lift a finger to help, they were happy enough to have as many British seamen as were available. Admiral Purvis was not, however, prepared to let the number rise above 300 always aware that, should the French Fleet put to sea from Toulon, his Squadron would have to go out and fight them, quite possibly with little prior warning. "You have your hands full and anxiety in abundance," Admiral Thornbrough wrote to him.

On 19th February the first of the Spanish ships, the *Leandro,* fully rigged, came down from the Carracas and moored in Puntales Road, the anchorage chosen by Admiral Alava for his refurbished Fleet. Two more were reported to be ready and awaiting a fair wind and several others were nearing completion. None of the ships, however, was watered. Admiral Purvis pointed out, with tact, to his Spanish counterpart that one of the first actions of an invading army would be to cut off the water supply to the Spanish Navy and it was therefore imperative that the ships were kept fully watered. Alava replied that it was: "completely out of his department", water being the concern of the Victualling Board to whom the appropriate representations should be made. By now Admiral Purvis was beginning to get their measure and, anticipating that the next area of procrastination would be a shortage of casks, he approached the British Consulate to requisition a supply immediately "for by what we have seen, nothing is thought of until it is wanted". He directed that if the casks required coopering the work should be put in hand immediately.

Though, on the surface, relations with the Spanish were cordial and cooperative, there was an underswell of reserve and hindrance which the Admiral could not fully understand. Certainly the bitterness of the preceding years of enmity between the two nations could not be expected to be healed in the first few months of alliance; nor total trust restored. And yet the Spanish authorities seemed intent on placing every obstacle in the way of the most simple actions which were so clearly necessary for their own interests let alone achieving what they had declared to be common objectives. If they were truly resolved to oppose a French attack, they would surely do everything to prepare themselves without constant prodding from their allies; this tended to sow the seeds of fear in Admiral Purvis's mind that, perhaps, they sought to keep their options open and to be in a position to negotiate terms with the French should they feel it would best serve their interests when the time came. "It is quite unnecessary," he wrote to Charles Stuart in the British Consulate in Cadiz, " for us to be working on these ships if there exists in the Spanish Government a determination on their part not to permit them to be finally prepared for sea; whether they suspect our integrity, or whether a worse motive influences them I cannot pretend to say, but certainly there must be some hidden cause for what appears such monstrous indifference."

On 22nd February seven Spanish ships of-the-line lay at the Puntales anchorage. Two more were fully rigged and waiting to come down from the Carracas. This just left the *Santa Ana* of the ships which Admiral Purvis considered restorable to seagoing condition; she still required a topmast and top gallant rigging but supplies were on the way and, if the need arose, she could be brought down under her foresail.

Ashore in Cadiz passions were running high: the arrival of an army corps consisting of Poles, Swiss and other foreign nationals invoked a public riot and the mob refused to allow the soldiers to be admitted to the city. At the same time several prominent citizens were accused of French sympathies and traitorous practices. The Marquis of Villel, the Civil Governor, and Don Josef Heredia were seized and their houses searched for incriminating evidence. Villel was later released but Heredia was put to death by the mob. The following day calm was restored and a Public Proclamation issued, with copies sent out to the British warships, acknowledging the debt and attachment of the citizens of Cadiz to Britain for the zeal it was showing in their cause; but it likewise, in express terms, declared that no foreign troops should be admitted to Cadiz. At this, Major-General MacKenzie, his troops still confined in the transports, announced his intention of returning with them to Lisbon where there was clearly work to be done.

Left: Admiral-of-the-Fleet Sir Francis Austen who was Captain Purvis's First Lieutenant in the *London* in 1798/99 and whose daughter, Mary-Jane, later married George Purvis's son. Admiral Austen was a brother of the author Jane Austen.

Right: Admiral the Hon. Sir William Cornwallis, 'Billie Blue' within the Service, who was Commander-in-Chief of the Channel Fleet in 1803/04 when Captain Purvis was commanding the *Dreadnought*.

Below: The massive 98-gun *Dreadnought* which Captain Purvis commanded in the Channel Fleet during the winter of 1803/04 until he was promoted to Rear-Admiral. There being a shortage of small ships, Admiral Cornwallis would sometimes send the *Dreadnought* with despatches to Rear-Admiral Collingwood's Inshore Squadron off Brest. This task would normally have been undertaken by sloops or brigs causing Collingwood to write to Purvis: *"I think when Bonaparte is informed that our packet boats carry ninety guns he will not look to the sea for his glory."* The picture shows the ship in about 1830 when she was moored off Greenwich and used as a hospital ship for seamen.

Vice-Admiral Lord Collingwood, Commander-in-Chief Mediterranean from Nelson's death at Trafalgar in 1805 until his own death five years later. In 1806, exhausted by the burdens of his command, he asked the Admiralty for his friend, Rear-Admiral Purvis, to be sent out to assist him and handed over the Mediterranean Command to him four days before his death in 1810. Revered by all who sailed with him, one sailor wrote: *"A better seaman — a better friend to seamen — a greater lover and more zealous defender of his country's rights and honour, never trode a quarter-deck . . . how attentive he was to the health and comfort and happiness of his crew! A man who could not be happy under him could have been happy nowhere; a look of displeasure from him was as bad as a dozen at the gangway from another man."*

Landsman Hay — Memoirs of Robert Hay 1789-1847.

Above: Cadiz from the air. The modern bridge can be seen connecting the Isle of Leon with the mainland between Trocadero and Matagorda.

Right: El Almirante Don Ignacio Maria de Alava; severely mauled by Collingwood at Trafalgar and appointed to liaise with Admiral Purvis on the refurbishment of the Spanish ships at Cadiz.

Below: A highly stylised contemporary Spanish engraving showing the French massed on the north shore, and pounding the city with its artillery, while the citizens dance contemptuously in the square.

Above: El Arsenal Militar de la Carraca. To the right can be seen the Carracas Channel, known today as Sancti Petri, in which the Spanish ships and prison hulks were moored together with the remnants of Villeneuve's French Fleet which had been trapped in Cadiz by the British blockade since Trafalgar. In the distance is the old Suaso Bridge which, at the time, was the only way on to the Isle of Leon.

Left: The Military Prison in the Arsenal. It is unused today but in 1810 was filled to capacity with French prisoners-of-war as was every available naval and military barracks in Cadiz.

Below: The magnificent Plaza de Armas in the Carracas Arsenal. The earliest buildings date from 1717; the archway at the end of the Plaza, leading to the dockside, was completed in 1792.

Above: The old Suaso Bridge, still in use for one-way traffic leaving the Isle of Leon.

Right: Looking across Trocadero Creek, some grassy mounds and stonework are all that remain today of Fort Louis and the mighty French emplacements of 1810.

Below: *"The City of Cadiz, faithful to the principles it has sworn, acknowledges no other King than the Señor Don Fernando VII."* The Spaniards' response to the French demand for their surrender to 'King' Joseph Bonaparte. The central characters are: Admiral Alava (black coat), the Duke of Albuquerque (white breeches) and General Venegas (arm raised). Detail from an oil painting by Ramón Rodriguez Barcaza in the Museo de Cadiz.

Above: The view from a gun embrasure in the ruins of the Castillo de Santa Catalina shows the command which the fort had on the harbour approaches and illustrates the necessity of its destruction. Had the French captured the fort, they could have denied the besieged city all supplies and communications from the outside.

Left: The concrete aprons of the Puerto Real shipyard now cover the site of Fort Matagorda.

Below: The ruins of Santa Catalina destroyed by the Royal Navy, on Admiral Purvis's insistence, as the French army approached. The scale can be appreciated by the two adult figures on the beach (far left).

Above: Vice-Admiral John Brett Purvis (1787-1857), elder son of Admiral John Child Purvis and father of Rear-Admiral Richard Purvis.

Above: Revd. Richard Fortescue Purvis (1789-1868), younger son of Admiral John Child Purvis (1) and father of Vice-Admiral John Child Purvis (2).

Above: Captain John Scott RN (1784-1867), widely believed to have been a natural son of Admiral John Child Purvis.

Left: Vice-Admiral John Child Purvis (2) (1832-1904).

Right: Sir William Purves, Bart (1623-1684) the Admiral's great-great-great grandfather.

Below: Darsham House, Suffolk, seat of the Darsham Purvises from 1712 to 1877.

Above: Vicar's Hill House, near Lymington, Hampshire, Admiral Purvis's home from his retirement from active duty in 1810 until his death in 1825. The house was a U.S. Army Air Force hospital during World War II and is today 'Southlands School'.

Below: St. Leonard's Church, Whitsbury, c.1865, of which Admiral Purvis was Patron and his younger son, Richard, was Vicar for forty-four years. The present Patron is William John Purvis, the Admiral's great-great-great grandson.

Though he seemed to have taken it very much for granted, Admiral Alava was not ungrateful for the help he had received and wrote to Admiral Purvis: "I give Your Excellency many thanks for the assistance which you have lent in fitting out the ships of His Catholic Majesty and I consider one of the principal helps the conduct of the officers who commanded the sailors among whom I beg to particularize Lieutenant Wormely whose zeal and activity have been conspicuous." He then gave his assurance that two English sailors who had been injured in the work would be attended to with particular care in the Spanish hospital on Leon.

The commendation for Lieutenant Wormely was particularly pleasing to the Admiral and one which he lost no time in endorsing and passing on to the Commander-in-Chief. Ralph Wormely was an American, a grandson of the Attorney General of Virginia;[1] he had started his career as a boy in the *London,* under Captain Purvis, and had become a close friend of his two sons John and Richard. His command, and the work of his men in the rigging parties, had been undertaken with great restraint: although the Spaniards would do nothing to assist, and "stood in great numbers looking on", while the British sailors laboured back and forth from the dockyard storerooms with supplies for Spanish ships, there had not been a single incident or complaint of improper conduct; the temptation to teach the Spanish seamen a lesson must, on occasions, have been almost overwhelming.

On 4th March the *Medusa* arrived in Cadiz Harbour with a message for the Admiral from Lord Gambier that nine French ships of-the-line had escaped from Brest. They had been sighted by Captain Beresford in the *Theseus* off L'Orient on 21st February. Beresford judged that their destination might be Cadiz having formed a junction with the French ships in L'Orient and Rochefort making a potential force of sixteen of-the-line and nine frigates. Admiral Purvis had six of-the-line — *Atlas, Ville de Paris* (designated as Lord Collingwood's Flagship), *Hibernia, Invincible, Eclair and Bustard.* With the nine Spanish ships at the Puntales, apparently ready for sea, and the *Santa Ana* which was still at the Carracas with British seamen on board, he could just scrape together a numerically equal force.

He immediately applied to General Jones to ensure that the shore defences towards the sea were alerted to the news and in proper order. He then moved the British ships into defensive positions in the outer bay and asked Admiral Alava if he would bring his ships out to complete a defensive line. Alava declined to do so, doubting that the French would try to force the harbour mouth and therefore considering the precaution unnecessary. In truth, the Spanish ships, though claimed to be ready for sea, did not have sufficient men on board to move them from their anchorage let alone to fight them.

With the French Brest Fleet at large and their position unknown, it would clearly not be prudent to despatch any of the prisoner-of-war convoys for fear they would run into, and be recaptured, by their own countrymen. It was, therefore, with considerable relief that Admiral Purvis received intelligence on 20th March that Lord Gambier had driven them into Rochefort and was able to advise Alava: "Rear-Admiral Purvis has the honour to acquaint Admiral Alava that the Fleet that lately put to sea from Brest is now blocked in the port of Rochefort by a British Squadron of thirteen ships of-the-line commanded by Admiral Lord Gambier." It was now back to the business of trying to get the Spanish to get their prison convoys under way: "Rear-Admiral Purvis would be obliged to Admiral Alava to inform him what number of transports are collected for the purpose of conveying the prisoners and when they will be prepared to sail — these moonlight nights being very favourable for their security."

On 23rd March Purvis was able to report to Lord Collingwood that fifteen Spanish transports had been assembled for the Balearics convoy which was due to sail on the 25th. The convoy would be under the direction of a Spanish frigate, the *Cornelia*, but Admiral Alava had declined to send any of his other ships, expecting the British to provide the escorts. Admiral Purvis had therefore agreed to send *Bombay, Norge, Ambuscade* and *Grasshopper* under the orders of Captain Cuming in the *Bombay* "who has full directions from me respecting the watchfulness so necessary to be observed by himself and the other Captains on this important service". Cuming was then to return to Cadiz for another batch.

The first convoy was to transport some 5,000 French soldiers and the French naval officers to the Balearics. The French seamen, separated from their officers and thus rendered less of a risk, it was thought, would later be sent to the Canary Isles. Lord Collingwood was deeply concerned fearing that the prisoners would mutiny during the voyage and repatriate themselves; but the alternative of leaving them in Cadiz until the French arrived was unthinkable.

Two days before the convoy was due to sail, Admiral Purvis was astonished to receive a request from Alava for one of the designated British escorts to be withdrawn to undertake some frivolous errand for the Junta. He refused point blank; Alava had sufficient ships of his own for such purposes: "I cannot lessen the force I have directed; and I trust Your Excellency will pardon my saying that with the ships you now have under your command there does not appear a necessity on the present occasion for an alteration in the arrangements I have made." Alava persisted: "I do not think depriving the convoy of this vessel will in any way hazard its safety. If Your Excellency approves of this proposal and it can be effected it will be another claim to my gratitude added to the many which you already have for your great assistance." Purvis still refused to weaken the escort but acrimony was avoided by the arrival of the sloop *Racoon* which he was able to divert for the Junta's purpose.

The 25th came and went with no sign of the convoy getting ready to leave; perhaps the Spanish might be spurred into action with a hint that the British escort might have to be withdrawn if they delayed much longer: "I have to beg Your Excellency will pardon me for mentioning the anxiety I feel respecting the sailing of the ships with the French soldiers for the Balearic Islands. Here is a very fine wind, a good moon, our ships are all ready — and no movements which indicate an early departure; and I beg to state that if I should receive instructions for the British ships to proceed to some other place, I shall be under the necessity of abandoning the plan which I had so readily concerted with you."

"My desire," Alava replied, "to see the convoy of prisoners bound to the Balearic Islands sail is no less than Your Excellency's. They are already embarked and I hope will not lose a moment in putting to sea." It was another week before the convoy eventually sailed on 3rd April.

The plan now was for the French sailors to be taken to the Canaries in three Spanish ships of-the-line which Admiral Purvis

agreed to match with British escorts. Though he could not wait to
see the seamen removed from Cadiz, he was now more or less
reconciled to the interminable delays and excuses for delays which
would inevitably precede their departure. On 9th April, the day they
were due to sail, one of the Spanish ships had its main mast struck
by lightning; this gave the Spanish a legitimate excuse for
postponement while a mast was removed from one of their old ships
to replace it. An operation which the Royal Navy would have
completed in twenty-four hours was strung out for six days; on the
15th Purvis wrote to Alava pointing out that he had to account to his
Government, and his Commander-in-Chief, for the unacceptably
long detainment of the British escort ships in Cadiz and pressing
him for a sailing date. "Owing to the scarcity of sailors," the
Spanish Admiral replied, "it is not easy for me to fix the day the
three ships ordered can proceed to sea but I am persuaded they will
be ready next week." One week later he requested that some of the
French prisoners should be transported in the British escort ships.
Aware that disease were now rife among them, Admiral Purvis
refused but confirmed that *Leviathan, Invincible* and *Conqueror*
were ready to sail as soon as the Spanish warships were ready.

   The sailing date was fixed for 26th April and Purvis warned his
escort Captains to stand by. The day arrived but no sign of activity
on board the Spanish ships. "The unaccountable delays," he wrote
to Lord Collingwood, "and contradictory orders which have taken
place in conducting the naval department of Spain in this port is
beyond any thing I have ever met with." At last, on 30th April two
of the Spanish ships, *Montanes* and *San Lorenzo* were ready; the
third, *Pluton*, was not. Admiral Purvis persuaded Alava to get the
two ships away, escorted by *Leviathan* and *Conqueror* and
promised that he would send *Bulwark,* which had just returned from
Gibraltar, with the *Pluton* when she was ready.

   Meanwhile, the first tranche of prisoners had arrived in Minorca
and, as Vice-Admiral Thornbrough reported, had received a less
than enthusiastic reception from the natives who were living in
dread that they would mutiny and take the island. Thornbrough,
also, had had dealings with the Spanish authorities and could well
understand the difficulties of the command at Cadiz: "You have a
most arduous task but you manage it well," he wrote encouragingly.

With the prison convoys now under way, Admiral Purvis turned his attention to the shore defences of the harbour. During the previous month he had asked Lieutenant-Colonel Landman of the Royal Engineers, an expert in fortifications, to inspect all the shore batteries and forts around the harbour and report back to him on their state of readiness to repel an attack by the French. The Colonel's report made gloomy reading.

Spaced roughly equidistantly along the shore of the Bay of Bulls, to the north side of the harbour, was a string of four forts designed to deny access to an enemy fleet. Their defences to the landward were minimal thus rendering them completely vulnerable to capture by an invading army. The most eastern of the forts, the Castillo de Santa Catalina, was also the most important; commanding a promontory directly opposite the city, its guns could deny access by sea to Puerto Santa Maria and the upper reaches of the harbour. Colonel Landman reported that all these forts were equipped with guns, big mortars, ammunition and furnaces for hot shot but were completely unmanned.

With the French Fleets effectively blockaded by the Royal Navy an attack from the sea was unlikely; but, with the progress the French armies were making in Spain, an attack on Cadiz from the land seemed a certainty. It was therefore clear to Admiral Purvis that all ordnance must be removed from these northern batteries, and their fortifications destroyed, before the enemy arrived. In his report to the Admiralty he expressed his confidence that the city itself could be held without difficulty; as the enemy advanced, Spanish forces in the field would fall back into Cadiz ensuring an adequate garrison of professional artillerymen to augment the very brave, but inexperienced, volunteers.

However, if, as they undoubtedly would, the French took possession of the northern forts, and they were in a condition in which they could be readily recommissioned, the enemy could deny access to allied ships at a time when, with the City of Cadiz cut off and under siege, it would be entirely dependent upon provisions and communications from the sea. The logic of his argument and the need to destroy the northern forts was readily accepted by the British Admiralty and Military Command; but to persuade the Spanish authorities would be a different matter.

Lord Collingwood was fully aware of the difficult task his second-in-command faced but he knew he had the right man in place; he had, after all, chosen him for the job. He wrote to Purvis at length on 26th March: "You observe the anxiety which Ministers have that the Spanish ships should not, in any event, fall into the hands of the enemy; and to prevent this, in case of affairs going to extremity in Spain, will require much delicacy of conduct and skill: but it cannot be in better hands than yours."

There were two possibilities, Lord Collingwood felt, if it became apparent that Cadiz would fall to the French: either, they would embark their Government and all the loyal citizens they could accommodate in their ships and sail for America. In this case, Cadiz would become the rendezvous for all loyal Spaniards who fled from the tyranny of the usurper: "Cadiz should be made impregnable, and the ships placed so as to defend and be defended by it. Whatever will inspire them with perfect confidence in us should be done. It is their cause in which we have no interest but their success." The second, less happy, scenario would be if the Spaniards felt that all was lost and sought to mitigate the violence of the enemy's conquest by coming to terms; such terms would inevitably include the handing over of their ships to the French and in this case, Lord Collingwood thought, they would, when the time approached, move the ships back to the Carracas to prevent their trump cards being removed, or destroyed, by the British. It was this uncertainty of their own intentions, and lack of a completely firm resolution, Admiral Purvis realised, that made the Spanish authorities so difficult to pin down to any course of action which might, conceivably, prejudice their bargaining position with the enemy at a later date.

The indecision and delays associated with the prisoner-of-war convoys, and the insistence of the Admiralty that sufficient ships must be retained at Cadiz for their security, gave rise to a slight contretemps between Vice-Admiral Berkeley, desperate for ships on the coast of Portugal, and Rear-Admiral Purvis, desperate for ships at Cadiz. The former, piqued that the latter had retained the *Norge* longer than he considered strictly necessary, and unaware of the Admiralty edict regarding prison convoy escorts, accused him of having disobeyed his orders. Of all the officers in the Royal Navy, John Child Purvis was probably the least deserving of such a charge: ". . . you may be assured, Sir," he replied, "I will send the *Norge* to you the instant she arrives for I never did, nor ever shall, disobey any orders notwithstanding I have been so unfortunate as to receive such a charge from you."

A further misunderstanding in May, this time on the part of the Spanish authorities, was to cause the Admiral considerable annoyance. The pressure he had been putting on the Spanish for the clearance and destruction of the northern forts had resulted in a printed report on the defensive state of the city being submitted by the Military Junta in Cadiz to the Government in Seville. In this report it was stated that the British Naval Commander, Rear-Admiral Purvis, had advocated the destruction of all the defensive works around the City of Cadiz. Whether this was the result of slovenly translation, gross lack of understanding or contentious mischief-making we shall never know; but whatever the cause, the Admiral was understandably furious and wrote to the Spanish Government immediately to point out the error and to ask for his name to be cleared publically from any association with such a dangerous and absurd proposal. What he did not tell them was that, prior to Colonel Landman's inspection of the northern forts, he had received an assurance from Governor Jones that all the forts and batteries on the northern side of the harbour, including Santa Catalina, had been completely dismantled and there was not a gun in them. Had this been the result of sheer incompetence, he was forced to wonder, or a direct lie to relieve the Governor of further demands from him for the destruction of the forts? A straightforward man of scrupulous honesty, he felt out of his depth in the midst of such intrigue for which a lifetime of service in the Royal Navy had done little to prepare him. But he knew his duty and must have been encouraged by his Commander-in-Chief's obvious faith in his ability to handle the situation.

On his return from escorting the Canaries prison convoy, Captain John Harvey of the *Leviathan* came on board the Flagship with some news for the Admiral. He reported that while his ship was in Tenerife he had received a message from the Marquis Villaneuva del Prado, President of the Junta of the Canary Islands, requesting a meeting with him ashore which he duly attended with Captain Fellowes as an interpreter. The Marquis wished him to apprise his Admiral of the fact that the inhabitants of the Canaries were staunchly loyal to the old monarchy and, in the event of Old Spain falling to the French, it was their wish that the Islands should be taken under the protection of Great Britain. He was most anxious to obtain a pledge from Britain to this effect and Captain Harvey assured him he would inform his Admiral immediately upon his return to Cadiz. It was heartening to know that an outlying province of Spain was so firm in its resolve to oppose Bonapartism.

Though becoming weary with the frustrations and responsibilities of a difficult command, there were events in his private life over the past year which gave the Admiral cause for good cheer. Richard, in India, seemed to have settled down and got himself out of debt; his wife, Elizabeth, who had been in Bath on the advice of her doctor, had now returned home showing a marked improvement in her health; and the financial worries from which he had always suffered in the past had recently been removed.

The Admiral's forenames 'John Child' had been chosen by his parents in recognition of his descent, through his mother's side, from one John Child — a member of the great Child mercantile empire which had amassed considerable wealth in trade with the East Indies. This tribute to his Child descent had reaped a rich harvest earlier in the year: a distant cousin, Thomas English, of the Child branch of the family, had died nominating John Child Purvis as his sole heir. Mr. English's fortune was substantial and, together with the prize-money the Admiral was now regularly receiving, he had become, for the first time in his life, extremely well off.

While going through a pile of correspondence from the Captains of his Squadron one day, his eye was caught by a Court Martial request for a seaman on one of his sloops who had imprudently stabbed the boatswain with a pair of compasses and called him a "Bloody Bugger". "I have therefore to request you will be pleased to direct a Court Martial to be held on the said John Hartnell for the above mentioned offences. I am, Sir, your most obedient, humble servant . . ." The sloop was the *Delight* and the Captain was his son John Brett Purvis. Of all his blessings, it was John's good character and progress in the Service which gave the Admiral greatest joy. He had heard nothing but good reports of him from his Captains and fellow Flag-Officers. His conduct, his manners and procedures were impeccable; his seamanship and professional competence beyond reproach; his sense of duty and commitment to his officers and men as strong as those of the father under whom he had learned his trade and under whose command he was now so proud to serve. Taking up his pen and a sheet of paper, he wrote to Lord Mulgrave, the First Lord of the Admiralty: "My Lord — My son, John Brett Purvis, having commanded the Delight, sloop-of-war, fifteen months and having been on the list of Commanders the prescribed time, I take the liberty of requesting your Lordship will be pleased to promote him to the rank of Post-Captain, and I believe I may assure your Lordship he will not discredit the Service."

John was to be promoted to Post-Captain in September — one month after his twenty-second birthday.

CHAPTER 12

Commander-in-Chief

Saturday 1st August 1809
Cadiz

On the morning of Saturday 1st August 1809 Lord Byron, the poet, was awoken at his lodgings in Cadiz by the sound of cannon fire in the city. Having attended a bullfight at Puerto Santa Maria the previous day and then spent much of the night in a whore house, it is probable that he was at first displeased by this rude awakening;[1] he may, however, have become more reconciled to it when he learned that the noise was in celebration of an Anglo-Spanish victory over the French, a few days previously, at a place called Talavera. The British Commander at Talavera had been Arthur Wellesley whose brother Richard, Marquess of Wellesley, Byron was to see being towed in his carriage through the streets of Cadiz by a jubilant Spanish crowd later on the same day.

The Marquess had previously been British Ambassador in Madrid and had now accepted the appointment of Ambassador to 'Free Spain' or, more particularly, to the central Junta in Seville. He was a statesman of immense ability and experience having, as Governor-General of India, restored the supremacy of British influence throughout the sub-continent in the face of a strong French Imperial threat. Great things were expected of him in Spain which was now, also, having problems with the Bonapartes.

The following day Lord Byron and his travelling companion, John Hobhouse, both declared admirers of Napoleon, dined on board the *Atlas* with Admiral Purvis who then arranged passage for them to Gibraltar with Captain Brodie in the frigate *Hyperion*.[2] Apart from the fact that Purvis, as a Lieutenant in 1778, had served in a squadron commanded by the poet's grandfather, it is unlikely that the two men found much in common.

It had been a summer of continual social activity. The Spanish, it seemed, needed little excuse to stage an endless succession of parades, processions and galas at which the British Admiral was naturally expected to attend as a guest-of-honour. Though he had more important matters on his mind, he could not give offence by refusing such invitations but, like Lord Collingwood, he drew the line when celebrations involved the profligate use of gunpowder; the Spanish were only too happy to blast off their cannons in support of any and every festivity with little thought that, within months, perhaps weeks, the powder would be required for more serious purposes.

To 'show the flag' and to repay some of the hospitality which was daily pressed upon him, he had held a Grand Ball on board the *Atlas* on 21st July. The Band of the City Volunteers augmented the ship's own musicians and the guest list read like a register of the Spanish nobility with over 100 titled and prominent citizens attending what was generally adjudged to have been the high point of the social calendar in Cadiz in the summer of 1809. The Admiral was not, of course, unaware that his acquaintanceship must be regarded as a valuable asset amongst a privileged community who might, before too long, be begging him for a passage for themselves and their families out of a doomed city. Nor was the Admiralty unmindful of this possibility; Admiral Purvis was instructed that, in the event of the Marquess of Wellesley and his suite requiring a sudden passage to England, they should be "accommodated in a line-of-battle ship if the service will permit. If not, a large frigate."

With the summer festivities behind him, Purvis again turned his attention to the task of trying to persuade the Spanish to move their ships from the Puntales into the outer harbour to form a defensive line with the British. Back in May he had written to Admiral Alava pointing out that, as from that time his own Squadron was likely to be greatly reduced, there could be occasions when he had only one ship of-the-line in Cadiz. It really was, therefore, incumbent on the Spanish Navy now to take over the defence of their own harbour.

Alava, who up to that point had maintained that his ships were ready for sea and required no further assistance from the British, then did an astonishing U-turn: apart from the *Pluton*, he replied, all the Spanish ships were unserviceable and not fit to move from the Puntales for want of men, rigging and sails.

Admiral Purvis had always considered it a part of his job to closely monitor the availability of naval matériel ashore. Only the week before he had passed on to Alava a letter from an English merchant in Cadiz advising that he had just received a large consignment of good quality sail canvas which he could offer at a very reasonable price. Purvis also knew that all forms of cordage could be readily purchased from the chandlers in the port.

He replied to Alava that it was "very regrettable" that men could not be raised to man the Spanish ships for such essential service but, as canvas and cordage were both readily available ashore, he could not understand why this was a problem. If, however, it was, and Alava would present him with a list of the sizes and types of ropes required, he would make the need known to the British Government. Not a week went by without a British merchantman arriving in Cadiz laden with money, clothing or other provisions for the Spanish patriots who could always, it appeared, find the cash to fund their own, often reckless and impetuous, designs; it seemed unbelievable to the British Admiral that they now appeared unwilling to pay themselves for fundamental preparations for the defence of their continued sovereignty; and this at a time when he was being plagued with correspondence and instructions regarding the transport to England of a flock of merino sheep — a gift from the Supreme Junta to King George — a gift which, in the event, consumed more administrative time, and generated more agitation and ill-humour than the movement of a division of troops halfway across the world would have done. On board one of the transports which carried them was Captain Edward Moncrieffe of the 50th Regiment, together with his wife and family. Moncrieffe did not object to the sheep but he did object to the "fourteen women of infamous character" who had been put on board by the authorities in Gibraltar and to whom he did not wish his family to be exposed. They were removed the same day on Admiral Purvis's orders.

Female passengers were also causing the Commander-in-Chief some anxiety: the Dey of Algiers had applied to him for a British warship to transport his ambassador to Constantinople together with gifts for the Sublime Porte; Lord Collingwood was concerned about the politically-incorrect nature of the gifts: "I have, in a civil way, put him off," he wrote to Purvis, "until the spring weather when the women, lions and other savage creatures that are presents to the Sultan may be conveyed with more convenience."

Nor could Lord Collingwood understand a request from James Green in Tangier for a British escort for the Emperor of Morocco's ships; Morocco was not at war with France, or any other of Britain's enemies, so from whom did he expect protection? "We have no right to protect the Barbary ships from any power with whom we are not at war," he wrote to Admiral Purvis, "the Emperor is not at war with Tunis nor with Sicily nor with Sardinia, I believe; but if he is, our being at peace with those states cannot give him protection from their hostility; or from any nation with whom we are not at war. — Perhaps the convoy they want is merely to show them the way to Tripoli," he added.

In the interior of Spain, in what had by now become the Peninsular War, General Wellesley was also finding the Spanish to be difficult allies. Jealousy, mistrust and political manoeuvring thwarted any form of effective, unified command and the Battle of Talavera, though technically a victory for the allies, had ended with a blazing row between Wellesley and the Spanish General Cuesta and the fracture of their allied force.

In November, Cuesta's successor, General Areizaga, with 53,000 men attempted a surprise strike at Madrid and was routed at Ocaña by a French army of 30,000 under Marshals Victor and Soult. The Spanish lost 5,000 killed and wounded and 20,000 were taken prisoner; French losses were less than 2,000. The Spanish fell back to the Sierra Morena to lick their wounds but this shattering defeat confirmed that nothing could now stop the French from driving into Andalusia for Seville and Cadiz — the remaining enclave of resistance in the south.

An Account of His Catholic Majesty's Ships remaining in Cadiz Harbour this 6th October 1809

Ships of the Line

Algeçiras	**76**	Lying near the *Atlas* in the lower part of the harbour. Arrived 17th ult. from Catalonia. Sails bent.
Santiago la America	**68**	Next to above. Arrived 4th inst. from Ferrol. Sails bent.
San Julian	**60**	Next to above. Arrived 18th ult. from Ferrol. Sails bent.
San Telmo	**76**	Next to above. Arrived 18th ult. from Ferrol. Sails bent.
Santa Ana	**114**	Next to above. Mizzen topsail bent. Bearing the Flag of Admiral Alava.
Glorioso	**76**	Next to above. Fore & mizzen topsails bent. Bearing the Flag of Rear-Admiral Mondragon.
San Francisco de Paulo	**76**	Next to above. No sails bent.
Montanes	**76**	Next to above. No sails bent. Mizzen topmast down.
Purisima Concepcion	**114**	Next to above. Arrived 21st ult. from Ferrol. No sails bent.
Pluton	**80**	Next to above. Off the Puntales. Topsails bent.
Principe de Asturias	**114**	Above the Puntales. Arrived 19th ult. from Ferrol.
Neptuno	**84**	Above the Puntales. No sails bent.
San Justo	**76**	Above the Puntales. Topsails bent.
San Pedro Alcantara	**68**	Sails bent.
San Fulgencio	**68**	At the Carracas. Yards and topmasts struck.

Frigates, etc.

Esmeralda	**38**	At the Carracas. Arrived 27th August from Ferrol. No sails bent.
Venganza	**38**	In the lower part of the harbour. Arrived 1st ult. from Ferrol. No sails bent.
Diana	**36**	In the lower part of the harbour. Arrived 4th ult. from Ferrol. Topsails bent.
Indagadora	**20**	Near the *Santa Ana*. Arrived 16th ult. from Ferrol. Sails bent.
Principe de Asturias	**16**	Inshore above the town. Arrived 15th ult. from Ferrol. No sails bent.

The *Santa Maria Magdalena*, **36,** arrived 1st ult. from Ferrol
and sailed 24th ult. under sealed orders.

In Cadiz, Admiral Purvis's difficulties remained much the same as they had been at the beginning of the year: the prisoners-of-war still constituted a serious security risk and the Marquess of Wellesley wanted to know the true extent of the problem which the Spanish were trying to conceal; they admitted to 5,000 in the hulks but Purvis had intelligence that there were a further 2,000 at Chiclana, south-east of the Isle of Leon, and 1,000-plus in and around Puerto Santa Maria. The latter, he understood, were not confined so would be free to rejoin their countrymen when they appeared. He had also received several representations from the French prisoners appealing for British intervention to alleviate the appalling conditions in which they were confined in the hulks — sometimes without food and water for several days on end and denied the means to keep themselves clean. Every morning before dawn the bodies of those unfortunates who had not survived the night were thrown overboard from the hulks; later the shoreline would be punctuated with clusters of shrieking gulls feeding on the morning's harvest of bloated corpses. Diplomacy would not allow the Admiral to reveal to the Spanish his true feelings — that the complaints were entirely justified and a stain on the honour of the Spanish Navy; instead, he had to request that Alava would investigate the complaints though he was "sure that the Spanish would not treat their prisoners-of-war in such a barbarous and neglectful fashion".

The Spanish had no plans to ship any more prisoners out of Cadiz, nor had any action been taken regarding the decommissioning of the harbour defences. Now that it was almost certain the French would come from the land and not the sea, the demolition of the northern forts, particularly Santa Catalina, was imperative.

As well as the need for continual reminders on the actions necessary for the defence of Cadiz, there was also the question of the Spanish ships at Cartagena which must also be safeguarded from falling into enemy hands. As early as April Lord Collingwood had urged the Junta to make arrangements for them to be moved to safety; now, with a French attack more certain, it was becoming urgent and he directed Admiral Purvis to enquire what arrangements had been made. Purvis knew the answer before he asked the question but, nevertheless, went through the motions of diplomatic enquiries and evasive answers and wrote to the British Chargé d'Affaires in Seville asking that official representations should be renewed with the Government.

On 25th October 1809 John Child Purvis was promoted to Vice-Admiral of the Blue. Vice-Admiral Felipe de Villavicencio, Alava's second-in-command, wrote to him: "The pleasing news of Your Excellency being promoted to the rank of Vice-Admiral of His Britannic Majesty's Squadron fills me with the utmost joy; as well because I see justly rewarded the merit of so worthy a General as for the particular esteem and friendship I profess for Your Excellency to whom I offer the most sincere congratulations."

Learning that his old friend Lord Collingwood was now in extremely poor health and hoped to return soon to England, Vice-Admiral Purvis decided he would like, if possible, to return with him. He had now been on station for nearly three and a half years and there were personal matters in England which required his attention. He wrote to Lord Mulgrave on 5th November: "I take the liberty of representing to your Lordship that business of much importance respecting my private fortune requires my being in England and I shall be very thankful if your Lordship will be pleased to make such arrangements as may admit of my retiring from active service until I shall have settled the business which at present obliges me to solicit your indulgence." He realised that if the Admiralty acceded to his request it would still be several months before he could be relieved and, in the meantime, there was still much work to be done.

Throughout November and December French forces were concentrating north of the Sierra Morena in preparation for their thrust into Andalusia. The Spanish ships at Cadiz, Purvis reported to the Admiralty, "far from getting into a state of better preparation at this particular time, are <u>unbending sails</u> and <u>striking yards and topmasts</u> for the winter as guardships in Britain would do in times of profound peace. Admiral Alava's Flagship, the *Santa Ana*, has not even topsail sheet blocks on the yards."

Yet again, at the Commander-in-Chief's direction, he requested the Chargé d'Affaires at Seville to urge the Junta "to give immediate and peremptory orders" for the Spanish ships at Cartagena to be moved. Yet again, he urged the Military Governor of Cadiz to demolish Santa Catalina and the northern forts and

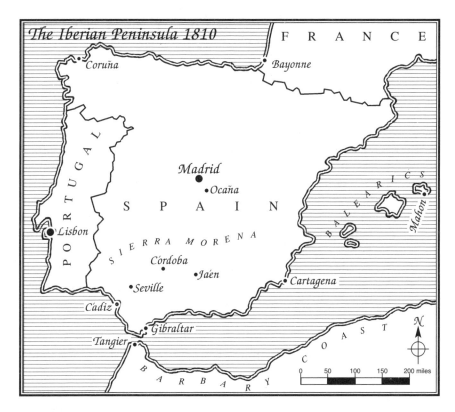

The Iberian Peninsula 1810

batteries while there was still time. Yet again, he pleaded with Admiral Alava to get his ships ready to move into a defensive position in the outer harbour. And yet again, he pressed for more of the French prisoners to be moved out of Cadiz. Only on this last matter was there any positive response — they intended sending further convoys to Ceuta in their own ships, they announced. He would believe that when he saw it!

On 8th December Admiral Purvis wrote to Lord Collingwood saying that he knew no more than he had a year ago regarding the intentions of the Spanish for their ships: ". . . by the Treaty between the two countries signed on 14th January last, the Spanish Government engages to take the most effectual measures for the preventing of the Spanish squadrons in all parts of Spain from falling into the power of France; but how far dependance can be placed on that Treaty at a time when they may possibly be making terms with the French regarding the City of Cadiz, is not for me to decide." The Commander-in-Chief had a pretty fair idea of how things would go, one way or the other: "If the Spaniards in the disportions they make intend that their ships shall leave the harbour," he replied, "they will have little difficulty in doing it. If they determine otherwise, their measures of security will be taken long before you can know their resolve."

At the end of the year an uneasy calm pervaded the city; travellers from the interior and Masters of arriving ships were immediately pounced upon and interrogated for the slightest shred of intelligence which might indicate where the French were and what they were doing. Then on 17th January it was reported that a large French army was gathering at Bayonne, on the Biscay coast just across the Franco-Spanish border, and on the same day the inhabitants of Seville were "put into a state of alarm" by news that a considerable body of the enemy was approaching the principal pass through the Sierra Morena. It was true: four columns, comprising 68,000 seasoned troops under Victor and Sebastiani, were moving south and by 21st January had forced the passes through the Sierra Morena. Jaén fell to Sebastiani the following day and Victor entered Cordoba on the 24th.

In Cadiz Admiral Purvis had the *Atlas, Renown, Triumph, Zealous* and *Minstrel*. The *Invincible* was on her way from Gibraltar with Captain Donnelly under orders to bring as much bread and wine for the Squadron as he could carry and "as much powder as her magazine will contain". In Lord Collingwood's opinion it was about all she was fit for; in common with several of the ships sent out from England she was in poor condition: "I find in general those ships that come from England want most," he wrote to Purvis. "That *Invincible* seems to have been in distress ever since she came from home; like to have sunk in the passage out and to have [overturned] for want of ballast; and now most of her masts and yards sprung without (I believe) ever having been once in chace."

With the availability of pilots likely to be uncertain once the enemy arrived, Admiral Purvis ordered his Captains to get their Masters to take soundings and to thoroughly familiarise themselves with the navigation of the harbour so they could enter and leave it without assistance; but, even at this stage, to avoid giving offence to the Spanish and "if observed, to discontinue the proceedings at that time".

Ships; forts; prisoners-of-war. Purvis, yet again, reminded the appropriate authorities; there was very little time left now, he pointed out. Of the fourteen Spanish line-of-battle ships only four were below the narrow passage of the Puntales; a few of the others were beginning to bend some sails in a leisurely fashion. "There can be no doubt," he urged Alava, "one of the first objects of the enemy will be to get possession of as many of the ships as possible and he will consequently endeavour to obstruct their coming down by every possible means. The wind is now fair for their moving which can be attended with no inconvenience." At last Alava agreed and asked for British help. Four hundred British seamen and their officers were immediately sent to move the Spanish warships and prison hulks.

It was by now apparent that the Spanish hoped, at best, to be able to hold the Isle of Leon against the enemy with a fall-back position at the narrow neck of land east of the Puntales. This was confirmed by the fact that they had, on their own initiative, removed the guns from Fort Matagorda on the assumption that the French would take the whole eastern side of the harbour. But the fortifications and furnace were still intact and it would be easy enough for the enemy to move in their own ordnance and have the fort in action against the Puntales in a very short space of time. There were also many guns at the Carracas Arsenal and "not much less than 100,000 shot" which would serve the enemy well if it was not moved beyond their reach. At last, General Venégas, the new Governor of Cadiz, gave permission for Matagorda, Catalina and the other batteries on the north and east sides of the harbour to be destroyed. Parties of British seamen spiked the guns and demolished the fortifications to the best of their ability in the time available. Admiral Purvis pointed out, however, that the work could have been done far more effectively if it had been done well in advance and under the supervision of officers of the Royal Engineers with experience in demolitions.

On the subject of the prisoners-of-war, the Spanish clearly had no intention of using their own ships to take them to Ceuta, as they had previously intimated. On 26th January the Count of Ayamans approached Admiral Purvis to enquire if they could not be sent to

England in British ships? No, they could not, the Admiral replied, and it was a great pity that the Spanish could not implement their original plan as there were far more Spanish ships than British available for the purpose. He would put the matter to the Commander-in-Chief but doubted that he would feel differently.

The next request was for British seamen to man the batteries which guarded the approach to the Suaso Bridge and Admiral Purvis, again, had to curb his exasperation for long enough to compose a civil reply: ". . . when I consider the trifling advantage which could be derived from the few men that could be spared from the four ships here," he explained, he must, with regret, decline their request. He did, however, remind them that it would be greatly to their advantage if they arranged for the guns and shot at the Carracas Arsenal to be removed before they fell into the hands of the enemy.

A Public Proclamation on 26th January announced that the Supreme Junta had been dissolved. The people, it seemed, had suspected it of being about to treat with the French. In its place, a group of trusted worthies had been appointed as a Regency to manage the affairs of Free Spain until such time as a newly-formed Cortes had structured a plan of government. Saavedra became Regent with Castaños and the petulant General Cuesta as his counsellors; the Marquess de la Romana became Captain-General of Valencia and its army and General Blake Captain-General of Andalusia and its army. The citizens of Cadiz were to form a 'Junta of Vigilance and Defence' which would consist of deputies elected by the people of each quarter of the city; the deputies were to be changed every four months before they succumbed to corruption or were coerced by French sympathisers. Advising Lord Collingwood of this on 31st January, Purvis wrote: "These changes and the great distrusts which prevail amongst themselves will be their ruin. How the Spanish armies are disposed of I cannot tell; but if only one-third of the people of Cadiz would do their duty, the town would hold out longer than might be convenient to the enemy." He still believed that regular Spanish troops would fall back into the city before the French advance and, on the following day, this is exactly what happened with the arrival of the Duke of Albuquerque at the head of 11,000 men. The city now had its professional garrison. On the same day Marshal Victor, accompanied by the triumphant 'King' Joseph Bonaparte, entered Seville.

The seat of the Government of Free Spain was now on the Royal Isle of Leon as it had become known. The Duke of Albuquerque was appointed Military Governor and it seemed to Admiral Purvis that there was considerable public confidence in the new Regency team even to the extent that it appeared to have motivated "great exertion in fortifying the Isle of Leon, particularly towards Sancti Petri". It was the first time the British had seen the Spaniards do anything briskly and with a will.

Intelligence suggested that the approaching French army comprised some 27,000 including 4,000 cavalry commanded by Victor. The Spanish garrison was now about 11,000 including 700 cavalry. There were a further 3,000-4,000 Spanish troops at Ayamonte, some seventy-five miles to the west, which the Regency had requested Admiral Purvis to collect and transport to Cadiz. In addition to the Spanish troops, Brigadier-General Bowes had just arrived at Cadiz to command a detachment of 1,000 men on its way from Gibraltar and the Spaniards had also appealed to Lord Wellington to send troops from Portugal.

Always anticipating the enemy's next move, something which his Spanish allies seemed incapable of doing, Admiral Purvis had cancelled his orders for the *Bulwark* to return to England and ordered her to remain at Gibraltar in a state of constant readiness to undertake whatever orders he might issue. "I have further to desire that all empty transports may be held in readiness to come here and that every exertion may be used to clear those which are unloading for the same purpose." He was also anxious about water: the Spanish appeared to have taken little heed of his warning that the enemy would cut the water supply as soon as they arrived and had done nothing to ensure an adequate supply of good casks and to keep their ships topped up. He had already cornered the market for casks in Cadiz and now turned to Gibraltar, writing to Mr. Cutforth, the Agent Victualler: "One of the enemy's first actions will be to put a stop to the means of our obtaining water . . . therefore, collect all water casks possible and start repairing those in need. If you require coopers, apply to the Senior Royal Naval Officer who will arrange coopers from the ships."

The Admiral was further embarrassed by a fresh spate of appeals from the French prisoners-of-war. The Spanish had moored one of the hulks very close to the *Atlas* which was not only a cause of some anxiety to the ship's company but made it easier for the prisoners to get messages and petitions over to the British Admiral whom they saw as their only chance of getting their conditions investigated. Having received no response or action from Alava on previous occasions, he this time referred it to the Governor, General Venegas: "I beg to inform Your Excellency that I have received several letters from the prisoners in the ships in the harbour representing their having been kept several days without provisions and, as their cases are more particularly described in that I have just received, I take the liberty of enclosing it to you."

French faith in British justice and fair play was not mistaken: there was a growing sense of outrage among all ranks of the British forces in Cadiz, both Navy and Army, at the inhumane treatment of the prisoners-of-war. Eventually, when Venegas failed to take action, Admiral Purvis took matters into his own hands and had fresh provisions distributed to the hulks for which he received a touching letter of thanks from the prisoners. There is also a case on record of British soldiers harbouring and rehabilitating an escaped French prisoner and repatriating him to his own lines — not without some risk to themselves.[3]

The Spanish authorities may have been slow to investigate maltreatment of their prisoners but Admiral Alava was quick enough to report a British Midshipman who, probably at the limit of his patience, had apparently been rude to a Spanish officer. Purvis, mindful of the need for diplomacy, even when the enemy was at the door, replied: "I am much concerned that any English officer should so forget the discipline of the Service and the respect due to the Spanish uniform and flag as to behave as Don Juan Topete has described in his letter." The Midshipman, he advised him, had been arrested and was awaiting Court Martial. It speaks highly for the discipline and restraint of Royal Navy personnel in Cadiz at the time that there were not more incidents of this kind. But while Admiral Purvis would go to great lengths to ensure that his officers and men did nothing to affront the dignity of his Spanish allies, he would brook no interference with, or misuse of, his men by them:

when a party of British seamen, which had been put aboard the *San Justo* specifically to work on her rigging, was appropriated by a Spanish officer for some other task, the Admiral's reprimand to Alava was firm and swift: "I was much disappointed to find the men under my command had been employed on a service which I had repeatedly assured Your Excellency was not consistent with the arrangements I had made and such as I cannot consequently allow. I have therefore to request you will be pleased to order men to supply the place of those now on board the *San Justo* belonging to me as I shall be obliged to send for them tomorrow morning."

The first sight of the enemy came on 4th February when small advance reconnaissance parties were observed on the eastern side of the harbour. The first skirmish took place near the ruins of Fort Matagorda where a boat from the *Invincible* landed and her seamen took a French corporal and nine soldiers prisoner.

The following day large bodies of French troops were seen marching towards Puerto Santa Maria and Puerto Real. Later the same day the water supply was cut off.

To observers on the British warships, who had become used to the ponderous transactions of the Spanish forces, the speed with which the French commanders appraised the situation and started work was astonishing. The day after their arrival a large body of men was at work constructing an artillery position behind the hill of rubble which had once been Fort Matagorda while, at the same time, French emissaries entered Cadiz under Flag of Truce with proposals of a surrender to 'King' Joseph and to treat on the means of securing the Spanish ships and arsenal. The Spaniards answered that the City of Cadiz, faithful to the principles it had sworn, acknowledged no other King than the Señor Don Fernando VII.

To impede the construction work behind Matagorda, Admiral Alava agreed to send a line-of-battle ship off the point to bombard the position and Admiral Purvis sent 200 seamen to act as gunners. Additionally, he commissioned a gunboat and a launch armed with a carronade from each of his ships to annoy the enemy from close inshore as circumstances might allow.

"I have never entertained a doubt," Purvis wrote to the British Chargé d'Affaires, "of Cadiz holding out against the enemy and putting him to defiance; the strength of its works, its natural defences and the patriotism of its people fully justify such an expectation. The only evil to be dreaded is the want of confidence and unanimity; but when the Spaniards reflect on what must be the consequences of yielding to the French, they must surely revolt at the idea of submitting themselves to the shocking insults, barbarity and revenge which such a people are in the habit of exercising over those they conquer."

The guns of the *San Justo* were having some success in delaying the enemy's works at Matagorda. The gunnery was good — the gunners were British seamen — but the damage inflicted would have been far greater if the Spanish naval officers had been more competent in the positioning and mooring of their ship. Admiral Purvis had little confidence in them and in a secret letter to the Admiralty of 17th February confided: "I place no dependance on their officers; they allow their sails to get rotten for want of loosing them to dry, and I am under the necessity of directing our men to clear hawse and serve the cables of the prison ships to prevent them from breaking adrift, perhaps to the enemy; and yet with all this, an apparent cordiality exists between me and the Spanish Admiral." He had hoped that, when faced with active service against the enemy, he might see some improvement in their attitude; but nothing was thus far evident.

Though the *San Justo* was not, technically, under his command, he could not, on occasions, resist the temptation of pointing out essential targets to her Captain, Don Josef Jordan, and gently encouraging him towards actions the need for which would have been immediately apparent to any British second-year Midshipman.

Observing the standard of gunnery on the *San Justo*, the Duke of Albuquerque approached Admiral Purvis to request that British gunners might be provided to man the batteries on Leon. He replied: "It is with great regret I feel myself obliged to assure Your Excellency that from the great number of our best men which are already employed in His Catholic Majesty's ships and gunboats, as well as in the English boats fitted with carronades, I have it not in my power to send those which you have asked for and if any of the enemy's ships should appear off the port, I should have difficulty in collecting men so far separated from me."

The gunboats and launches were proving reasonably effective in harassing the enemy from close inshore and from the narrow channels to the east and south-east sides of the island; the Admiral therefore heartily concurred with a suggestion by the Spanish, received at midnight on 13th February, that a further four gunboats should be commissioned. Each would be manned by a British Lieutenant, ten British seamen and twenty Spanish seamen; the gunboats were to proceed to the Puente Suaso as soon as they were manned and equipped. However, the equipment of all these gunboats had drained the Squadron of small arms and it was necessary for the Admiral to order 500 stand of arms to be delivered to the gunner of the Flagship for distribution among the ships of the Squadron.

Between the Matagorda promontory and Puntales Roads lay the Caño del Trocadero. A single island at low water, it became a group of four boggy islets when the tide was in. The French, under continual pressure from the *San Justo* in their works at Matagorda, decided to switch their effort to Trocadero. An artillery emplacement here would be almost as well placed for bombarding Fort Puntales and its construction less vulnerable to the attentions of Spanish ships of-the-line. It would also be a good position, Purvis pointed out to Alava, for the French to assemble vessels for a landing near the Puntales should they have such a venture in mind. The gunboats would be an effective means of harassing the enemy works on Trocadero but, if the allies were now to occupy Matagorda, they could also engage them with some heavier ordnance from the north-west across Trocadero Creek. This was proposed for the consideration of the Naval and Military Commands of both nations.

The Cadiz Garrison was swelled with the arrival of 2,400 British and 1,394 Portuguese troops from Lisbon and Admiral Purvis received an urgent request from the Spanish to arrange collection of the 4,000 Spaniards at Ayamonte who were, in due course, brought to Cadiz in eleven British transports escorted by the *Rota*. The coffers were recharged with the arrival of the *Undaunted* and *Ethalion* from Porto Rico carrying $3 million for the Spanish government and the huge fortification on the isthmus, already called Fort Fernando, was going ahead fast with thousands of men employed on the site. The *San Julian,* which had been in dock at the Carracas, was warped out for use as a floating battery. The Spanish were now clearly determined to dig in and fight.

The French, also, were clearly determined to take Cadiz: within days of their arrival work had started to establish batteries on the ruins of the fortified positions on the north and east sides of the harbour, from Rota to the mouth of the Carracas, with particular emphasis on Trocadero and Santa Catalina. Work on the former was proceeding at an alarming rate despite the efforts of the *San Justo*. Admiral Purvis knew that much greater damage could be achieved if the ship was handled and moored properly. He had himself been involved in bombardment from close inshore in the *Princess Royal* at Toulon sixteen years earlier, he told Alava, and the secret lay in mooring the ship firmly broadside on to the target so there was no waste of time or shot. The following day the ship was still swinging ineffectually, delivering the occasional broadside when the target presented itself; he could watch this incompetence no longer: "I beg leave again to solicit your interference regarding the San Justo," he wrote to Alava, "Your Excellency must be well aware that . . . unless you direct suitable anchor lighters to moor her properly immediately, the enemy will get so forward in his works that it will be difficult to dislodge him."

When it became apparent that the enemy's works at Santa Catalina demanded the attention of a line-of-battle ship, he was determined to avoid a repeat performance. He would send British officers and seamen to move and moor the ship and British gunners to fight her; but with thirteen Spanish and only five British line-of-battle ships in the outer harbour it must, of course, be a Spanish ship. He wrote to Frere for the necessary order from the Regency to be issued: ". . . I will immediately send officers and men to move her and afterwards to fight her guns whereby all the enemy has done will be quickly overthrown. The Spaniards may possibly propose an English ship being placed there but I'm certain I need not point out to you the impossibility of admitting such a measure when there are so many of their own in the harbour."

Alava then pleaded that the reason the *San Justo* could not moor herself properly was that she required a further anchor; could the British supply one? Brought up in a discipline where a Captain would never dream of abandoning an anchor, and with memories of having to recover buoyed anchors himself, sometimes under heavy fire from the enemy, Purvis's reply was laconic: "I beg leave to mention that there are no less than four buoys over anchors from which some of the Spanish ships have slipped in the channel leading to the Carracas any of which will serve for the San Justo."

On 22nd February Admiral Purvis advised the Admiralty that he had visited the defences which had been thrown up to the east of the Suaso Bridge and "from the judicious construction of the batteries and the natural marshy ground, intersected with multitudes of canals, there appears no risk of surprise from that quarter". He reported that similar defences were now being constructed along the canal towards Sancti Petri in which many gunboats patrolled and kept the enemy in check. Four of these gunboats, and another four off Matagorda, were commanded by British Lieutenants. One of the British gunboats had been sunk on the 18th by enemy fire.

The plan for the British to occupy Matagorda had now been approved and Purvis sent a party of seamen and marines to assist the soldiers already there. With this, and the British personnel already employed in gunboats and on board Spanish ships, his crews had been very much reduced and he asked the Admiralty for more ships. He also related a daring escape by a group of French officers from the prison hulk moored close to the *Atlas*. A boat had come alongside the hulk with provisions and the prisoners leapt into her, hoisted a sail and threw the Spanish crew overboard as they got under way. "Our launches gave chase and fired their carronades at the boat but could not stop her. No notice was taken of this boat by any of the Spanish ships although she passed just under their guns and completely made her escape to the eastern side of the bay."

On 24th February two of the *San Justo*'s guns burst killing two British seamen and wounding twelve. Captain Hunt of the Royal Artillery went on board and, having examined the remainder, reported them totally unfit for service. It later became known that they had been condemned in 1807 "notwithstanding which she was allowed to be placed against the enemy's works". Little wonder that the Spanish Navy was reluctant to man her guns. Officers of the Royal Artillery surveyed the guns in the *Glorioso* which were found to be the same; those in the *San Francisco de Paulo,* however, were deemed to be sound. Admiral Purvis approached Frere to prevail upon the Spanish to order Alava to replace the *Justo* with the *Paulo*. Time was of the essence; to change the guns in the *San Justo* would take too long; "nor can we entertain Alava's hint that a British ship should be sent. If the French fleet appear off the port, all the British ships will be required to oppose them."

On 2nd March Vice-Admiral Purvis wrote to Lord Collingwood advising him that the 88th Regiment had just arrived from Gibraltar increasing the British troops in Cadiz to 2,862. He also reported, evidently with some relief, that Admiral Alava had left to take up the appointment of Naval Commander in the Havannah; his place in Cadiz had been taken by Vice-Admiral Villavicencio with whom, as Alava's second-in-command, Purvis had already established a reasonable rapport. Official visits had been exchanged and he was hoping for "a cordial and determined joint endeavour".

Lord Collingwood never read this letter as he died before it reached him and on the following day, 3rd March 1810, although he would not know it until the end of the month, Vice-Admiral Purvis became Acting Commander-in-Chief Mediterranean.

CHAPTER 13

The Great Storm

Saturday 3rd March 1810
Cadiz

T here is a remote bay on the west coast of Sutherland, in the
     Scottish Highlands, called Sandwood Bay. It is served by no
     road and to reach it entails a walk of several miles along a
rough track through the heather. It is, consequently, seldom visited.
    A travel writer in Victorian times recorded that many skeletons of
long-dead ships lay stranded on this beautiful stretch of coast. Over
the next 150 years successive generations of travel writers, rather
than walk to the place themselves, repeated the information they
had read though the long-dead ships had long-since disappeared —
if, indeed, they had ever existed in the first place. A myth was thus
perpetuated through writers copying other writers rather than
checking the facts for themselves at source.
    In 1824, William James in his great 5-volume work *'The Naval
History of Great Britain'* incorrectly stated that, before his death,
Lord Collingwood handed over the Mediterranean Command to
Rear-Admiral George Martin. This mistake was repeated by Sir
William Laird Clowes in his definitive 7-volume work *'The Royal
Navy'* published 1897-1903 and by every one of Collingwood's
biographers before and since. Though Lord Collingwood's letter to
the Admiralty of 3rd March 1810 is available in the National

Archives for all to see[1], it was not until 2003 that the error was corrected by Captain C.H.H. Owen RN in his preface to a collection of Collingwood letters in *'The Naval Miscellany Volume VI'* published by the Navy Records Society.

So, to set the record straight once and for all, Rear-Admirals Martin and Sir Samuel Hood were left in command of the squadrons in the Eastern Mediterranean and Balearics respectively, both under the overall command of Vice-Admiral Purvis at Cadiz.

Vice-Admiral Cuthbert Collingwood, Baron Collingwood, was one of the great naval commanders in the greatest period of the Royal Navy's history. Like his friend John Purvis, he had lacked active patronage in his early days at sea and had had to wait until the age of twenty-seven for a Lieutenant's commission and thirty-one to make Post. Thereafter, among several other ships, he had commanded the *Barfleur* at 'The Glorious First of June', the *Excellent* at Cape St. Vincent and had flown his Flag in the *Royal Sovereign,* at Trafalgar. On the death of Lord Nelson he succeeded him as Commander-in-Chief Mediterranean. In 1810, the year of his death, he had not seen his family in England for seven years.

Totally committed to the service of his country and with a sense of duty which impelled him to involve himself personally in every aspect and level of his command, the strain soon started to tell. By 1806 when he had requested Rear-Admiral Purvis to be sent out as his second-in-command, he was exhausted — "worn to a shadow sometimes with fatigue and otherwise with anxiety,"[2] he told Purvis. By 1808 he had become physically ill and had written to Lord Mulgrave asking to be relieved. This and subsequent requests were refused; Prince William, Duke of Clarence, who was completely unfit for any command of importance, had been lobbying the Admiralty to succeed Collingwood in the Mediterranean; the easiest way to deflect such a potentially-disastrous proposal, without giving offence to a royal prince, was to keep the poor, dying Collingwood at his post.

In his last letter to Admiral Purvis, written on 21st January 1810, six weeks before his death, he was clearly in low spirits: "I hope you have seen Captain Purvis [John] and that he is gone to England to get a ship. Give my best compliments to Mrs. Purvis, I am glad to hear she is recovered — my family were pretty well when I heard from them which I do sometimes." He was also concerned about the calibre of officers being sent out to him from England: " . . . to be sure there is such a selection of Commanders as if it was expected the ships were to take care of themselves. Here is a gentleman a Mr. Shaw sent out to be made a Captain who cannot do the duty of Lieutenant; he has only been 48 hours in the Sultan. And poor [West] is in distress he has been most of his life in french prison [Collingwood never dignified france and french with an initial capital!] and is not a bit of an officer or a seaman. These things are the cause of much anxiety to me; I see the Navy going retrograde every day and cannot help it. The existence of Order is maintained by not more than two officers in each ship — many ships have not one — it is the seamen who are preservers of Order not the tasselled boys who fill the quarter decks and who are scraped from every filthy place on shore — as instance the party who attacked the Master of the Triumph at Gibraltar; that Mr. Owen Williams should have been sent to prison at Gibraltar and punished by the civil law."

The advanced state of his illness at this point must have caused Purvis deep concern: "This complaint in my stomach does not amend. I cannot bear to eat anything and drink only two wine glasses full of water in a day and this little throws my stomach into convulsions and it works as if it was full of young cats." Yet, ill as he was, he was still hoping for one last encounter with the enemy: "I am not without hope that I may meet those frenchmen again. I do not expect to take them; their object seems to be got on shore — prevent their ships falling to us and keep themselves from Prison."

It was not until 9th April 1810, the Clarence threat having long since passed, that the Admiralty appointed Admiral Sir Charles Cotton to relieve him; but it was too late — he had died five weeks earlier (although news of his death had not yet reached England) having been left with no alternative but to hand over his command to Vice-Admiral Purvis on 3rd March and sail for England in the *Ville de Paris*. He died on board four days later.

The body of Lord Collingwood was transferred to the frigate *Nereus* at Gibraltar and Captain Thomas in the *Ville de Paris* proceeded to Cadiz to report to the new Commander-in-Chief who on 30th March reported to the Admiralty:

It is with the greatest sorrow I am to acquaint you for their Lordships' information that my late valuable friend Lord Collingwood died on the 7th inst. On the 24th ult. His Lordship finding his health fast declining he parted from the Fleet and went to Mahon but not finding relief there he yielded to the persuasions of the medical gentlemen and determined to return to England in the Ville de Paris but survived only one day after leaving Mahon. Captain Thomas of the Ville de Paris made the best of his way to this harbour and, as Rear-Admiral Pickmore is here and was intended by Their Lordships to remain here, I shall shift my Flag to the Ville de Paris and proceed to join the Fleet at present under the orders of Rear-Admiral Sir Samuel Hood, leaving with Rear-Admiral Pickmore all such papers and instructions as are necessary for his guidance.

Two days later he heard that his request to return to England had been granted and that Admiral Sir Charles Cotton would be out shortly to take over as Commander-in-Chief Mediterranean and would be hoisting his Flag in the *San Josef*. Admiral Purvis therefore decided not to transfer his own Flag but to wait for Admiral Cotton at Cadiz where he could brief him and hand over the command. Meanwhile he ordered the *Ville de Paris* to join Sir Samuel Hood's Squadron which had "only one 3-decker fit for service".

March had been a busy month at Cadiz: during the first few days the French had sent in several emissaries under Flag of Truce with the intention, it was thought, of dividing public opinion and weakening resolve. But the citizens stood firm and some of the papers submitted by the French had been burned publically in the street by the common hangman.

On 2nd March *Achille* and *Tonnant* had joined the Squadron and the *Antelope* had arrived carrying Henry Wellesley to replace Frere; his official title was 'Envoy Extraordinary and Minister Plenipotentiary to His Catholic Majesty Ferdinand VII'. He was the fourth of the five Wellesley brothers with whom Admiral Purvis had had dealings — Arthur (later 1st Duke of Wellington), Richard (later 2nd Earl of Mornington), William Wellesley-Pole (who had been Secretary to the Admiralty until 1809 and a regular correspondent, later 3rd Earl of Mornington) and, now, Henry (later 1st Baron Cowley). Wellesley proved considerably more communicative than his predecessor. He held a meeting at his house on Leon the day after his arrival, with Admiral Purvis and Major-General Stewart, the Military Commander, so he could be fully briefed on the up-to-date naval and military position. By now the French were well entrenched on Trocadero; a plan had been discussed for its storming by British troops but had been abandoned in view of the very high casualties which could be expected.

The prisoners-of-war were still of major concern; a proposal by General Stewart for an exchange scheme for the French sailors had been vetoed by the Admiral: to allow French sailors to be at liberty at this time, he had pointed out, "would fill the seas with swarms of privateers to the devastation of British trade." They must, nevertheless, be got away from Cadiz somehow.

Then, on 7th March, the day Lord Collingwood died, almost as if the heavens were showing their displeasure at the great man's martyrdom to expediency, a mighty gale from the west-south-west, more violent than any of the residents could remember, struck Cadiz. It blew unabated for three days and wreaked havoc in the harbour. Three of the Spanish line-of-battle ships, the *Purisima Concepcion, Montanes* and *San Ramon,* broke their moorings and drove ashore on the east side of the harbour which was occupied by the enemy. They were shortly followed by the Portuguese seventy-four *Maria Primera* and by no less than twenty merchantmen — British, Spanish and American. It was high water spring tide and there was no chance of their ever being refloated. The French immediately opened fire with hot shot on the stranded ships and many were soon burning fiercely. Admiral Purvis sent in all the boats of the British Squadron to take off the crews.

The *Pluton* and the frigate *Paz* were driven up the Carracas where they stuck in the mud. The *Paz* was soon burnt to the water's edge by hot shot and the French then turned their guns on the *Pluton.*

Many Spanish boats were carried away to the enemy in the gale and a troop transport with 140 men of the 4th Regiment was driven ashore and the soldiers taken prisoner but not before they had burned their Regimental Colour to prevent its being taken by the enemy.[3] Several of the merchant ships as they were driven, out of control, across the harbour, ran aboard British warships causing extensive damage to spars and rigging.

At high water the next day, with the gale still blowing, the allied gunboats kept the enemy off the wrecks while the boats of the British Squadron, and such as the Spanish could muster, went in to salvage what stores they could. Then, at the height of the gale, Admiral Purvis received intelligence of a plot among the prisoners to overpower their guards and cut their moorings so the hulks would be driven ashore, causing yet more damage to the allied warships as they passed through the anchorage. Guards were doubled and the Admiral sent a message to Wellesley asking him to renew pressure on the Spanish authorities for removal of the prisoners: "Various situations could be fixed upon where they could not have the power to create alarm . . . each Spanish line-of-battle ship would take 600 with 300 seamen to sail the ship and a guard of 100 soldiers."

On the fourth day the gale abated leaving a scene of utter devastation: burnt-out wrecks lined the eastern shores of the harbour and there was hardly a ship afloat that did not have men in the rigging and over the side repairing storm or collision damage. Naturally, the French took advantage of the situation to further the construction of their works at Trocadero; the attentions of the *San Paulo* had been no more effective than those of the *San Justo* before it; the Spanish officers seemed devoid of all motivation and enthusiasm. In his confidential briefing to his second-in-command, Rear-Admiral Pickmore, Admiral Purvis hit upon what was perhaps the principal cause: "The Spanish ships are in a bad state for want of energy in their officers who, though perhaps not disposed to favour the views of France, are so dejected by their pay being long withheld from them that there appears in most of them a total disregard of all points of duty, and neglect in the care of their ships is marked in every instance."

Even among the most fervent patriots, morale cannot be maintained indefinitely where men are not paid for the work they do. In this case there seemed no reason for such neglect: ships laden with treasure from the Americas and money from England were continually arriving and would often lie at anchor for several weeks before the Spanish could be persuaded to unload them; at this moment the *Ethalion* was in the harbour, unable to undertake any other duty, still loaded with the money she had brought in a month previously.

According to Lord Balgonie, who had taken over command of the *Delight* from John, the same difficulty existed in Cartagena from where he had just returned. He told the Admiral that the seamen there had so much back pay owing to them that they were unlikely to move the ships even if the Spanish authorities could be persuaded to give the order. The Spanish authorities, meanwhile, continued to sidestep the regular British pleas for them to move the ships to Gibraltar or Minorca to get them out of the reach of the enemy.

By now Admiral Purvis was reconciled to the fact that the French could not be prevented from completing their massive fortification at Trocadero. The gunboats had harassed the work continually with as much success as could be expected from such lightly-armed vessels; but what had really been needed was round-the-clock bombardment from the 32- and 24-pounders of a well-moored ship of-the-line. All previous attempts, through Alava, to get the Spanish officers to moor their ship effectively had failed. On 22nd March, though he realised it was by now too late, he had one final attempt through Admiral Villavicencio: excusing himself for taking such a liberty, and explaining that it would not have been proper for him to approach the ship's Captain direct, and pointing out that his officers on board the *San Paulo* were under orders "to be observant to the instructions they may have from her Captain", he requested that the ship should be properly moored for bombardment.

To his surprise, Villavicencio readily agreed and, moreover, gave his permission for an officer of the Royal Engineers to go on board to advise on "the best possible position to do maximum damage to the enemy's works". The French responded to the improved bombardment which resulted by increasing the intensity of their own destructive fire on the British position at Matagorda.

While war ravaged the Iberian Peninsula, Thomas Bruce, 7th Earl of Elgin, diplomat and art connoisseur, had purchased from the Ottoman authorities in Greece some of the 5th century BC decorated sculptures on the Parthenon at Athens to save them from wilful damage and destruction. On 29th March Admiral Purvis, on directions from the Admiralty, ordered Rear-Admiral Martin to arrange for a transport from Malta to proceed to Athens to collect the "antiquities collected in Greece by the Earl of Elgin". And so the 'Elgin Marbles' were transported to England and later sold to the nation for £35,000 the Admiral little realising at the time the excitement they would cause when first placed on public display nor the contentious political issue they would later become.

No action had been taken by the Spanish on the prisoners-of-war and the likelihood of any arrangements now being made was further reduced by a growing hostility between the Regency and the Military Junta. Following a violent disagreement, the Duke of Albuquerque was relieved of the Spanish military command with General Castaños appointed in his place. For less theatrical reasons, Lieutenant-General Graham (later 1st Lord Lynedoch), who had recently commanded a division in the disastrous Walcheren Expedition, took over from Major-General Stewart in command of British land forces in Cadiz.

Henry Wellesley, a new broom sweeping clean, made it clear that he was not prepared to sink beneath the blanket of Latin torpor which smothered every initiative in the city nor to put up with any further procrastination over the prisoners. Calling a meeting of the Spanish and British naval and military commanders, he proposed a deal: Britain would remove 4,000 of the prisoners and ship them to England, using British resources, if Spain would undertake to remove the balance, perhaps a further 2,000, to the Canaries or the Balearics. The offer was conditional upon both sides acting immediately and was readily accepted by the Spaniards.

Within a week, true to the spirit of the agreement, Admiral Purvis had acquired five transports and on 12th April was able to report to the Admiralty that they were loaded with the first tranche of French seamen and ready to sail for Plymouth, where a large new prison had recently been completed, escorted by three frigates — *Iris, Rota* and *Ethalion* — under the orders of Captain Shortland in the *Iris*. The transports being full to capacity, some of the prisoners had even been taken on board the *Ethalion*. The convoy sailed the following day. Needless to say, the three Spanish line-of-battle ships detailed to take their share of the prisoners to the Canaries were not ready. They would sail, the Spanish Admiral assured Wellesley, within the next few days and, having landed the prisoners-of-war on Tenerife, would proceed to the Havannah.

Admiral Purvis might have been excused a wry smile as he waited for the next round of delaying tactics. A week later, under pressure from Wellesley, the Spanish reported that the *San Lorenzo* and *San Fulgencio* were loaded with 400 prisoners each and were ready to sail but awaiting provisions; they also enquired if Britain would be able to provide an escort for the convoy.

Next came a letter from Don Thomas de Isturiz, Commissioner for the Superior Junta in Cadiz: the Spanish ships could not sail unless the British could supply them with 131 water casks. Purvis had long since anticipated this need and had been collecting casks from wherever he could obtain them over the course of the past six months. He had them taken to the Spanish ships the same day.

Next: they could not sail until they had more cables. Purvis replied that he had already supplied them with "no less than thirty-four cables beside cablets and a large quantity of cordage by which the stores in the arsenal at Gibraltar are very much reduced and may occasion distress to the ships of His Britannic Majesty". He did not add that there were also cables attached to the several anchors which Spanish ships had left on the bottom since the Great Storm and which he had been urging them, ever since, to recover; since the storm the British Squadron had been forced to anchor in shoal water to avoid fouling the abandoned Spanish anchors.

When it seemed that all the deficiencies had been made good, all the objections overcome and nothing remained to prevent the convoy from sailing, Wellesley received a letter from the Spanish Government. Admiral Purvis had agreed to send the *Bulwark* to escort the prison convoy to Tenerife and then to escort the two Spanish ships across the Atlantic to the Havannah. As the *Bulwark* was going to the Havannah anyway, the Spanish wanted to know, could she not also convey quicksilver to Vera Cruz and then return to Cadiz with treasure from Vera Cruz?

At that point, it is likely that Admiral Purvis would have agreed to almost anything to get the convoy to sea; he replied to Wellesley: "Although quicksilver is not one of those articles which is allowed to be taken into His Majesty's ships of war, yet under the peculiar circumstances in which the affairs of Spain are placed, and the pointed manner in which the application has been made by the Spanish Secretary of State for Foreign Affairs to you, . . . I will direct Captain Fleeming to perform the service which is required of him." At last the convoy sailed.

At 0300 on the morning of 21st April the French opened fire from three new batteries on Trocadero containing twenty heavy guns and eight large mortars. These positions had been constructed behind a cluster of Spanish houses which formed the village of Saint Louis and which had masked the activity from British observers. Once the batteries were ready, the French demolished the flimsy houses with their first volley which opened a clear field of fire to Fort Matagorda.

The British garrison comprised some 160 sailors, marines and soldiers of the 94th Regiment of Foot (Scots Brigade), formerly a regiment of Scottish mercenaries in the Dutch service, commanded by Captain (later Lieutenant-General Sir) Archibald Maclaine. Admiral Purvis sent a message to Maclaine reminding him that, should it become necessary to abandon the position, which was becoming increasingly likely, it was essential that all the guns should be destroyed and the works rendered unfit for use by the enemy before evacuation. He promised him whatever assistance the Navy could provide. If his position became desperate a blue/white/red flag by day, or a blue light repeated until it was answered by a blue light from the *Atlas* at night, was to be the signal for "position no longer tenable". Boats would be placed near the fort during the night ready to receive the garrison if necessary and Captain Sir Richard King of the *Achille* was directed to stand by accordingly.

Captain Maclaine brought his main battery into action and returned the ferocious enemy fire from his seven 24-pounders until they ran out of powder. Lieutenant McMeekan of the *Atlas,* who was in the fort with the naval contingent, took boats to Fort Puntales to collect some of the powder which had been deposited there by the Royal Artillery for this eventuality. To his amazement, the Spanish refused to release it. Maclaine reported to Admiral Purvis: "We are breached in several places; our magazine shot through and through with cannon shot. We shall want almost everything particularly sandbags, powder and shot for our Spanish 24- and 16-pounders." He also requested a party of seamen armed with cutlasses as he believed the enemy would attempt to storm the fort that night. "Almost every officer in the fort has received contusions. I have 3 killed and 19 wounded — and obliged to leave off for want of powder," he told the Admiral.

Purvis and the Spanish Rear-Admiral Cayetano Valdés, Villavicencio's new second-in-command, decided to try and draw the enemy fire by moving the allied gunboats in closer to Trocadero — the Spanish boats to the south-east of the position and the British on the Matagorda side. In the ensuing crossfire the *San Paulo* was set on fire by enemy hot shot. The wind being easterly, she cut her cables and ran down to leeward of the British Squadron which immediately sent boats to her assistance and the fire was extinguished. The British contingent at Matagorda, however, was now clearly in serious trouble.

The bombardment of the fort continued throughout the night with the gunboats in attendance though, to the Admiral's disgust, there was little support from the Spanish batteries at Puntales. He wrote to Graham: "You will be surprised when I tell you there were very few guns fired from Fort Puntales and, in consequence of that mark of inattention, the English gunboats were directed to keep up a fire most part of last night." Graham replied: "I earnestly partake of the disappointment you feel on account of the unpardonable slackness of the fire from the Fort of Puntales." The General had, by now, become aware of the Spanish propensity for leaving everything to the British: "They wished the English would drive away the French, that they might eat strawberries at Chiclana,'" he later said.

At 0800 on the 22nd Maclaine wrote to Admiral Purvis: "Since 6 this morning we have not had a cartridge. The enemy has had the cannonade all to themselves. I am now a complete ruin and can defend the place no longer; although I am perfectly of opinion it might have been defended if prompt measures had been taken from the first. I shall therefore request your assistance in carrying off the garrison and blowing up the guns and fort at dark."

Purvis and Graham decided that the position must be evacuated as soon as the ordnance and works had been destroyed. The fire upon the British position was crippling and unremitting; six times within a single hour the flagstaff flying the Spanish flag was hit by enemy shot but, true to the prevailing spirit of diplomacy, Maclaine would not accede to the frequent requests from his men to replace it with a British ensign. Several stories of great courage during the

bombardment of Matagorda passed into the traditions of the 94th
Foot; not least the actions of a Sergeant's wife, Mrs. Reston, which
were immortalised by the great Scottish non-poet, William
McGonagall, whose tribute *"A Humble Heroine"* is reproduced at
Appendix 'F'.

Major Le Febvre of the Royal Engineers was landed at Matagorda
to assess the situation and immediately confirmed that the position
was no longer tenable. The guns were spiked and thrown down into
a mine which had been prepared for the purpose, the mine was
detonated and the remnants of the battered garrison taken off by the
boats of the Squadron. Captain Maclaine and his party had defended
the position with extreme gallantry until there was no further hope
of holding it. Of his 160 officers and men twenty were killed and
fifty wounded. Major Le Febvre, an officer of great ability and
promise, was the last man killed as he boarded one of the boats.

"The conduct of Captain Maclaine," Purvis later wrote to the
Admiralty, "and the whole of the detachments both Navy and Army
was meritorious and highly praiseworthy. Lieutenant I.F. Chapman
and Midshipman G. Dobson, both of the *Invincible,* have been
particularly noticed for their bravery, zeal and activity."

General Graham, not unnaturally, demanded an explanation for
the shortage of powder and ammunition. It transpired that Major
Duncan, the Royal Artillery Commander, had ensured a more than
adequate supply by stocking the fort with as much as its battered
magazines could accommodate and depositing a further quantity
with the Spanish at Puntales upon which the British Garrison could
draw. Lieutenant William Brierton, the Royal Artillery officer at
Matagorda, reported that much of the powder in the fort had been
used by the Royal Engineers, for construction of the mine, and he
had consequently sent boats to Puntales to draw on the reserve
supply. The Spaniards, he confirmed, had refused all requests to
release it. Both Lieutenant Brierton, who had fought with great
gallantry and had been seriously wounded, and Major Duncan were
exonerated by General Graham of all blame; it was simply another
painful and costly example of Spanish caprice.

A request from Graham to Purvis for the recovery of Major Le
Febvre's body was complied with immediately. The General was
also anxious to recover the dead sapper's watch so he could return

it to his family; he feared it had probably been "stripped by the first French that got to the fort", but, according to a soldier on the spot, it had actually been looted by a British soldier who had also torn the epaulettes off the dead officer's shoulders during the evacuation.[5] Graham offered a £10 reward for its return and the watch was eventually recovered but without its gold chain and seals.

Also commended to their Lordships by Admiral Purvis after the evacuation of Matagorda was Lieutenant McMeekan of the *Atlas* who had played a major part in the defence of the fort and "who has commanded the detachment of gun and mortar boats the whole time since the enemy came into this neighbourhood and his exertions, daring, enterprise and judgement have been remarked by every officer as well as by myself". The manning of the gunboats in Cadiz harbour was a hazardous business. Working close inshore to the enemy's batteries, several had already been destroyed, with much loss of life, and the gun in another had burst after which Admiral Purvis had insisted that all guns used in the boats must be of brass.

One of the gunboats was commanded by twenty year-old Lieutenant Samuel Leeke who had started his career, aged ten, under Captain Purvis and had been with him ever since, apart from the Admiral's time ashore. Together with Fairfax Moresby (later Admiral-of-the-Fleet) and Ralph Wormeley (later Rear-Admiral) he was one of a group of special friends of John's and Richard's, all of whom had been boys in the *London* and would remain in correspondence throughout their lives.Wormeley, after the excellent work he had done in the preparation of the Spanish ships, had been promoted to Commander in February and was now commanding the sloop *Minstrel*.

Admiral Purvis had, for months, been trying to get the Spanish to move their three ships of-the-line at Cartagena. Now, with the French almost upon the town, the need was imperative. Henry Wellesley appealed to the Admiral who agreed to send the *Invincible* and to direct Sir Samuel Hood to render such assistance as he was able. "But, I beg leave to suggest to Your Excellency," Purvis warned, "the necessity of the Regency sending by the *Invincible* such distinct and peremptory orders to the Spanish officer commanding the ships that there may no longer exist those hindrances which have been so very manifest."

By now Wellesley was beginning to understand the patience, cajoling and, ultimately, physical intervention which was necessary to convert any Spanish resolution into action. Could the British not provide crews from Cadiz, he asked, but the Admiral would not consider weakening the Squadron to this extent. He would transport Spanish seamen from Cadiz to Cartagena in the *Invincible* if necessary but: "If the Government of Spain will not on this very particular occasion send men in the *Invincible* to save their own ships, I have only one expedient left which is to desire Sir Samuel Hood to send what assistance he can spare from his Squadron."

Nothing was straightforward when dealing with the Spanish; good intentions melted in the heat of reality; optimism stifled reason and common sense; the desire for short-term appeasement suppressed the knowledge that problems must, in time, be faced; and, at the end of the day, Britain was always there for whatever Spain was unable, or unwilling, to undertake herself. "I must beg leave to suggest," Purvis spelt out to Wellesley, "how necessary it will be that some Spanish naval officer of long standing, active mind and approved character should be sent in the *Invincible* with full powers to enforce the orders for the immediate removal of the ships and that if pay is due to the seamen that they may be assured and convinced that they shall receive it on their arrival at Mahon. If measures of this nature are not adopted at this critical time, the English officer who is directed to give assistance will have all sorts of difficulties to contend with and possibly not succeed after all his exertions."

On 27th April the Admiral heard that the first two Spanish ships, the *San Carlos* and the *San Fernando*, were ready to sail from Cartagena for Cadiz under the escort of *Northumberland* and *Hibernia*. "Do not bring them here," he instructed Captain Hargood of the *Northumberland,* "take them to Gibraltar." This only left the third ship, when she was ready, to be escorted to Port Mahon by the *Invincible*.

In Cadiz Harbour, the French fieldworks on Trocadero, having cleared all opposition from Matagorda and chased off the *San Paulo* in flames, was exacting a heavy toll on Puntales and the other allied batteries on the north-east shore of Leon.

Admiral Valdés, who was something of a firebrand, had the answer: all it required, he said, was a few ships of-the-line, British of course, to moor close inshore and blast the enemy into submission with their broadsides; it would all be over in four hours, he argued, with: ". . . several vessels, united, well-served and well-manoeuvred, as are those of the English. I do not see the slightest risk with the exception of that which naturally attends the operations of war."

The proposal, of course, was laughable: the enemy now had over thirty heavy guns on Trocadero, their gunnery was excellent and they had the furnaces to maintain a continuous curtain of hot shot across Puntales Roads. Their fortifications, moreover, were extremely strong; the only chance the allies had had was at the construction stage when the works might have been indefinitely delayed, or even aborted, by sustained and accurate gunnery; but this chance had been wasted by the Spaniards' inept shiphandling.

Though hardly worthy of serious consideration by the British command, Admiral Purvis discussed it with Rear-Admiral Pickmore, who agreed with him that the only outcome of such a reckless action would be the almost immediate destruction of the British ships by hot shot. In his opinion, Purvis wrote to Wellesley, "an attack of the well constructed fieldworks of Trocadero by the British ships cannot have the effects which Admiral Valdés states in his plan whilst the ships must be exposed to almost certain destruction from the effects of the enemy's hot shot."

However, he had a counter-proposal: trying, perhaps, to match the frivolous absurdity of the challenge underlying the Valdés proposal, he added: "If, however, the Spanish officers continue to be of opinion that great good will result from placing ships against the enemy's works; or that a few ships, well managed, will in a few hours destroy these works with little loss to the ships and great dismay to the enemy, I will cause the necessary number of officers and men to be put into as many Spanish ships as may be deemed sufficient for the purpose and I will answer for it the men will do what may be expected from them in as good a style as if they were fighting in their own ships." Admiral Valdés did not reply.

The following day, 28th April, Admiral Sir Charles Cotton arrived in the frigate *Lively* and took over as Commander-in-Chief Mediterranean. The Valdés proposal was referred to him and he immediately and wholeheartedly endorsed Purvis's decision.

Meticulous to the last, Admiral Purvis briefed his successor on every current aspect of the command, closed his own files and reported to the Admiralty: "Herewith you will be pleased to receive a Return of the Disposition of His Majesty's Ships and Vessels employed on the Mediterranean Station and an Abstract of the state and condition of those at Cadiz and its vicinity together with a list of His Catholic Majesty's Ships remaining at Cadiz being duplicated reports of those delivered by me of this day's date to Admiral Sir Charles Cotton on his taking command of this Station."

There were tears in Lieutenant Leeke's eyes as he said goodbye to the Admiral whom he had known for half his life; from whom he had learned everything he knew and who had been like a father to him. He promised to visit him when he was next in England and the Admiral told him he would always be pleased to see him or hear from him. It was not to be: Leeke was killed in action in Cadiz Harbour six months later. Dr. Little, who had also been with him since *London* days, had no wish to remain in the Mediterranean and had obtained permission to return to England with the Admiral.

"I should not think I should have fulfilled one of the most flattering of my duties, nor with my own sentiments," Villavicencio wrote to Purvis on 20th April as he prepared to leave Cadiz, "if I did not inform Your Excellency how much I feel satisfied with the gallant conduct of those subjects of His Britannic Majesty, and of the friendships and good harmony with the Spaniards all the time they were in that position."

On 30th April the Admiral transferred his Flag to the frigate *Leda* which sailed for England on 2nd May and anchored in Spithead on the 10th. *The Times* of 15th May reported:

> Admiral PURVIS, who arrived at Portsmouth, in the *Leda,* from Cadiz, has been absent nearly five years. The *Leda* was only eight days on her passage. Sir C. COTTON arrived at Cadiz on the 29th ult. and shifted his Flag into the *San Josef.* There were besides lying in the harbour the *Hibernia* (Admiral PICKMORE), *Caledonia, Téméraire, Eagle, Atlas, Achille, Zealous, Tonnant, Triumph* and *Bulwark,* all of the line; and the *Undaunted* and *Lively* frigates, four bombs, and several smaller vessels. The *Invincible*

had sailed for Cartagena. The Spanish ships of war at that port were about to be removed to Minorca. The *Rota* and *Iris* had sailed for Plymouth, with the French prisoners under convoy that were taken in the ships at Cadiz. The *Undaunted* was expected to sail soon with the Duke of ALBUQUERQUE, for England, as Ambassador to our Court.

All his principal objectives had been achieved and on 10th May Purvis wrote to the Admiralty: "I beg you will be pleased to acquaint My Lords Commissioners of the Admiralty that having been nearly four years on the Mediterranean Station and having important business to settle which respects my private fortune, I am induced to solicit their Lordships' permission to strike my Flag that I may be at liberty to get the same accomplished."

And so, on Sunday 13th May 1810 Vice-Admiral John Child Purvis struck his Flag in the *Leda* and, on a fine spring morning with the sun shining and a gentle breeze from the south-west, was pulled ashore for the last time.

CHAPTER 14

Sunset

19th November 1810
Vicar's Hill House, near Lymington, Hampshire

The Siege of Cadiz was to continue for a further two years. The only serious attempt to break the French stranglehold came in February 1811 when 4,900 British troops under General Graham and 9,500 Spanish under General Count Manuel La Peña landed at Algeçiras with the intention of taking the enemy from the rear. The enterprise was blighted from the start by Spanish incompetence and apathy. When La Peña began to procrastinate about moving towards the French, General Graham told him that unless the Spanish moved immediately, he would march the British force in the opposite direction, to Gibraltar, and leave La Peña to get on with it by himself.

The next part of the plan was for the Cadiz garrison under General Zayas to break out across the Sancti Petri and attack the French from the front while Graham and La Peña's force struck from the rear. Zayas bungled his orders and came out too soon thus enabling the enemy to drive him back into Cadiz before turning and confronting the allied force to their rear at full strength. The resulting Battle of Barossa was a bloody, hand-to-hand affair in which the British drove the French from their commanding position astride the Torre Barossa Ridge with brute force and fixed bayonets;

there were some 2,000 British killed and about the same number of French. It was doubtless no surprise to Admiral Purvis, when he later read of the battle, to learn that the Spanish army had stood by and done nothing.

Then, instead of exploiting the British victory, by which the Siege might well have been broken, La Peña refused to cooperate and marched back into Cadiz in a sulk. General Graham was so disgusted with his behaviour that he refused the honour of 'Grandee First Class' offered to him by the Cortes, resigned his appointment at Cadiz and, leaving the Spanish to eat strawberries at Chiclana, rejoined Wellington's army in Portugal.

The French eventually withdrew of their own volition on 24th August 1812 as their situation in the north deteriorated. At no stage of the Siege had any of the Spanish ships fallen into the hands of the enemy except the remains of those wrecked in the Great Storm of March 1810.

Having put his financial affairs in order, Admiral Purvis, now a rich man, sold his house in Wickham and bought Vicar's Hill House, Boldre, near Lymington in Hampshire. It was a white stucco mansion, built about 1767, with extensive grounds, stabling and coach houses and enjoying a pleasant, elevated position above the Lymington River. Here, he and Elizabeth settled in with a staff of eight — a butler, footman, coachman, groom, housekeeper, cook and two housemaids. Also living with them was Ann Porter, who had cared for the boys after Mary Garrett's death; she was now eighty years of age and in poor health.

"It is pleasantly situated and only twenty-nine miles from Wickham," he wrote to Richard on 19th November. He had just received the sad news of Samuel Leeke's death earlier in the month; he had not disgraced his patron: "Your poor friend Leeke was lately killed in Cadiz Harbour in a very gallant attack on some French gunboats which were passing from one port to another; Wormeley is Captain of the Minorca, brig, up the Mediterranean and Mr. Little came home with me and is now Surgeon of the Guard Ship at Plymouth under the Flag of Sir Robert Calder." [1]

John was staying with them and was in hopes of getting a frigate very soon. In the meantime, he was "amusing himself with his gun", an activity at which he did not apparently excel having recently shot his dog instead of the partridge he was after.

"I have had a long and fatigueing station off and in Cadiz Harbour and had calculated to come home with my late friend Lord Collingwood and for which purpose I applied for leave but before Lord Collingwood could be relieved, he sunk under the illness which induced him to wish to retire" [2] the Admiral told Richard.

The air at Vicar's Hill seemed to suit them and Elizabeth, who had suffered from poor health for several years, and had periodically been sent by her doctor to take the waters at Bath, showed a significant improvement at their new home. They entertained regularly and fulsomely, as befitted a retired Admiral and his lady, and were seldom without house guests. The Admiral was a courtly and indulgent host to the Lymington society but, having lived all his life in the confined social coterie of naval ships, he found that he missed the male companionship and conversation it afforded. He was therefore never happier than when another officer was staying in the house, whether serving or retired, Navy or Army, and would press such guests to stay longer. Then, old campaigns would be refought and the military and political situation in Europe debated. On 19th October 1812, the same day that Bonaparte ordered the evacuation of Moscow, he wrote to Richard in India with this perceptive summary of the European situation:

"The fate of all Europe is now depending on the result of two vast Armies in the heart of Russia: Bonaparte has headed one to overthrow the Government of Russia and they have had some desperate battles already and, each being determined to persevere, there is every reason to expect there will be very hard fighting. The French have possessed themselves of Moscow but not before the greater part of that fine City was reduced to ashes; it is said Bonaparte has made offers of peace to the Russians but their Emperor has declared he never will directly or indirectly enter into any negotiation until the Enemy shall have quitted [Russian soil]; the season of the year, the difficulty of obtaining Provisions and Ammunition and the very great distance Bonaparte has to look for his supplies of men and necessities of all kinds, gives us hopes that his Army will, by desertion and sickness, crumble away and be no more formidable either to Russia or any other country; the French are said to have lost in one Battle 40,000 men and the Russians not a great deal less. Lord Wellington has done wonders in Spain: the Armies of France in that country have been very roughly treated by that great

General and please God to spare his life and bless him with health; he will be the happy means of relieving the Peninsula from the oppressions of a faithless Enemy. Cadiz is relieved from the Siege, and many of the great Towns are evacuated by the hated French; Lord Wellington has shewn Bonaparte his soldiers are not Invincible and what they are to expect if ever they should visit this Country; the deep rooted [hatred] of Bonaparte against this Nation is beyond any calculation and, should he succeed in his views against Russia, nothing can satisfy him short of the [total] destruction of our Navy, and our complete humiliation, but I trust we shall continue to frustrate all his wicked views and not only save our own Country but spur up others to a sense of their degraded situation and induce them to shake off the tyrannic yoke they have so long submitted to. America you will find has [recognised] also the danger of Bonaparte and has been induced through him to make war against us; but as the great Body of the people in that Country are completely against the measure I think peace with them will soon be established." [3]

The battle in Russia to which he referred was Borodino where two great armies of 120,000 men apiece engaged each other some sixty miles west of Moscow. The Russians lost 40,000 and the French 28,000. The Admiral's reasons for the war with America were, perhaps, a little partisan: more culpable, it must be admitted, were Britain's continual interference with American shipping and her impressment of over 6,000 American sailors into the Royal Navy!

There was a window in a room on the second floor of the house which afforded a view of the Needles on the Isle of Wight. The Admiral kept his telescope by the window at which he would sit for long periods of time watching the shipping in the Solent. He was beginning to suffer from gout but, apart from that, he kept in good health, riding frequently and, according to Elizabeth, "amusing himself with what he calls his Farm". [4]

The great change in lifestyle was eased for the Admiral's first year of retirement by the company of his son; but in October 1811 John was appointed to the *Gannymede,* "a nice little frigate, mounting twenty-eight guns with 185 men. She is at Portsmouth and he writes he is very much pleased with her," [5] the Admiral told Richard.

Employed initially in Cadiz Harbour, John then came under the orders of one of his father's old Captains, Benjamin Hallowell, now a Rear-Admiral commanding the British Squadron on the east coast of Spain. He took part in the Siege of Tarragona and in an attack on some French privateers in the Grao de Murviedro, just north of Valencia, where the *Gannymede* ran aground and fought a seventeen-hour duel with a French shore battery until she was refloated with five men killed and fourteen wounded. John also captured his first prize — the French privateer *Vauteur*. In 1813 *Gannymede* was ordered to the North American Station where she cruised, with some success but no prize-money, until the peace of 1815.

The Admiral wrote regularly to John and Richard. Since his early days of penury he had been determined to divide whatever he had to leave equally between his sons. This was now considerable and he reminded them both, repeatedly, of his intention — always, of course, subject to their continuing good character: "It has ever been my intention, my dear Richard, to divide my attentions equally between you and your brother and whilst your conduct continues fair and honourable I shall not in any way change my plan." [6]

He had used his influence to the full and had given John the best possible start in the Navy: Lieutenant at eighteen; Commander at twenty-one and Post-Captain at twenty-two. However, he had no contacts or influence in the East India Company and felt keenly his inability to assist Richard in his military career even though it was one which had been insisted upon by Richard himself. Through acquaintances of Elizabeth's, he attempted to bring Richard to the attention of Sir George Nugent, the Commander-in-Chief in India, but little came of it and Richard became more and more disenchanted with his life and prospects in the Bengal Army.

The Admiral's brother, George, also a rich man as a result of his prize commission, was now a magistrate in Fareham and actively engaged in local government. He and his wife, Renira, lived in their idyllic 'Blackbrook Cottage' on the outskirts of the town with their two daughters, Renira and Georgina, and their son, George Thomas Maitland, who was destined for the Navy. The two brothers had always been close, as far as their service at sea had permitted, and visits between Vicar's Hill and Blackbrook were frequent.

On the peace of 1815 John returned to England and announced his intention of marrying the elder Blackbrook daughter, his first cousin, Renira. His uncle George disapproved of the match and his father was taken by surprise, not being aware that any sort of attachment existed between them. John had been appointed to command the frigate *Magicienne* in the East Indies and the Admiral advised him strongly to postpone his marriage until he returned to England at the end of the commission. John, however, was determined to marry immediately and told his father that he would take his bride to sea with him when he sailed — "a measure which I think very imprudent and such as I fear he will himself be convinced of when it is too late," [7] the Admiral warned.

In the event, Renira took well to shipboard life and gave birth to two sons during their four years in the East Indies. As Senior Officer off the Mauritius, John was concerned principally with suppression of the slave trade, but also received high praise, and some handsome cash rewards, for his part in rescuing the passengers and crews off two wrecked ships — a free trader and an East Indiaman. Between 1817 and 1819 he was Acting Commodore Ceylon: a senior appointment for an officer not yet thirty.

Richard came home from India on furlough in 1818. He had last seen his father when he was aged fourteen; he was now twenty-nine. He had taken part in the Nepal War of 1816 and after fourteen years service in the Bengal Army had failed to obtain any form of preferment and had only just been promoted to Captain — the equivalent of Lieutenant RN, a rank which his brother had obtained at the age of eighteen. Added to this, the mortality rate among the Honourable Company's employees in India was horrific: only one in seven lived to enjoy their pension and Richard's health had suffered grievously in its service. His three first-cousins who had been brother officers in the Bengal Native Infantry all died before they were thirty.

Richard was determined not to return to India but it was six months from his arrival at Vicar's Hill before he summoned up the nerve to tell his father. The Admiral was initially outraged but eventually agreed to help his son establish himself in a new career and to support him while he studied for it. Richard went up to Jesus College, Cambridge, to read law with a view to the Ministry. He was ordained a priest in the Church of England in 1821 and graduated the following year with a first class Bachelor of Law degree.

With the system of patronage as entrenched in the Church of England as in the Navy and, indeed, in most other walks of life, it would not be easy for Richard to find a living. The Admiral had no influence in ecclesiastical circles and no clerical tradition in the family; but he did have the money to buy an opening for his son and saw in this the means by which he could make up to Richard for the help he had been unable to give him in his military career. Accordingly, when the advowson for St. Leonard's Church at Whitsbury, a small village near Fordingbridge in Hampshire, became available in 1823, the Admiral bought it. This granted him and his heirs, in perpetuity, the right to appoint the vicar and on 10th March 1824 he presented Richard to the living.

Richard, meanwhile, after an abortive courtship of his Blackbrook cousin, Georgina, married Elizabeth Baker, eldest daughter of Revd. Thomas Baker, Rector of Rollesby in Norfolk. The couple settled in to the Parsonage House at Whitsbury where they raised eight children and where Richard remained as vicar until his death forty-four years later.

John returned to England in July 1819 when the *Magicienne* was paid off and a career which had thus far been marked by such rapid advancement then ground to a temporary halt with the greatly reduced requirements of the peacetime Navy. He was not to be employed afloat for the next twenty-two years but the most important part of his career still lay ahead of him.

The following month, on 12th August 1819, John Child Purvis was promoted to Admiral of the Blue — the highest rank that any member of this distinguished branch of the Purvis family had ever achieved. During the final five years of his life he seldom ventured far from Vicar's Hill. He regularly attended divine service at Boldre Church, where he subscribed to a private pew, and made several visits to St. Leonard's, Whitsbury, of which he was Patron, to attend services conducted by Richard. His brother, George, and his family were regular guests at Vicar's Hill and he received many visits from Captains and Flag-Officers with whom he had served and from young officers whose footsteps he had guided. He died peacefully, secure in his faith, on 23rd February 1825, aged seventy-eight, and was buried four days later in Boldre Churchyard after a service conducted by the vicar, the Revd. C. Shrubb.

True to the promise he had so regularly made, John and Richard were equal and principal beneficiaries of his Will. Richard received the farms in Upminster, which the Admiral had inherited from his cousin, Thomas English, and John those in Ringwood, Wooton-under-Edge and Edwardston. His widow, Elizabeth, received the income from £20,000 capital and the Admiral's personal and housegold goods. She also had the use of Vicar's Hill for the rest of her life, or until such time as she wished to live elsewhere, when it would pass to John and Richard to dispose of as they thought best. He had, for some time, been making an allowance to his sister, Emma, who was very badly off and married to a retired army officer who was a chronic invalid. The Will made provision for this allowance to be continued until her death.

A codicil relating to the Whitsbury advowson had not, unfortunately, been drafted by the lawyers in the clear, unambiguous style in which the Admiral had always written his orders and memoranda. This later led to a dispute between John and Richard each of whom put a different interpretation on what had been their father's wishes.

But the most surprising bequest, which must have caused much speculation among his family at the time, was the subject of a further codicil: "To Captain John Scott of the Royal Navy now living at Bishop's Waltham in the County of Southampton, £2,000 sterling as a legacy from me." John Scott had been a boy in the *London* and the Admiral had followed his career closely ever since. There is a universal tradition among Scott's descendants all over the world that he was a natural son of John Child Purvis, conceived before his first marriage when he returned from America as a recently-appointed Post-Captain. All attempts, in recent years, to establish this for certain, or to identify the mother, have failed but the evidence certainly supports the belief; not least the Admiral's bequest of £2,000 — around £86,000 ($150,000) in today's terms — a fortune by any standard and far in excess of what might have been expected as a remembrance gift to a former protégé.

Scott was a gallant officer who had distinguished himself with great bravery both as a Midshipman and later as a Lieutenant in 1815 during the American War for which he had been promoted to Commander. However, in common with many other excellent officers, he was put on the half-pay list after the peace of 1815 and never received another seagoing appointment. His legacy from the Admiral, ten years later, enabled him to buy a house in Odiham, to support his twelve children and to live in greater comfort than the income of a half-pay Commander would ever have permitted.

John Brett Purvis, after twenty-two years ashore, was in 1841 appointed Commodore South American Coasts and Republics and hoisted his Broad Pendant aboard the *Alfred,* 50. He sailed for 'The Brazils' in the spring of 1842 where, over the next two years, he played a major role in the establishment of the infant Republic of Uruguay which had thrown off the yoke of Spain during the Napoleonic Wars, had since been annexed in turn by the Argentine and Brazil, and was now racked by civil war as it struggled for independence. A testimonial to Commodore Purvis, expressing the gratitude of the Government for the assistance of his Squadron during "the most difficult and hazardous period" of the country's history is lodged in the Uruguayan State Papers.

John returned to England in 1845 and was promoted to Rear-Admiral the following year. In 1852 he was appointed as Commander-in-Chief Ireland and hoisted his Flag in the *Ajax.* During this command he had as his secretary his first cousin and brother-in-law, Commander George Thomas Maitland Purvis of Blackbrook. This George Purvis had first married Mary Jane Austen, niece of Jane Austen the author and daughter of Admiral-of-the-Fleet Sir Francis Austen who had been his distinguished uncle's First Lieutenant in the *London* in 1798/99. This was John Brett Purvis's final appointment in the Navy; he was promoted to Vice-Admiral in 1853 and retired to Bury Hall, his impressive mansion in Gosport, from where until his death in 1857 he served as a Justice of the Peace and as Deputy Lieutenant for the County of Southampton.

On the accession of King William IV, the former Prince William, Duke of Clarence, in 1830, John had attended one of his first levees. When his name was called, the King came straight to him and, according to family tradition, said: "Ah Purvis, Purvis. How do you do? So the poor old Admiral your father is dead. Left you very well off I understand — ah, very well off indeed." He was less popular with the next monarch. At a reception held by Queen Victoria, John, highly critical of the Queen's marriage, turned his back on Prince Albert. The snub did not escape the Queen's attention who made it known that Admiral Purvis would no longer be welcome at Court. This incident, again according to family tradition, remained one of John's favourite after-dinner stories for the rest of his life.

Richard's eldest surviving son, Fortescue Richard Purvis, took holy orders and succeeded his father as vicar of Whitsbury from 1868 to 1885. The Patronage of St. Leonard's is still in the family and the present Patron is William John Purvis, a great-great-great-grandson of the Admiral.

Richard's third son was christened John Child Purvis, after his illustrious grandfather, and entered the Navy. He did not dishonour the name being the first officer ashore in the Siege of Fort Kinburn during the Crimean War and the first officer to hoist the Royal Standard on the shores of India after the transfer of government to the Crown in 1858. He died in Germany, having attained the rank of Vice-Admiral, in 1904.

John also sent a son into the Navy. The youngest of his four sons, Richard, became a Rear-Admiral and himself had four sons the third of whom, Richard Brett Purvis, emigrated to America and gave rise to a large and widespread tribe of descendants in the United States. One of these, a great-great-great-granddaughter of John Child Purvis, married a U.S. Navy officer, Captain Alan Bean, who became an astronaut and was the lunar module pilot in the Apollo 12 Mission, the second lunar landing, during which he walked on the moon. This, one can be reasonably certain, would have delighted, if confused, the old Admiral.

The City of Cadiz has changed considerably since Admiral Purvis's time there. A great bridge, the Puente José León de Carranza, now spans the harbour from the Isle of Leon to the mainland which it meets at the site of the violent artillery duel between the British and the French across Trocadero Creek. To the right, on the marshlands of Trocadero, can be seen some grassy mounds and stonework which is all that remains of Fort St. Louis and the French positions. To the left, the site of Fort Matagorda, where Captain Maclaine and his gallant contingent made their stand, is lost beneath the concrete aprons of the Puerto Real shipyard. It is still, however, referred to as the Matagorda Shipyard.

The narrow streets and alleys of the old town are unchanged and it is easy to picture the Admiral passing along them on his way to yet another frustrating meeting with his Spanish counterparts. The theatre where he and Lord Collingwood were cheered by the audience for fifteen minutes was replaced by the present Gran Teatro Falla in the late 19th century as was the bullring at El Puerto Santa Maria where Byron attended his first bullfight before dining with Admiral Purvis on board the *Atlas*. Fort Puntales is still standing and houses a Spanish military establishment and the northeast shore from here to the point of the old town, which once bristled with batteries, is now a huge commercial docks complex.

The old Suaso Bridge, once the only access to the island, is still in use carrying one-way traffic to the mainland; a modern bridge alongside it takes traffic the other way. The remains of the batteries which guarded it, and which the Duke of Albuquerque was so anxious should be manned by British gunners, can be seen on either side. From here one can understand the Admiral's confidence that Leon could not be stormed from the east: apart from the road to the Suaso Bridge, the whole area is still as he described it to the Admiralty — a bog intersected by multitudes of unnavigable canals.

The Arsenal de la Carraca is still a major Spanish naval establishment and I am grateful to the Spanish Navy for giving me a full guided tour. Its beautiful 18th-century administrative buildings and impressive storehouses are much the same as in 1809 when they contained many guns and some 100,000 rounds of shot — much to Admiral Purvis's consternation. The military prison, packed to capacity with French prisoners-of-war during the Siege, now stands empty although it was in use until fairly recently.

Beyond the Arsenal the channel of the Carracas flows up to the Suaso Bridge and one can visualise the sinister line of prison hulks and decaying galleons moored up its centre which the Admiral discovered when he went up the Carracas in his barge on 17th December 1808, three days after his arrival at Cadiz. From here, one can see quite clearly, from the narrowness of the channel and its accessibility from the Suaso approaches that, had the Spanish and captured French ships remained at this anchorage, they would have been taken by the French with comparative ease.

The site of the Battle of Barossa has been buried beneath a tourist development and the town of Chiclana is largely industrialised. The state of the lavatories in the bar at which I had lunch was enough to kill one's appetite for any sort of food let alone strawberries.

The most impressive footprint left by the Royal Navy is on the north side of the bay. Here the ruins of the Castillo de Santa Catalina, the destruction of which Admiral Purvis pressed for so hard and so long, remain massive and majestic on a little-populated stretch of coast. The top of the great circular tower, its stonework intact and hardly disturbed, lies across the beach where it fell 200 years ago. Because there has been little building in the area, stone from the ruins has not been removed, as so often happens, and the entire layout of the fortress can be seen. As the Admiral explained, had he been given more time for the demolition, for which he did not receive permission from the Spanish authorities until the French were almost upon Cadiz, he would have ensured a more thorough job under the supervision of a Royal Engineers officer. Looking through the great gun embrasures across the water to Cadiz, one can see the complete command this fort had of the harbour approaches and can understand Admiral Purvis's insistence on its destruction.

From the top of Mont Faron, to the north of Toulon, one gets a magnificent panoramic view of the harbour from which every important landmark connected with the Siege of 1793 may be identified. The little town of La Seyne to whose inhabitants "much mischief was done" by Captain Purvis's 32-pounders, is now known as La Seyne-sur-Mer and is a thriving tourist resort. Its esplanades and an extensive complex of boatyards and marinas to the north of the town have entirely changed the contour of the shoreline and now cover the sites of the first batteries constructed by Captain Buonaparte to engage the *Princess Royal* moored close inshore.

However, Fort L'Eguillette and La Tour de la Balaguier remain where they were, and as they were, and La Grosse Tour still dominates the point on the opposite side of the harbour. L'Eguillette remains a French military establishment and Balaguier, which has altered little since it was built in 1636, stages seasonal exhibitions during which it is open to the public. An hourly waterbus service between Toulon and La Seyne passes over the spot where the *Princess Royal* was moored.

In 1821 the French built a vast fort over the remains of Fort Mulgrave, or 'Petit Gibraltar' as they knew it. It was called, not unsurprisingly, 'Fort Napoleon'. Today, its defensive role long past, it is used as a cultural centre for concerts, art exhibitions and the like. There is no trace of Buonaparte's batteries to the west of Mont Caire, including the Batterie des Hommes-Sans-Peur, as the whole area has been covered by modern housing.

Corsica, still relatively undeveloped, has changed little in 200 years and most of the major landmarks associated with Lord Hood's liberation of the island in 1794 can be readily identified. Some sixty of the Genoese towers which circle the coast can still be seen — some in an almost perfect state of preservation.

The Citadel at Bastia is little changed from the time that the naval contingent under Captain Nelson, including officers and men from *Princess Royal,* bombarded it from the north. The marks of their shot can still be seen. But even the bulk of the Citadel is overshadowed when the flagship of the ferry company Société Nationale Corse Méditerranée is in port; this enormous ferry with 555 cabins, four restaurants, four bar/lounges and a swimming pool measuring 11 x 5 metres towers above the town when it lies at its berth. It is called, again not unsurprisingly, the *Napoleon Bonaparte*.

On the western side of this once, albeit briefly, British island is San Fiorenzo, or Saint Florent as it is now called; it is easy to imagine Lord Hood's Fleet lying at anchor in this spectacularly-beautiful bay surrounded by the rugged mountains and dramatic cliffs of Cap Corse and with the unique scent of the maquis drifting across the moorings.

Captain Purvis's prize, the *Ça Ira*, was brought here after her capture in March 1795. This ship had been built at Brest in 1781 as an 80-gun ship of-the-line and was originally called the *Couronne*. In 1791 her name was changed to *La Revolution* and again in 1793 to *Ça Ira,* a phrase taken from the refrain of a cheerful revolutionary song: *"Ah! Ça Ira. Ça Ira. Ça Ira. Les aristocrates on les pendra."* (All the aristocrats will be hanged.) The ship was in the Old Basin at Toulon during the Siege, had thus escaped destruction in the haste of the evacuation and had put to sea again in Admiral Martin's Fleet in 1795.

After her capture off Genoa, the Royal Navy put her into service as a hospital ship serving the warships and military establishment at San Fiorenzo under the command of a newly-promoted Post-Captain — Charles Dudley Pater. However, one year later, on 11th April 1796, she caught fire and sank at her moorings.

In 1989 a sub-aqua team led by Monsieur Pierre Villié located the wreck lying in nine fathoms in San Fiorenzo Bay. The clarity of Corsican waters, with underwater visibility in summer ranging between twenty-five and forty metres, is well known. The wreck of Captain Purvis's prize has therefore become a favourite expedition for amateur shallow-water divers.

APPENDIX A

The Purvis Papers at the
National Maritime Museum

Throughout his commissioned service, John Child Purvis kept meticulous records and on his retirement was in possession of all his logs, order-books, letter-books and an enormous amount of loose correspondence mainly relating to his command of the Cadiz Squadron between 1806 and 1810. For Hotham's actions off Genoa and Hyères in 1795, he had augmented the records in his log with detailed schedules of ship movements and signals.

After his death in 1825 the Papers remained in the cellars of his house, Vicar's Hill, near Boldre in Hampshire, for several years where they became very damp and suffered some deterioration. They were discovered there by his elder son, Admiral John Brett Purvis, during a visit to the empty house in 1831; he brought them up to the drawing room, lit fires, dried them out, listed them and stored them in a dry cupboard.

From here they were passed down through the family, each generation preserving them intact, until 1954 when a great-great grandson of the Admiral (whom I shall not identify) broke up the collection, selling off individual letters of particular value and offering the balance to the highest bidder. The collection was thus split into three main parts the first of which was bought through Sotheby's by the National Maritime Museum in April 1955.

The second part, comprising some twenty-six bound volumes, was purchased by the Museum from Mr. Weinreb of Great Russell

Street in November 1959; then in May 1973 the third part, consisting of some 150 Peninsular War documents, came on the market and was bought by the Museum through Spinks of St. James's. Though many of the valuable letters, notably from Lord Collingwood, were dispersed to private collectors and the remaining files of loose correspondence had been opened and were much confused, the bulk of Admiral Purvis's Papers are now reunited and, thanks to the foresight and diligence of the National Maritime Museum, preserved for posterity. Together, they provide a uniquely comprehensive record of the career of a sea officer of the late-18th / early-19th centuries.

Other Purvis Papers, including letters from Lord Nelson and Lord St. Vincent, were passed down through the descendants of the Admiral's younger brother, George, who was secretary to Lords Howe and St. Vincent and, for a short time, Nelson's Prize-Agent. These were presented to the Museum in 1946 by Mrs. G.F.G. Purvis, the widow of George Purvis's great-grandson and the last in the male line of the Blackbrook branch of the family.

An extensive collection of personal correspondence, including many letters between Admiral Purvis and his younger son, Richard, has been preserved by Richard's descendants and is still in the possession of the family; much of this was reproduced in Richard's biography *"Soldier of the Raj"*. There is also a large collection of personal letters between Richard Purvis and his brother officers in the Bengal Army. Most of these are in the possession of the family but, at some stage in the past, part of the collection appears to have been subjoined to the Admiral's professional papers and is therefore now at the National Maritime Museum under reference PRV/101.

All extracts in this book from the Purvis Papers at the National Maritime Museum are reproduced by kind permission of the Trustees and can be readily located by reference to the schedule which follows:

Books and manuscripts at the National Maritime Museum may also be located through their online catalogue:
http://www.nmm.ac.uk/librarycatalogue

LOG-BOOKS 1762-1810

PRV/1	29 Dec 1762	to	19 Aug 1763	*Arrogant*	Mid.
PRV/2	11 Feb 1778	to	31 Mar 1779	*Invincible*	Lieut.
	2 Apr 1779	to	22 Oct 1779	*Britannia*	Lieut.
PRV/3	23 Oct 1779	to	20 May 1781	*Britannia*	Lieut.
	22 May 1781	to	11 Jun 1781	*Duc de Chartres*	M&C
PRV/4	12 Jun 1781	to	10 Apr 1783	*Duc de Chartres*	Capt.
PRV/5	1 Feb 1793	to	4 Apr 1793	*Amphitrite*	Capt.
	5 Apr 1793	to	25 Dec 1794	*Princess Royal*	Capt.
PRV/6	26 Dec 1794	to	24 Feb 1796	*Princess Royal*	Capt.
PRV/7	25 Feb 1796	to	10 Nov 1796	*Princess Royal*	Capt.
	15 May 1797	to	19 Apr 1798	*London*	Capt.
PRV/8	20 Apr 1798	to	20 Jun 1799	*London*	Capt.
PRV/9	27 Jun 1799	to	20 Sept 1800	*London*	Capt.
PRV/10	21 Sep 1800	to	10 Feb 1801	*London*	Capt.
	11 Feb 1801	to	3 Apr 1801	*Royal George*	Capt.
PRV/11	4 Apr 1801	to	24 Apr 1802	*Royal George*	Capt.
PRV/12a	8 Sep 1803	to	4 May 1804	*Dreadnought*	Capt.
	2 Jun 1806	to	27 Jun 1806	*La Chiffone*	R-Adml.
	28 Jun 1806	to	3 Aug 1806	*Minotaur*	R-Adml.
PRV/12b	2 Jun 1806	to	27 Jun 1806	*La Chiffone*	R-Adml.
	27 Jun 1806	to	5 Aug 1806	*Minotaur*	R-Adml.
PRV/13	4 Aug 1806	to	22 Sep 1806	*Minotaur*	R-Adml.
	22Sep 1806	to	9 Dec 1806	*Queen*	R-Adml.
	9 Dec 1806	to	31 Dec 1806	*Atlas*	R-Adml.
PRV/14	1 Jan 1807	to	26 Jun 1807	*Atlas*	R-Adml.

PRV/15		27 Jun 1807	to	31 Dec 1807	*Atlas*	R-Adml.
PRV/16		1 Jan 1808	to	10 May 1808	*Atlas*	R-Adml.
PRV/17a		11 May 1808	to	24 Oct 1809	*Atlas*	R-Adml.
		25 Oct 1809	to	30 Apr 1810	*Atlas*	V-Adml.
		30 Apr 1810	to	13 May 1810	*Leda*	V-Adml.
PRV/17b	i)	30 Aug 1808	to	31 Dec 1808	*Atlas*	R-Adml.
	ii)	1 Jan 1809	to	30 Apr 1809	*Atlas*	R-Adml.
	iii)	1 May 1809	to	24 Oct 1809	*Atlas*	R-Adml.
		25 Oct 1809	to	31 Dec 1809	*Atlas*	V-Adml.
	iv)	1 Jan 1810	to	30 Apr 1810	*Atlas*	V-Adml.

ORDER-BOOKS AND LETTER-BOOKS 1781-1810

PRV/18	9 Apr 1781 to 4 Dec 1782	*Duc de Chartres*	Orders Recd.
	25 Jul 1781 to 9 Apr 1783	*Duc de Chartres*	Letters Out
PRV/19	31 Jan 1793 to 4 Apr 1793	*Amphitrite*	Letters Out
	5 Apr 1793 to 10 Nov 1796	*Princess Royal*	Letters Out
	5 Jun 1793 to 10 Mar 1794	*Princess Royal*	Orders Issued
PRV/20	31 Aug 1793 to 3 Oct 1795	*Princess Royal*	Orders Recd.
	16 Apr 1793	*Princess Royal*	Standing Orders
PRV/21	4 Oct 1795 to 20 Oct 1796	*Princess Royal*	Letters In
			Orders Recd.
PRV/22	25 May 1797 to 21 Mar 1799	*London*	Orders Issued
	15 May 1797 to 23 Mar 1799	*London*	Orders Recd.
PRV/23	15 May 1797 to 15 Apr 1800	*London*	Letters Out
	3 Jul 1797 to 4 Apr 1800	*London*	Letters In
PRV/24	25 Mar 1799 to 10 Feb 1801	*London*	Orders Recd.
	11 Feb 1801 to 21 Apr 1802	*Royal George*	Orders Recd.
	1 May 1799 to 10 Feb 1801	*London*	Orders Issued
	11 Feb 1801 to 12 Apr 1802	*Royal George*	Orders Issued

PRV/25	15 Apr 1800 to 10 Feb 1801	*London*	Letters In
	11 Feb 1801 to 24 Apr 1802	*Royal George*	Letters In
	8 Sep 1803 to 4 May 1804	*Dreadnought*	Letters In
	2 Jun 1806 to 27 Jun 1806	*La Chiffone*	Letters In
	28 Jun 1806 to 22 Sep 1806	*Minotaur*	Letters In
	22 Sep 1806 to 9 Dec 1806	*Queen*	Letters In
	9 Dec 1806 to 9 Oct 1807	*Atlas*	Letters In
	17 Apr 1800 to 10 Feb 1801	*London*	Letters Out
	11 Feb 1801 to 24 Apr 1802	*Royal George*	Letters Out
	8 Sep 1803 to 4 May 1804	*Dreadnought*	Letters Out
	2 Jun 1806 to 27 Jun 1806	*La Chiffone*	Letters Out
	28 Jun 1806 to 22 Sep 1806	*Minotaur*	Letters Out
	22 Sep 1806 to 9 Dec 1806	*Queen*	Letters Out
	9 Dec 1807 to 27 Dec 1807	*Atlas*	Letters Out
PRV/26	2 Nov 1803 to 4 May 1804	*Dreadnought*	Orders Issued
	28 Jun 1806 to 22 Sep 1806	*Minotaur*	Orders Issued
	22 Sep 1806 to 9 Dec 1806	*Queen*	Orders Issued
	9 Dec 1806 to 1 Sep 1807	*Atlas*	Orders Issued
	10 Sep 1803 to 4 May 1804	*Dreadnought*	Orders Recd.
	28 Jun 1806 to 22 Sep 1806	*Minotaur*	Orders Recd.
	22 Sep 1806 to 9 Dec 1806	*Queen*	Orders Recd.
	9 Dec 1806 to 15 May 1807	*Atlas*	Orders Recd.
PRV/27a	20 Jun 1807 to 2 Mar 1810	Letters recd. by Adml. Purvis for Lord Collingwood to whom the originals were forwarded.	
	25 Apr 1801 to 28 Apr 1802	Out letter-book of Adml. Sir Archibald Dickson Bart. (Purvis's third father-in-law).	
PRV/27b	5 Aug 1800 to 21 Apr 1802	Orders Issued by Adml. Sir Archibald Dickson and directions for navigating the Black Sea.	
PRV/28	2 Sep 1807 to 23 Nov 1808	*Atlas*	Orders Issued
	21 Jul 1807 to 7 Jul 1808	*Atlas*	Orders Recd.
PRV/29	20 Nov 1807 to 9 Mar 1810	*Atlas*	Secret Letters Out
	19 Dec 1808 to 16 Apr 1809	*Atlas*	Secret Letters In

PRV/30	23 Nov 1808 to 2 Nov 1809 *Atlas*	Orders Issued
PRV/31	25 Nov 1808 to 7 Jul 1810 *Atlas*	Letters Out
PRV/32	3 Nov 1809 to 30 Apr 1810 *Atlas*	Orders Issued
PRV/33	26 Nov 1809 to 28 Apr 1810 *Atlas*	Secret Letters

MISCELLANEOUS ITEMS

PRV/34	Ms. notes on the Azores and Directions for Entering the Harbour of Cadiz, 17 Mar 1808.
PRV/35	A bound copy of *"Hardy's List of Captains"* 1673-1783 by Rear-Admiral John Hardy. Published in 1784.
PRV/36	A bound book of thirty-six French charts of Mediterranean ports 1727-1730, which belonged to Captain J. C. Purvis.

LOOSE PAPERS

PRV/37	1795-1805	General Correspondence.
PRV/38	1806	General Correspondence.
PRV/39	1807	General Correspondence.
PRV/40 a&b	1808	General Correspopndence.
PRV/41 a&b	1809	General Correspondence.
PRV/42 a&b	1810	General Correspondence.
PRV/43	1807-1808	Original Admiralty Letters.
PRV/44	1808-1810	Original Letters from the Junta and Governor of Cadiz.

PRV/45	1810	Original Captains' Letters.
PRV/46		Undated correspondence and some later papers.
PRV/47	1807-1810	Selected Letters.
PRV/48		An autobiographical sketch written by Admiral Purvis after his retirement.
PRV/101	1806-1810	Letters connected with Admiral Purvis's younger son, Richard, whilst serving with the 21st and 30th Bengal Native Infantry.
PRV/102		Collection of holograph letters with distinguished signatories. Unconnected with Admiral Purvis or the Royal Navy.
PRV/103		Holograph letter from Sir John Jervis (later Lord St. Vincent) to his secretary, George Purvis, younger brother of Admiral Purvis.

OTHER PURVIS MANUSCRIPTS
(Presented to the Museum in 1948 by Mrs G. F. G. Purvis)

BGY/P/4	Miscellaneous papers concerning Captain George Purvis (1680-1740), Captain George T. M. Purvis (1802-1883) and Rear-Admiral Francis R. Purvis (1833-1895).
AGC/23/3	Letter from George Purvis to his brother Captain J. C. Purvis Victory, Lagos Bay, 16 Feb 1797.
AGC/23/6	Letters to Rear-Admiral J. C. Purvis from Duke of Wellington and Lord Collingwood. Letter to George Purvis from Sir John Jervis, 24 Jan 1791.
AGC/N/13	Holograph letter from Nelson to George Purvis 19 Jun 1797.
AGC/N/14	Holograph letter from Nelson to George Purvis 3 May 1798.

APPENDIX B

Other Principal Sources Consulted

Baugh, Daniel A., [Ed.] *Naval Administration 1715-1750.* Navy Records Society, Vol. 120, 1977.

Clowes, William Laird, *The Royal Navy: a History from the Earliest Times to the Present.* First published 1897-1903. 1996 paperback edition, London, Chatham Publishing, 7 vols.

Collingwood, G.L.N. [Ed.], *Correspondence and Memoir of Lord Collingwood.* 4th edition, 1828.

Cronin, Vincent, *Napoleon.* Collins, London, 1971.

Donaldson, Joseph, *Recollections of the Eventful Life of a Soldier.* First published 1852. Spellmount edition, Staplehurst, 2000.

Duffy, Michael, [Ed.], *The Naval Miscellany Vol. VI.* Ashgate, Aldershot 2003 for Navy Records Society.

Fraser, Edward, *The 'Londons' of the British Fleet.* John Lane, The Bodley Head, London, 1908.

Hughes, Edward, [Ed.], *The Private Correspondence of Admiral Lord Collingwood.* Navy Records Society, Vol. 98, 1957.

Humble, Richard, *Napoleon's Peninsular Marshals.* Purcell, London, 1974.

Hylton, Lord, [Ed.] *The Paget Brothers 1790-1840.* John Murray, London 1918.

James, William, *The Naval History of Great Britain.* London, 1886 (7th edition), 6 vols.

James, Admiral Sir William, *Old Oak: The Life of John Jervis, Earl of St. Vincent.* Longmans, Green, London 1950.

King-Hall, L. [Ed.] *Sea Saga: the Naval Diaries of Four Generations of the King-Hall Family.* Victor Gollancz, London, 1935.

Laughton, Sir John Knox, [Ed.], *Letters and Papers of Charles, Lord Barham, Admiral of the Red Squadron, 1758-1813.* Navy Records Society, 3 vols. Vol. 32, 1907; Vol. 38, 1910; Vol. 39, 1911.

Lavery, Brian, [Ed.], *Shipboard Life and Organisation 1731-1815.* Ashgate, Aldershot, 1998 for Navy Records Society, Vol. 138.

Marioné, Patrick, *The Complete Navy List of the Napoleonic Wars 1793-1815.* CD-ROM, Brussels, 2003. www.ageofnelson.org

Morriss, Roger, [Ed.], *The Channel Fleet and the Blockade of Brest 1793-1801.* Ashgate, Aldershot 2001 for Navy Records Society, Vol. 141.

Murray, Geoffrey, *The Life of Admiral Collingwood.* Hutchinson, London, 1936.

Napier, William, *History of the War in the Peninsula and the South of France from the year 1807 to the year 1814.* Boone, London, 1840-47, 6 vols.

Parkinson, C. Northcote, *Britannia Rules: The Classic Age of Naval History 1793-1815.* Wiedenfeld & Nicolson, London, 1977.

Rodger, N.A.M., *The Wooden World: an Anatomy of the Georgian Navy,* Collins, London, 1986.
— *The Command of the Ocean: a Naval History of Britain 1649-1815.* Allen Lane, London, 2004.

Tucker, Jedediah Stephens, *Memoirs of Admiral the Right Hon. the Earl of St. Vincent.* Richard Bentley, London, 1844.

APPENDIX C

Notes

NMM   National Maritime Museum, Greenwich
PFP   Purvis Family Papers
PRO   National Archives (formerly Public Record Office)

Preface
1. http://www.royal-navy.mod.uk/
   static/pages/2204.html
2. Clowes Vol. 5, P.10
3. Ibid. P. 9
4. NMM AGC/23/6(i)
5. Tucker, *Memoirs of Admiral the
   Right Hon. Earl St. Vincent, etc.*
6. Collingwood. *Correspondence
   and Memoir of Lord Collingwood*
   P. 508
7. PFP JCP/RFP 1816/08/30
8. Gordon, *Soldier of the Raj,* Leo
   Cooper, Barnsley, 2001

Chapter 1. Early Days
1. NMM BGY/P/4
2. Ibid.

Chapter 2. Toulon
1. Cronin, *Napoleon,* P.75

**Chapter 3. Corsica, Genoa and
Hyères**
1. Marioné, *The Complete Navy List
   of the Napoleonic Wars 1793-
   1815*
2. Clowes, Vol. IV. P.272 Note (i)

**Chapter 4. The Mediterranean
Discipline**
1. NMM PRV/103
2. NMM AGC/23/3

Chapter 5. The Pursuit of Bruix
1. NMM ORD/11
2. Ibid. 46 MS 9266
3. PFP DG/JCP 1800/01/20
4. Ibid.

Chapter 6. Royal George
1. NMM ORD/11
2. PFP JCP/RFP 1803/05/15
3. Ibid. CP /JCP 1803/10/17

Chapter 7. Dreadnought
1. PFP CP /JCP 1803/10/17
2. Ibid. DG/JCP 1803/09/22
3. Hughes, *The Private
   Correspondence of Admiral Lord
   Collingwood* P.148-149
4. PFP DG/JCP 1803/10/07
5. Ibid. JCP/RFP 1803/11/02
6. Ibid. DG/JCP 1804/01/01
7. Ibid. JCP/RFP 1804/01/29
8. Ibid. DG/JCP 1804/02/04
9. Ibid. JCP/RFP 1805/04/21
10. Ibid. JCP/RFP 1806/04/28
11. NMM 46 MS 9266/2

Chapter 9. Vivan los Ingleses!
1. Hylton, *The Paget Brothers 1790-
   1840,* P. 81-82
2. Ibid.
3. PFP JCP/RFP 1807/09/08
4. Ibid.
5. Ibid. RFP/EP 1809/02/20
6. Clowes, Vol V, P. 25, Note (i)

Chapter 11. Cadiz
1. Marioné, *The Complete Navy List of the Napoleonic Wars 1793-1815*

Chapter 12. Commander-in-Chief
1. MacCarthy, Fiona, *Byron: Life and Legend*, P.96
2. Ibid.
3. Donaldson, *Recollections of the Eventful Life of a Soldier*, P. 68-70

Chapter 13. The Great Storm
1. PRO ADM 1/416/100
2. NMM 46 MS 9266/2

3. Donaldson, *Recollections of the Eventful Life of a Soldier*, P.65
4. Napier, *English Battles and Sieges in the Peninsula*, P.62
5. Donaldson, *Recollections of the Eventful Life of a Soldier*, P.77

Chapter 14. Sunset
1. PFP JCP/RFP 1810/11/19
2. Ibid. JCP/RFP 1812/10/19
3. Ibid.
4. Ibid. EP/RFP 1815/01/10
5. Ibid. JCP/RFP 1811/11/24
6. Ibid. JCP/RFP 1810/11/19
7. Ibid. JCP/RFP 1815/10/04

APPENDIX D

Ministries 1762-1812

PRIME MINISTER		
1762-1763	John Stuart, Earl of Bute	Tory
1763-1765	Hon. George Grenville	Whig
1765-1766	Charles Watson-Wentworth, Marquess of Rockingham	Whig
1766-1768	William Pitt, Earl of Chatham	Whig
1768-1770	Augustus Fitzroy, Duke of Grafton	Whig
1770-1782	Frederick North, Lord North	Tory
1782-1783	William Petty, Earl of Shelburne	Whig
1783-1801	William Pitt, the Younger	Tory
1801-1804	Henry Addington	Tory
1804-1806	William Pitt, the Younger	Tory
1806-1807	William Wyndham Grenville, Lord Grenville	Whig
1807-1809	William Cavendish-Bentinck, Duke of Portland	Tory
1809-1812	Spencer Perceval	Tory

APPENDIX E   THE DESCENDANTS OF CAPTAIN GEORGE PURVIS RN 1680-1740

George Purvis
1680-1740
Captain RN, Commissioner of the Navy and MP for Aldeburgh, Suffolk
=1712 Elizabeth Allen

Martha Purvis
1713-1762
=1739 Captain Thomas Pearce RN
1 son, 1 daughter (Pearce)

Charles Wager Purvis
1715-1772
Rear-Admiral
= 1741 Amy Godfrey
3 sons, 4 daughters

George Purvis
1718-1773
Admiralty Official
=1742 Mary Oadham

Harvey Purvis
1721-1740
Lost at sea from 'Princess Caroline' returning from Portobello with Admiral Vernon

Richard Purvis
1743-1802
Captain RN
=1780 Lucy Leman

John Child Purvis
1747-1825
Admiral of the Blue
=1. 1784 Elizabeth Sowers
=2. 1790 Mary Garrett
=3. 1804 Elizabeth Dickson
CONTINUED ON NEXT PAGE

George Purvis
1751-1826
Secretary to Lord Howe and Lord St Vincent
= 1791 Renira Charlotte Maitland
CONTINUED ON NEXT PAGE

4 Daughters
Mary Oadham b.1745
Elizabeth b.1748
Lissey Anna b.1755
Emma b.1757

Richard Oadham Purvis
1785-1804
Lieutenant RN
Died on service in West Indies

John Leman Purvis
1786-1805
Lieutenant Bengal Army
Died on service in East Indies

George Thomas Purvis
1789-1819
Captain Bengal Army
Died on passage home from East Indies

Barrington Purvis
1792-1822
Lieutenant Bengal Army
=1820 Amy Laetitia Colville

2 Daughters
Mary Anna b.1781
Lucy Anna b.1783

Frances Laetitia Purvis
1821-1873
=1841 Edward John Kelso
Captain 72nd Highlanders
3 sons, 2 daughters (Kelso)

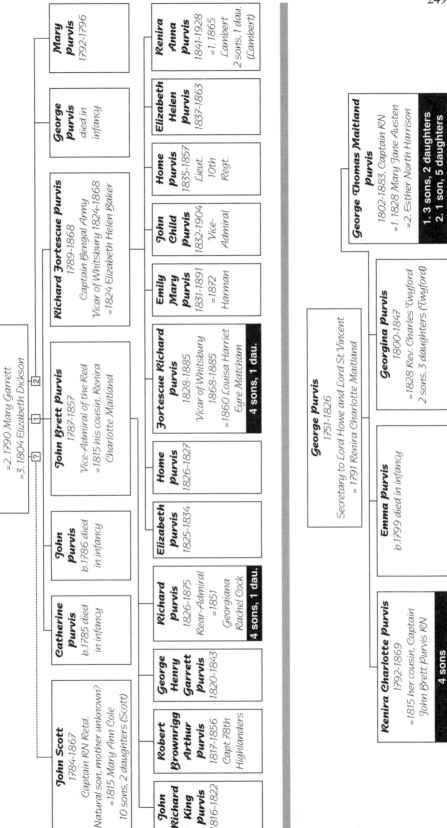

John Child Purvis
1747-1825
Admiral of the Blue
=1. 1784 Elizabeth Sowers
=2. 1790 Mary Garrett
=3. 1804 Elizabeth Dickson

John Scott
1784-1867
Captain RN Retd.
Natural son, mother unknown?
=1815 Mary Ann Cole
10 sons, 2 daughters (Scott)

Mary Purvis
1792-1796

George Purvis
died in infancy

Richard Fortescue Purvis
1789-1868
Captain Bengal Army
Vicar of Whitsbury 1824-1868
=1824 Elizabeth Helen Baker

John Brett Purvis
1787-1857
Vice-Admiral of the Red
=1815 his cousin, Renira
Charlotte Maitland

Catherine Purvis
b.1785 died in infancy

John Purvis
b.1786 died in infancy

John Richard King Purvis
1816-1822

Robert Brownrigg Arthur Purvis
1817-1856
Capt 78th Highlanders

George Henry Garrett Purvis
1820-1843

Richard Purvis
1826-1875
Rear-Admiral
=1851
Georgiana
Rachel Cock

4 sons, 1 dau.

Elizabeth Purvis
1825-1834

Home Purvis
1826-1827

Fortescue Richard Purvis
1828-1885
Vicar of Whitsbury
1868-1885
=1860 Louisa Harriet
Eyre Matcham

4 sons, 1 dau.

Emily Mary Purvis
1831-1891
=1872
Harman

John Child Purvis
1832-1904
Vice-Admiral

Home Purvis
1835-1857
Lieut.
10th Regt.

Elizabeth Helen Purvis
1837-1863

Renira Anna Purvis
1841-1928
=1.1865
Lambert
2 sons, 1 dau.
(Lambert)

George Purvis
1751-1826
Secretary to Lord Howe and Lord St Vincent
= 1791 Renira Charlotte Maitland

Renira Charlotte Purvis
1792-1869
=1815 her cousin, Captain
John Brett Purvis RN

4 sons

Emma Purvis
b.1799 died in infancy

Georgina Purvis
1800-1847
=1828 Rev. Charles Twyford
2 sons, 3 daughters (Twyford)

George Thomas Maitland Purvis
1802-1883, Captain RN
=1.1828 Mary Jane Austen
=2. Esther North Harrison

1. 3 sons, 2 daughters
2. 1 son, 5 daughters

APPENDIX F

A Humble Heroine

by William Topaz McGonagall

' Twas at the Siege of Matagorda, during the Peninsular War,
That a Mrs. Reston for courage outshone any man there by far;
She was the wife of a Scottish soldier in Matagorda Fort,
And to attend to her husband she there did resort.

' Twas in the Spring of the year 1810,
That General Sir Thomas Graham occupied Matagorda with 150 men;
These consisted of a detachment from the Scots Brigade,
And on that occasion they weren't in the least afraid.

And Captain Maclaine of the 94th did the whole of them command,
And the courage the men displayed was really grand;
Because they held Matagorda for fifty-four days,
Against o'erwhelming numbers of French, therefore they are worthy of praise.

The British were fighting on behalf of Spain,
But if they fought on their behalf they didn't fight in vain;
For they beat them manfully by land and sea,
And from the shores of Spain they were forced to flee.

Because Captain Maclaine set about repairing the old fort,
So as to make it comfortable for his men to resort;
And there he kept his men at work day by day,
Filling sand-bags and stuffing them in the walls without delay.

There was one woman in the fort during these trying days,
A Mrs. Reston who is worthy of great praise;
She acted like a ministering angel to the soldiers while there,
By helping them to fill sand-bags, it was her constant care.

Mrs. Reston behaved as fearlessly as any soldier in the garrison,
And amongst the soldiers golden opinions she won;
For her presence was everywhere amongst the men,
And the service invaluable she rendered to them.

Methinks I see that brave heroine carrying her child,
Whilst the bullets were falling around her, enough to drive her wild;
And bending over it to protect it from danger,
Because to war's alarms it was a stranger.

And while the shells shrieked around, and their fragments did scatter,
She was serving the men at the guns with wine and water;
And whilst the shot whistled around, her courage wasn't slack,
Bacause to the soldiers she carried sand-bags on her back.

A little drummer boy was told to fetch water from the well,
But he was afraid because the bullets from the enemy around it fell;
And the Doctor cried to the boy: "Why are you standing there?",
But Mrs. Reston said: "Doctor, the bairn is feared, I do declare."

And she said: "Give me the pail, laddie, I'll fetch the water.",
Not fearing that the shot would her brains scatter;
And without a moment's hesitation she took the pail,
Whilst the shot whirred thick around her, yet her courage didn't fail.

And to see that heroic woman the scene was most grand,
Because as she drew the water a shot cut the rope in her hand;
But she caught the pail in her hand dexterously,
Oh! The scene was imposing and most beautiful to see.

The British fought bravely as they are always willing to do,
Although their numbers were but few;
So they kept up the cannonading with their artillery,
And stood manfully at their guns against the enemy.

And five times the flagstaff was shot away,
And as often it was replaced without dismay;
And the flag was fastened to an angle of the wall,
And the British resolved to defend it whatever did befall.

So the French were beaten and were glad to run,
And the British for defeating them golden opinions have won.
All through brave Captain Maclaine and his heroes bold,
Likewise Mrs. Reston, whose name should be written in letters of gold.

William Topaz McGonegall (1825-1902), Poet and Tragedian of Dundee, is generally credited with having produced the worst poetry ever written in the English language. Yet during his lifetime he was lionised by the academic community and gave public readings of his work to packed audiences in Scotland, London and New York. The awfulness and disarming innocence of his verse, where historical accuracy was often sacrificed to the needs of patriotism (as with the ending of the Matagorda saga) has ensured him a place in literary history and he remains a cult figure to this day.

Index

Adml.	Admiral.	mar.	Marine.
A.D.S.	Armed Defence Ship.	Mid.	Midshipman.
Capt.	Captain.	Min.	Minister.
Cdr.	Commander.	Neap.	Neapolitan.
Col.	Colonel	Port.	Portuguese.
Dip.	Diplomat.	R.A.	Royal Artillery.
Fr.	French.	R.E.	Royal Engineers.
Genl.	General.	R.M.	Royal Marines.
H.E.I.C.	Hon. East India Co.	Sard.	Sardinian
H.M.S.	His Majesty's Ship.	sm	Seaman.
Hosp.	Hospital Ship.	Sp.	Spanish.
Lieut.	Lieutenant.	t	Appears in table.
Maj.	Major.	U.S.S.	United States Ship.